THE GOSPEL OF MATTHEW
IN CURRENT STUDY

William G. Thompson, S.J.

THE GOSPEL OF MATTHEW IN CURRENT STUDY

Studies in Memory of
William G. Thompson, S.J.

Edited by

David E. Aune

WILLIAM B. EERDMANS PUBLISHING COMPANY
GRAND RAPIDS, MICHIGAN / CAMBRIDGE, U.K.

Wm. B. Eerdmans Publishing Co.
255 Jefferson Ave. S.E., Grand Rapids, Michigan 49503 /
P.O. Box 163, Cambridge CB3 9PU U.K.

Printed in the United States of America

06 05 04 03 02 01   7 6 5 4 3 2 1

Library of Congress Cataloging-in-Publication Data

The Gospel of Matthew in current study: studies in memory of
William G. Thompson, S.J. / edited by David E. Aune.
        p.   cm.
    Proceedings of a colloquium held June 12-14, 1998 at the
Lake Shore Campus of Loyola University.
    Includes bibliographical references (p.   ).
    ISBN 0-8028-4673-4 (pbk.: alk. paper)
    1. Bible. N.T. Matthew — Criticism, interpretation, etc. — Congresses.
I. Thompson, William G., 1930-   II. Aune, David Edward.

    BS2575.52.G67   2001
    226.2'06 — dc21

                                        00-047638

www.eerdmans.com

Contents

v

CONTENTS

Preface

I first met Bill Thompson at the Catholic Biblical Association annual meeting in Albany, New York, in 1970, and he was present and supportive 20 years later when I presented lectures to the Department of Theology at Loyola University prior to my appointment there as Professor of New Testament in the fall of 1990. Preparations for a colloquium in Bill's memory began shortly after his premature death at the end of September 1996 after a lengthy illness. After sounding out a number of colleagues on the advisability of honoring Bill's memory in a suitably academic way, early in 1997 I assembled a committee of four colleagues to formulate plans for the event, two from the Department of Theology (Wendy Cotter, C.S.J., and myself), and two from the Institute for Pastoral Studies (Camilla Burns, S.N.D., and Peter Gilmour). In view of Bill's life-long preoccupation with the Gospel of Matthew, that seemed an obvious focus for the colloquium. It was also our desire to invite some of the foremost Matthean scholars to present papers and to emphasize the pastoral as well as the academic aspects of the study of Matthew. Eighty participants attended "The Gospel of Matthew in Current Study: A Colloquium in Memory of William G. Thompson, S.J.," which took place on June 12-14, 1998, at the Lake Shore Campus of Loyola University. Earlier versions of the papers assembled in this volume were presented in the order in which they appear here. One segment of the program could not be represented in this volume, and that is the stunning dramatic reading of the Sermon on the Mount by David Rhoads, Professor of New Testament at the Lutheran School of Theology in Chicago. I well remember the 30 minutes of motionless, reflective silence which followed Professor Rhoads's moving presentation and the awkwardness I felt in finally having to formally conclude that session.

A brief biographical sketch of the honoree is appropriate here; Tom Tobin, S.J., contributes additional personal reflections in the first article. After graduating from high school in Detroit, Bill entered the Society of Jesus on July 24, 1948. In 1953 he graduated from Loyola University in Chicago with a B.A., followed by an M.A. in philosophy in 1956. He earned an S.T.L. (Licentiate in Sacred Theology) from West Baden College in West Baden, Indiana, in 1962, and an S.S.L. (Licentiate in Sacred Scripture) from the Pontifical Biblical Institute in Rome in 1965, followed by an S.S.D. (Doctor of Sacred Scripture) in 1969. In 1966 he took final vows in the Society of Jesus. He taught at the Jesuit School of Theology in Chicago from 1967 to its closing in 1981. Bill has been associated with the Institute of Pastoral Studies at Loyola University since 1971, and taught there full time from 1981 until some months before his death on September 24, 1996. He authored several books, including *Matthew's Advice to a Divided Community (Mt 17,22–18,35)* (Rome: Pontifical Biblical Institute, 1970), the published version of his S.S.D. dissertation; *The Gospels for Your Whole Life* (Minneapolis: Winston, 1983); *Paul and His Message for Life's Journey* (New York: Paulist, 1986); *Matthew's Story: Good News for Uncertain Times* (New York: Paulist, 1989); and *Matthew's Jesus* (London: Sheed & Ward, 1989), as well as numerous articles.

I want to thank the institutional sponsors of the Colloquium, for it would not have taken place witihout the generous financial support of the Loyola Jesuit Community, the Chicago Province Jesuit Community, and several divisions of Loyola University, including the Graduate School, the Endowment for the Humanities of the College of Arts and Sciences, the Department of Theology, and the Institute of Pastoral Studies. The Rev. John Piderit, S.J., President of Loyola University, opened the Colloquium with a tribute to Bill Thompson, and a number of colleagues at Loyola graciously chaired the sessions, including Richard Ascough; Camilla Burns, S.N.D.; Wendy Cotter, C.S.J.; Eugene Szarek, C.R.; Franz Josef van Beeck, S.J.; Cam von Wahlde; John White; and Daniel Williams. I also want to express my gratitude to Jim Smith, a Ph.D. student in the Graduate Program of Theology, for helping me successfully surf the thousand-and-one details which attend such projects.

Bill, your ministry continues in the hearts and lives of those you influenced!

DAVID E. AUNE

Abbreviations

AB	Anchor Bible
ABD	*Anchor Bible Dictionary,* ed. David Noel Freedman
AnBib	Analecta Biblica
ANRW	*Aufstieg und Niedergang der römischen Welt*
ATDan	Acta theologica Danica
BASOR	*Bulletin of the American Schools of Oriental Research*
BETL	Bibliotheca ephemeridum theologicarum lovaniensium
BEvT	Beiträge zur evangelischen Theologie
BJRL	*Bulletin of the John Rylands University Library*
BTB	*Biblical Theology Bulletin*
BZNW	Beihefte zur *ZNW*
CAH	*Cambridge Ancient History*
CBQ	*Catholic Biblical Quarterly*
CBQMS	CBQ Monograph Series
CIL	*Corpus inscriptionum latinarum*
ConBNT	Coniectanea biblica, New Testament
EKK	Evangelisch-katholischer Kommentar zum Neuen Testament
EvT	*Evangelische Theologie*
ExpTim	*Expository Times*
FRLANT	Forschungen zur Religion und Literatur des Alten und Neuen Testaments
GRBS	*Greek, Roman, and Byzantine Studies*

HSM	Harvard Semitic Monographs
HTKNT	Herders theologischer Kommentar zum Neuen Testament
ICC	International Critical Commentary
IG	*Inscriptiones graecae*
IGLAM	*Inscriptions grecques et latinae en Asia Mineure,* ed. Philippe LeBas and William Henry Waddington
ILS	*Inscriptiones Latinae selectae*
Int	*Interpretation*
JAAR	*Journal of the American Academy of Religion*
JAC	*Jahrbuch für Antike und Christentum*
JBL	*Journal of Biblical Literature*
JECS	*Journal of Early Christian Studies*
JES	*Journal of Ecumenical Studies*
JRS	*Journal of Roman Studies*
JSNT	*Journal for the Study of the New Testament*
JTS	*Journal of Theological Studies*
KEK	Kritisch-exegetischer Kommentar über das Neue Testament
LEC	Library of Early Christianity
LSAM	*Lois sacrées de l'Asie Mineure,* ed. F. Sokolowski
MM	Moulton and Milligan
NCBC	New Century Bible Commentary
NovT	Novum Testamentum
NTAbh	Neutestamentliche Abhandlungen
NTOA	Novum Testamentum et Orbis Antiquus
NTS	*New Testament Studies*
OGIS	*Orientis Graeci inscriptiones selectae*
RHPR	*Revue d'histoire et de philosophie religieuses*
RNT	Regensburger Neues Testament
SANT	Studien zum Alten und Neuen Testament
SBL	Society of Biblical Literature
SBLASP	SBL Abstracts and Seminar Papers
SBLDS	SBL Dissertation Series
SBS	Stuttgarter Bibelstudien
SIG	*Sylloge inscriptionum graecarum*
SJT	*Scottish Journal of Theology*
SNTSMS	Society for New Testament Studies Monograph Series
Sup	Supplement
TAM	Tituli Asiae Minoris
TDNT	*Theological Dictionary of the New Testament,* ed. G. Kittel– G. Friedrich

TS	*Theological Studies*
TU	Texte und Untersuchungen
WBC	Word Biblical Commentary
WUNT	Wissenschaftliche Untersuchungen zum Neuen Testament
ZNW	*Zeitschrift für die neutestamentliche Wissenschaft*
ZPE	*Zeitschrift für Papyrologie und Epigraphik*
ZTK	*Zeitschrift für Theologie und Kirche*

Ancient writings
Quintilian *Inst. or.* *Institutionis oratoriae*

Inscriptions and Papyri

IDelos	*Inscriptions de Délos,* ed. A. Plassart, et al.
IEphesos	*Die Inschriften von Ephesos,* ed. H. Wankel, et al.
IKios	*Die Inschriften von Kios,* ed. T. Corsten
IPriene	*Die Inschriften von Priene,* ed. F. Hiller von Gaertringen
PLond	*Greek Papyri in the British Museum III,* ed. Frederick E. Kenyon and H. I. Bell
PMich teb	*Michigan Papyri 2: Papyri from Tebtunis I,* ed. A. E. R. Bonk
PParis	*Le papyrus grecs de musée de Louvre*

The Legacy of William G. Thompson, S.J.

THOMAS H. TOBIN, S.J.

Bill Thompson was a man of parts. At six-feet-six he was the center for the University of Detroit High School basketball team in 1947-48. With all due respect to Professor Graham Stanton, Bill would have been hard-pressed to choose between Professor Stanton's paper and the Chicago Bulls basketball game, both of which begin at 8:00 this evening.

Bill also liked to think of himself as contributing to the work of the Second Vatican Council. From 1963 to 1967 he was a student at the Pontifical Biblical Institute in Rome, from which he earned both S.S.L. (1965) and S.S.D. (1969) degrees. Thus his time in Rome overlapped with all the Council sessions under Pope Paul VI. It was during this period that the Council debated what was eventually to become the decree *Dei Verbum*, the Decree on Revelation. The first draft of the decree was awful and was sent back to committee for revision. The professors at the Pontifical Biblical Institute were involved in various ways in the draft's revision and especially in explaining the revised version to groups of bishops. Bill's contribution was to drive professors from the Pontifical Biblical Institute around Rome to brief these groups of bishops on the decree and explain to them how the decree was not a surrender to modernism but rather reflected the best of Catholic biblical thought and was in continuity with Pope Pius XII's 1943 encyclical, *Divino Afflante Spiritu*. Bill liked to explain how, given the habits of Roman drivers, being "wheel-man" in such circumstances was no small contribution to the Council. All of his passengers got to their destinations on time and in one piece.

1

Bill returned from Rome to the United States in the fall of 1967, in the middle of writing his dissertation, to begin teaching scripture to the Jesuit seminarians at the Jesuit School of Theology, which was then in Aurora, Illinois, but which was soon to move to the south side of Chicago near the University of Chicago. The Jesuit students had just run two other scripture professors out of town, and so Bill began this assignment with some trepidation.

I first met Bill that autumn of 1967. I was beginning my philosophy studies as a Jesuit, and several philosophy students who knew Greek were allowed to take Bill's seminar on the Gospel of Matthew. It turned out to be one of the grandest educational experiences of my life. The course was not a required course, and all the students in the class knew Greek and Latin, French and German. Bill was in the process of completing his dissertation on Matthew 18 and so was playing at the top of his game. We first went through Rudolf Bultmann's *History of the Synoptic Tradition* (Oxford: Blackwell, 1963) and then turned to the Gospel of Matthew. What I remember most about the course was its liveliness and intensity. Bill had a tremendous capacity both to push and to encourage us at the same time, to push us to understand in detail how to interpret a New Testament text in its historical and cultural context and to encourage us to see those texts as part of a wider theological and religious world.

Since I was interested in going on in biblical studies, Bill became for me from that time on an example of what it meant to be a scholar, a teacher, a mentor, and above all a friend. Bill taught me New Testament again when I was a theology student from 1970-73 at the Jesuit School of Theology. Most of what I know about New Testament exegesis I learned from Bill, since as graduate students at Harvard we looked at the New Testament only sporadically. During my Harvard studies from 1973-1980, I returned to Chicago almost every summer; and during several summers Bill and I team-taught courses at the Institute of Pastoral Studies here at Loyola. Shortly after I began teaching New Testament in the Theology Department at Loyola, the Jesuit School of Theology in Chicago closed in the summer of 1981, and Bill joined the faculty of the Institute of Pastoral Studies full time. From 1981 until shortly before his death in 1996, he taught at the Institute. Bill and I also lived in the same small Jesuit community here at Loyola, Ignatius House. It is within the context of this friendship of almost 30 years that I want to say something about Bill's legacy both as a scholar and as a teacher.

A large part of Bill's scholarly attention was devoted to the Gospel of Matthew. It is, of course, this particular interest that has sparked this conference. Bill's dissertation, which was published as *Matthew's Advice to a Divided Community (Mt 17,22–18,35)*, was marked by a clear, careful, and nuanced analysis of this section of Matthew's Gospel, both redaction-critically and form-critically. But he also moved the discussion forward by insisting that one needed to look at the passage as a whole, as a Matthean composition, and not only piecemeal in terms of what Matthew may have done with his sources. Bill thought of himself much more as a "composition critic" than as a "redaction critic." He carried this same kind of care and insight into several other articles he published in the early 1970s, especially "Reflections on the Composition of Mt 8:1–9:34" (*CBQ* 33 [1971]: 365-88) and "An Historical Perspective in the Gospel of Matthew" (*JBL* 93 [1974]: 243-62). While Bill later changed his mind about the relationship of the Matthean community to contemporary Judaism, the latter article is still, in many ways, one of the most perceptive I have ever read on how Matthew understood different stages in the history of the Matthean community. During this time Bill was also a pivotal figure in the Matthew Seminar at the Catholic Biblical Association meetings. This seminar was surely one of the most productive in the CBA's history. In addition to Bill, its membership included Jack Dean Kingsbury, Douglas Hare, John Meier, Donald Senior, and Daniel Harrington.

In the second half of the 1970s Bill's interests turned in a somewhat different direction. He became more and more interested, in part as a result of his teaching at the Jesuit School of Theology and at the Institute of Pastoral Studies at Loyola, in the pastoral implications and applications of the study of scripture. This resulted in a number of books: *The Gospels for Your Whole Life* in 1983; *Paul and His Message for Life's Journey* in 1986; and two further books on Matthew: *Matthew's Story: Good News for Uncertain Times* and *Matthew's Jesus*, both published in 1989. Bill saw these books not as less "scholarly" than his previous work but as scholarly in a different way. He liked to think of his work in terms of what Bernard Lonergan referred to as the "functional specialty" of communications, because he took the best of more traditionally "scholarly" work and made it accessible to a wider audience. Bill sometimes found this transition difficult, and he sometimes worried that he had not lived up to his "scholarly" potential in a narrower sense. Although this ambivalence was hard on Bill personally, it was of great benefit to his readers, in that he was careful to keep up with developments in the study of scripture, could critically evaluate them, and communicate them in a non-technical way to a much wider audience.

As a teacher Bill had the capacity to be both challenging and encouraging at the same time. I had the privilege of being both Bill's student and his colleague. In the mid-1970s we team-taught several summer courses at the Institute of Pastoral Studies. Bill approached teaching with the same intensity he approached everything else; and when you are six-feet-six, that is very intense. He had the capacity to combine clarity of presentation with the capacity to challenge students to take seriously issues in the interpretation of scripture in ways they would not have done otherwise. Whatever else they did in his classes, they engaged the text. Bill relished what he called "clear points of disagreement." Because he did this in a way that took students' thoughts on issues seriously, he also enkindled in them their own critical and creative abilities. I and others learned a great deal about teaching from Bill, or, in my case, as much as a true introvert could learn from a real extrovert.

I should like to conclude with two other reflections. The first has to do with the way Bill saw himself. He saw himself first and foremost as a Jesuit, as a member of the Society of Jesus. He saw all of the various activities he was involved in, whether as a scholar or teacher or whatever, as part of the broader work of the Society of Jesus. As most of you know, the history of the Jesuits is both colorful and checkered. But I think Bill represented and sought to represent the work of the Society of Jesus at its best — intense, intellectually serious, open to dialogue and the differences that dialogue brings to the surface.

Bill both lived and died as a Jesuit. And this brings me to my final reflection. Several years before Bill's death in 1996, he was diagnosed with non-Hodgkin's lymphoma of the liver. He underwent several kinds of chemotherapy, the first of which seemed to work. But the cancer returned, and the subsequent chemotherapy did not work. Through most of it, Bill continued to teach and was always interested in what other people were doing. Although sometimes depressed and often exhausted by the therapy, he always remained convinced that his life and even what he was experiencing in his sickness, what Teilhard de Chardin called the "passivities of diminishment," was still part of God's overarching love for him.

His life was marked by both the love of God and the desire for learning. I'm sure that he would be pleased with this conference, not primarily because it is a colloquium in his memory but because it is an opportunity to explore those "clear points of disagreement" he so relished over the years.

Directions in Matthean Studies

DONALD SENIOR, C.P.

My task is to offer an overview of Matthean studies in recent years and to chart some possible directions for the future. In many ways, William Thompson's own life of scholarship spanned a significant period in Matthean studies. His doctoral dissertation, *Matthew's Advice to a Divided Community*, appeared in 1970 just as redactional studies of Matthew were beginning to blossom, inspired by the groundbreaking work of German scholars such as Bornkamm, Barth, and Held, among others.[1] Redactional critical studies would dominate Matthean scholarship for the next 20 years — and in most instances still do.[2] My first close acquaintance with Bill Thompson and his exuberant scholarship came at the Catholic Biblical Association's meetings in the mid- to late 1970s. The Matthew Task Force that developed there managed to attract several young scholars whose work would have significant influence on interpretation of the Gospel:

1. See Günther Bornkamm, Gerhard Barth, and Heinz-Joachim Held, *Tradition and Interpretation in Matthew* (Philadelphia: Westminster, 1963).

2. See the essay of Graham N. Stanton, "Introduction: Matthew's Gospel: A New Storm Centre," in *The Interpretation of Matthew*, 2nd ed. (Edinburgh: T. & T. Clark, 1995), 1-18; and the introduction to *A Gospel for a New People: Studies in Matthew* (Louisville: Westminster John Knox, 1992), 1-49; also David R. Bauer and Mark Allan Powell in the introduction to *Treasures New and Old: Recent Contributions to Matthean Studies.* SBL Symposium Series 1 (Atlanta: Scholars, 1996), 1-26; and Donald Senior, *What Are They Saying about Matthew?* rev. ed. (New York: Paulist, 1996).

Lamar Cope, Douglas Hare, Daniel Harrington, Jack Dean Kingsbury, John Meier, and James Reese — to name a few. All of us had completed our dissertations at about the same time and were able to bring that enthusiasm to our yearly meetings. For me it was one of the most satisfying educational experiences of my life and left a lasting imprint not only about the depth and richness of this Gospel, but also about the quality of those who were devoted to studying it.

Thompson's insistence on "composition criticism," with its attention to the narrative structure of the Gospel, anticipated the current growing emphasis on literary critical methodologies such as reader response criticism and narrative criticism, approaches that have played a major role in the past decade of biblical studies. While the assumptions of literary criticism, especially in its more ideological forms, about auctorial intent and the possibility of access to the historical context through the narrative are decisively different from those of historical criticism, nevertheless the attention given to literary and narrative structures of the Gospel by Thompson and other redaction critics paved the way for later methodological developments.

Thompson's work as a Matthean scholar roughly coincides with that of the eminent British scholar W. D. Davies. Davies' monumental work, *The Setting of the Sermon on the Mount,* appeared in 1964 while Bill was working on his dissertation, and he employed Davies' hypothesis about the context of Matthew in his own thesis.[3] The summit of Davies' own extraordinary scholarly career is likely to be the three-volume commentary on Matthew, co-authored with Dale C. Allison, Jr., in the International Critical Commentary Series.[4] The first volume was published in 1988 and the final volume appeared in 1997.

Davies and Allison note in the preface to their first volume that there was a dearth of major commentaries on Matthew as they began their task in the mid-1980s. But they also predicted that the mushrooming number of studies on Matthew at that time foreshadowed a "renaissance" in Matthean scholarship. In the preface to their concluding volume, written a

---

3. See William G. Thompson, *Matthew's Advice to a Divided Community (Mt 17,22–18,35).* AnBib 44 (Rome: Pontifical Biblical Institute, 1970); W. D. Davies, *The Setting of the Sermon on the Mount* (Cambridge: Cambridge University Press, 1964; repr. Atlanta: Scholars, 1989).

4. W. D. Davies and Dale C. Allison, Jr., *A Critical and Exegetical Commentary on the Gospel According to Saint Matthew.* ICC (Edinburgh: T. & T. Clark; 1: 1988; 2: 1991; 3: 1997).

decade later, Davies and Allison could note that indeed the renaissance had come. If major commentaries are a barometer for the vitality of scholarship and the need to consolidate some of it, then there truly has been a renaissance. One could cite English-language works such as the excellent commentaries of Eugene Boring, Robert Gundry, Donald Hagner, Daniel Harrington, and Augustine Stock, and on the continent, the superb works of Joachim Gnilka, Ulrich Luz, Alexander Sand, and others.[5]

Few commentaries, even in this distinguished list, can match the size and scope of Davies' and Allison's work. In reading the "retrospect" at the end of their third volume, it struck me that this might be a helpful starting point for our colloquium, a way of culling some major gains from recent decades of Matthean scholarship — even though admittedly from one vantage point and one classic methodology. At the same time, on the basis of their "retrospect," we could hazard a "prospectus" or some suggestions about future directions for the sake of discussion in this colloquium.

Retrospect

Davies and Allison organize their retrospect under five major headings. I will summarize each of them and offer some assessment.

Matthew's Jewish Setting

Perhaps no issue has been more dominant in the past decade of Matthean studies than this: the relationship of Matthew's Gospel to 1st-century Pal-

---

5. M. Eugene Boring, "The Gospel of Matthew," *The New Interpreter's Bible* 8 (Nashville: Abingdon, 1995): 87-505; Donald A. Hagner, *Matthew 1–13*. WBC 33A (Waco: Word, 1993); *Matthew 14–28*. WBC 33B (Waco: Word, 1995); Daniel J. Harrington, *The Gospel of Matthew*. Sacra Pagina 1 (Collegeville: Liturgical, 1991); Augustine Stock, *The Method and Message of Matthew* (Collegeville: Liturgical, 1994); Joachim Gnilka, *Das Matthäusevangelium*. HTKNT (Freiburg: Herder, 1988); Ulrich Luz, *Matthew 1–7*. Continental Commentary (Minneapolis: Augsburg, 1989; the German original in the EKK series continues through vol. 2, including chs. 8–17, but has not yet been translated into English); Alexander Sand, *Das Evangelium nach Matthäus*. RNT (Regensburg: Pustet, 1986). My own contribution to this list is Donald Senior, *Matthew*. Abingdon New Testament Commentaries (Nashville: Abingdon, 1998).

estinian Judaism. And while remaining an area of sharp debate, this is an issue in Matthean scholarship where there have been measurable gains.

Davies' and Allison's commentary holds a refined view of the hypothesis first asserted by Davies in his magisterial work more than 30 years ago. Matthew's Gospel was written in direct response to the situation created by the aftermath of the Jewish Revolt of A.D 66-70 and the subsequent emergence of Pharisaic Judaism as the dominant force within the Palestinian Judaism of this period. The experience of discontinuity created by the revolt and its brutal Roman suppression, climaxing with the destruction of the temple and Jerusalem, as well as the seduction posed by such divergent groups as pagans, Jewish apocalyptics, and Jewish Christians in the chaotic period following the war, led to a consolidating movement on the part of the Pharisaic leadership. The Pharisees strove for greater unity among themselves, began a collection of oral laws, gave normative force to certain defining practices, and attacked the legitimacy of deviant groups within the community. Davies admits that he may have given an overemphasis to the so-called council of Jamnia, as many subsequent critics have noted, but he still holds to the importance of the Pharisaic reform as an immediate and direct context for Matthew's Gospel.

Matthew's community was probably a "group of house churches," probably located in Antioch of Syria, perhaps fairly prosperous and urban, possibly associated with a group of teachers, mainly Jewish in make-up but remaining in contact with local Gentile Christian groups. The Matthean community was, in Davies' and Allison's view, unable to "leave" Judaism. Similar to the thesis of Anthony J. Saldarini but without fully adopting his sociological categories, Davies and Allison believe that Matthew's community was a "deviant" Christian Jewish group. Matthew's Christians were, in a sense, torn in two directions. While they remained psychologically and spiritually "within Judaism," there is evidence of some differentiation from the rest of Judaism taking place. Matthew's use of the term "their synagogues" (Matt. 4:23; 9:35; 10:17; 13:54; 23:34 ["your"]), his negative view of the term "rabbi" (23:8; see also 26:25, 49), his incessant critique of the Jewish leaders (see, especially, the discourse of ch. 23), his severe sanctions on internal dissent (18:15-17), and above all, his overwhelming emphasis on the legitimacy of belief in Jesus and his messianic authority — all these factors set in place a distinctive identity within a broader Jewish context.

But even with such idiosyncrasies, Matthew emulates the "dominant" or "parent" group. Note, for example, the prominent role given to scribes and wise men within the community, the emphasis on righteous-ness, the commitment to proselytizing in the manner of the Pharisees, and the evidence of rudimentary organizational structures.

Davies and Allison suggest that the Pharisees faced four key ques-tions in this critical post-war period:

1. Without state or temple, what is the identity of the people of God? For the Pharisees that identity had to be built on renewed obedience to the Torah.
2. What is Torah? For the Pharisaic movement, the answer was the cen-trality of the written Torah as interpreted according to Hillel.
3. What is the relation of Jew and Gentile? For the Pharisees, the proper course was increased isolation from and rejection of Gentile ways.
4. What should one think of the Messiah and eschatology? The Phari-saic response: the Messiah had not come and apocalyptic enthusiasm was to be dampened.

Matthew's community, too, had to deal with the same types of ques-tions, but in each instance, Matthew's response would be christological in emphasis. The story and teaching of Jesus became the medium for an un-derstanding of and obedience to the Torah. While Matthew retained strong roots in Judaism, he sought reconciliation between Jew and Gentile within the community. Matthew, Davies and Allison believe, remains si-lent on Paul the champion of Gentile Christianity while the figure of Peter emerges in the Gospel as a model of reconciling leadership within the community. Finally, belief in Jesus as the Messiah gives the Gospel a strong eschatological dimension.

The past 30 years of Matthean scholarship have seen a wide range of views about the relationship of Matthew's Gospel to formative Judaism. For example, John Meier, following a tradition proposed long ago by Poul Nepper-Christensen, continues to espouse the view that the author of Matthew's Gospel in fact was a Gentile, citing what he considers erroneous or uninformed views on Matthew's part about Jewish practice and belief.[6]

---

6. Poul Nepper-Christensen, *Das Matthaüsevangelium: Ein judenchristliches Evangelium?* ATDan 1 (Aarhus: Universitetsforlaget, 1958); John P. Meier, *Matthew.* New Testament Message 3 (Wilmington: Michael Glazier, 1981); "Matthew, Gospel of," *ABD* 4:622-41.

Somewhat less radical, yet believing that Matthew has made a definitive break with Judaism, are such authors as David E. Garland, Douglas Hare, Ulrich Luz, Graham N. Stanton, and Georg Strecker.[7] Donald A. Hagner attempts a mediating view, situating Matthew's community in a kind of "no man's land" between Rabbinic Judaism and Gentile Christianity, although he speaks of Matthew's Jewish Christians being aware that they had "broken with their unbelieving brothers and sisters."[8] Yet the Davies-Allison perspective has a growing number of allies, such as Daniel Harrington, J. Andrew Overman, and perhaps most emphatically, Anthony J. Saldarini.[9]

A question underlying this debate is one raised by literary criticism. To what extent can one deduce specific knowledge about the circumstances of the author and his audience from the contours of a narrative? Does, for example, the Gospel's emphasis on the negative role of the Pharisees in its story of Jesus tell us anything at all about the relationship of Matthew's community to Pharisaic Judaism? Both literary criticism and historical criticism are becoming more self-critical about their differing assumptions on this question. If I can admit a bit of prejudice, I believe that literary texts do have the capacity to provide, if not a window on the world behind the text, then at least a translucent screen through which we can see some defined characters.

In addition, supposing that one can deduce some of the circumstances of the Matthean community from leads in the Gospel text, more critical reflection is still needed on other assumptions of our debate. For example, what does a "break with Judaism" mean in the context of the 1st century? Or conversely, what constituted "belonging" for Jewish communities in the region of Syria, the probable location of Matthew's commu-

7. See David E. Garland, *The Intention of Matthew 23*. NovTSup 52 (Leiden: Brill, 1979); Douglas R. A. Hare, *The Theme of Jewish Persecution of Christians in the Gospel According to St. Matthew*. SNTSMS 6 (Cambridge: Cambridge University Press, 1967); Luz, *Matthew 1–7; The Theology of the Gospel of Matthew*. New Testament Theology (Cambridge: Cambridge University Press, 1995); Stanton, *A Gospel for a New People*; Georg Strecker, *Der Weg der Gerechtigkeit: Untersuchung zur Theologie des Matthäus*, 3rd ed. (Göttingen: Vandenhoeck & Ruprecht, 1971).

8. Hagner, *Matthew 1–13*, lxv-lxxi.

9. Harrington, *The Gospel of Matthew*; J. Andrew Overman, *Matthew's Gospel and Formative Judaism* (Minneapolis: Fortress, 1990); *Church and Community in Crisis: The Gospel According to Matthew* (Valley Forge: Trinity, 1996); Anthony J. Saldarini, *Matthew's Christian-Jewish Community* (Chicago: University of Chicago Press, 1994).

nity? These questions are not easily answered, particularly when we are dealing with a turbulent period in Jewish and Christian history and with traditions that often used conflictual and even violent rhetoric to denounce rival factions.

Despite apparent differences, Matthean scholarship is not in full disarray here. First of all, the level of discussion about 1st-century Judaism has greatly matured over the past quarter century, and this is evident in the debate of the scholars mentioned above. Christian scholars generally recognize that Second Temple Judaism was not monolithic and hesitate to take Gospel characterizations of the Jewish leadership and Jewish practices at face value — while nevertheless recognizing that the Gospels are prime sources for our knowledge of Palestinian Judaism of this period. There is also increasing attention to archaeological data and its implications for our understanding of conditions in 1st-century Palestinian Judaism and the social world in which Matthew's Gospel was composed.[10]

Also, the scholarly instinct to differentiate one's views from others can mask converging similarities on some disputed points. For example, virtually every commentator on Matthew will affirm that this Gospel has strong roots in Judaism and is concerned with issues of traditional importance to Judaism, such as the authority of the scriptures, the interpretation of Torah, obedience to God's will, and the destiny of God's people. Can one call a community "Jewish" that appeals to Jewish history, uses Jewish language, Jewish symbols, and Jewish tradition, and may even be organized along Jewish traditional structures — even if that community has a core belief so idiosyncratic that it is strange or abhorrent to the rest of the Jewish community? The debates going on in contemporary Judaism — or contemporary Catholicism, for that matter — offer some intriguing insight into how complex this question can be, and suggest that the views of the dominant group about identity do not always coincide with the self-identity of deviant groups.

Similarly, all would agree that faith in Jesus as the Messiah and authoritative interpreter of the law, as one uniquely endowed with God's authority and as one risen from the dead, is the fundamental basis for tension between Matthew's community and other contemporary Jewish groups. And even if Matthew's community did not yet think of itself as distinct

---

10. E.g., David L. Balch, ed., *Social History of the Matthean Community* (Minneapolis: Fortress, 1991).

from Judaism, its belief in Jesus as Messiah and Son of God would ultimately be the ground for the distinct religious identity of that community. Add to these religious perspectives the cultural and social impact of an increasing Gentile membership in the Hellenistic Jewish community of Matthew — a membership ultimately sanctioned by the community's interpretation of Jesus' teaching and mission — and one has in hand the ingredients for an eventual parting of the ways.[11]

This broader framework tempers the divergent views of most scholars about Matthew's relationship to Judaism. Luz may argue that the break with Judaism is past history and that Matthew's interest is christological, yet the christological categories of Matthew and the issues addressed in Jesus' teaching and ministry are still thoroughly Jewish in tone and content. Saldarini, on the other hand, may view Matthew's community as a Christian Jewish deviant group completely within Judaism, but he must also concede that the authority and status given to Jesus by Matthew's Gospel has no precedent or analogy in any other known Jewish group of the period. And Overman and Saldarini also concede that if Matthew's community is still within the orbit of Judaism when the Gospel is written, the break with Judaism and entry into "the mainstream of the non-Jewish, second-century Christian church [would come] soon after it was written."[12]

Theology and Salvation History

Davies and Allison characterize Matthew as a "pastoral theologian" rather than a systematic thinker.[13] Given the fact that Matthew wrote a narrative and not a theological treatise, this seems to be an obvious point. Along with the majority of Matthean scholars, Davies and Allison accept the two-source theory as a working hypothesis. While some attempts to reaffirm Matthean priority are still made and some studies continue to assert that

11. I have found particularly helpful on this point the work of James D. G. Dunn, *The Parting of the Ways: Between Christianity and Judaism and Their Significance for the Character of Christianity* (Philadephia: Trinity, 1991); also Stephen G. Wilson, *Related Strangers: Jews and Christians 70-170 C.E.* (Minneapolis: Fortress, 1995).

12. Saldarini, 113.

13. See similarly, Mark Allan Powell, *God With Us: A Pastoral Theology of Matthew's Gospel* (Minneapolis: Fortress, 1995).

behind the Greek Matthew stands an original Hebrew or Aramaic version, most scholars believe Matthew drew on Mark as his principal source, along with Q and some special Matthean traditions which may represent a distinct source or constitute evidence of Matthew's own literary creativity.[14]

Davies' and Allison's interest in the question of Matthew's sources is more theological than historical. Matthew should be viewed as a creative yet faithful interpreter of the tradition available to him. His intent was not to innovate as much as to retell the founding story of the community "with commentary" (3:705). Parenthetically, we might ask if Matthew intended to supplement Mark's Gospel or supplant it altogether.[15] Yet Matthew does have some characteristic theological interests; among these would be the emphasis on obedience to God's will and some attempt to schematize history, with Jesus as the pivotal figure. Earlier studies had attempted to chart the precise demarcations in Matthew's view of "salvation history." Rolf Walker and Georg Strecker had proposed, with some variations between them, that Matthew envisaged a three-stage view of salvation history, with an initial period from Abraham to the Messiah, then the period of Jesus the Messiah, and finally a projected period for the life of the Church until the consummation of the world.[16] Kingsbury, however, detected a two-stage period, that of Israel leading up to the birth of the Messiah, and then a second period that enveloped not only the earthly ministry of Jesus but continued into the ongoing life of the Church since in Matthew's perspective the Risen Christ abides with the community until the end of time.[17]

These attempts to chart Matthew's theology of history have not

---

14. For a state of the question on the source issues, see Senior, *What Are They Saying about Matthew?* 21-37.

15. In discussing the emergence of the fourfold canonical Gospels, Graham N. Stanton speculates that Matthew actually intended to replace Mark's version with his own fuller account; see "The Fourfold Gospel," *NTS* 43 (1997): 317-46.

16. See Rolf Walker, *Die Heilsgeschichte im ersten Evangelium.* FRLANT 91 (Göttingen: Vandenhoeck & Ruprecht, 1967); Georg Strecker, "Das Geschichtsverständnis des Matthäus," *EvT* 26 (1966): 57-74; trans. "The Concept of History in Matthew," *JAAR* 35 (1967): 219-30.

17. Jack Dean Kingsbury, *Matthew: Structure, Christology, Kingdom* (Philadelphia: Fortress, 1975), 1-39. John Meier added to the discussion by noting that within the lifetime of Jesus as presented by Matthew, the moment of the death and resurrection is an apocalyptic demarcation signaling the beginning of a new age; see John Meier, "Salvation-History in Matthew: In Search of a Starting Point," *CBQ* 37 (1975): 203-15.

proven decisive, however, and scholarly interest in them seems to have waned. As Davies and Allison suggest, one reason may be the ongoing reassessment of Matthew's relationship with Judaism. If Matthew's community continued to see itself as authentically Jewish, what implications does this have for a schematized theology of history, particularly one that presumes a self-conscious parting of the ways with Israel? And perhaps another theological issue is also at work to complicate this question: the messianic status attributed to Jesus by Matthew's community may have defied all attempts to schematize history.

Literary Genre and Moral Instruction

Attempts to identify the genre of Matthew's Gospel have been part of a larger discussion in New Testament studies. Davies and Allison suggest that Matthew's Gospel is a mix of genres. It is orderly and has biographical characteristics without strictly qualifying it as a "biography" according to the canons of ancient Hellenistic literature.

However, here too the underlying interest of Davies and Allison is in the ultimate theological significance of Matthew's literary characteristics. Matthew's choice of the narrative and quasi-biographical form is ultimately related to his "christocentric" focus as distinct from what Davies and Allison call a "theocentric" approach found in Qumran and Rabbinic literature.

Matthew's characteristic insistence on linking words and deeds — the ultimate principle that, in their view, underlies the overall structure of the Gospel — has deep roots in Jewish tradition, even while perhaps reflecting some similar traits in Hellenistic literature.[18] In Jewish tradition specific teaching is linked with a specific person, such as the Pentateuch with Moses or sayings with Rabbis. In the context of this tradition, Jesus' words required "biography."

The social context of Matthew's community also fueled his decision to write a "biography" of Jesus rather than a summation of his teaching.

---

18. Dale C. Allison, "Matthew: Structure, Biographical Impulse and the *Imitatio Christi*," in *The Four Gospels, 1992*, ed. Frans van Segbroeck et al. BETL 100 (Leuven: Leuven University Press, 1992), 1203-21. For a thorough discussion of the structure of Matthew, see David R. Bauer, *The Structure of Matthew's Gospel*. JSNTSup 31 (Sheffield: Almond, 1989).

The issues of identity, authority, and legitimacy acutely raised by the debate with Pharisaic Judaism in the chaos of the times led Matthew to focus on Jesus as a model to be emulated. Jesus was the model of authentic righteousness as well as its teacher. At the conclusion of the Gospel the Risen Christ would commission his disciples to teach and do everything that he commanded. Here Davies and Allison are allied with the view of Luz, who emphasizes the profound christological focus of Matthew's Gospel. Jesus, as Luz notes, is both the *Urbild* and the *Vorbild* of the Christian community.[19] Matthew's negative portrayal of Jesus' opponents as "hypocrites," as those who teach but do not act, is the flip side of this portrayal of Jesus as authoritative teacher and model of righteousness. As Davies and Allison note, "hypocrisy is the homage that vice renders to virtue."

It should be noted that the more traditional redactional, historical, and theological interests of Davies and Allison tend to discount the important gains concerning Matthew's narrative strategies that have come from literary critical approaches. For example, the work of David B. Howell on the narrative rhetoric of Matthew (which is not cited in their commentary although it appeared in time for the third volume) traces the "emplotment" of Matthew's story, including its notion of salvation history and the relationship of word and action, and relates it cogently to the overall strategy of the Gospel to "include" the world of future readers into the world of the text.[20] Janice Capel Anderson has also attended to the narrative structure of the Gospel, noting how the segments of the story are woven together through Matthew's characteristic literary techniques, particularly that of verbal and thematic repetitions.[21] More bridges should be built between literary critical approaches of this nature and the classic approaches represented by Davies and Allison.

Messianism and Christology

Davies and Allison affirm what is surely a strong consensus of virtually all modern interpreters of Matthew: the conviction that Jesus is the Messiah is

---

19. See Luz, *Matthew 1–7*, 44; also *The Theology of the Gospel of Matthew*, esp. 142-59; and *Matthew in History* (Minneapolis: Fortress, 1994), 48-49.

20. David B. Howell, *Matthew's Inclusive Story: A Study in the Narrative Rhetoric of the First Gospel*. JSNTSup 42 (Sheffield: Sheffield Academic, 1990).

the conceptual foundation of Matthew's Gospel and explains much of the Gospel's characteristic content. The liberal use of the Old Testament and fulfillment quotations, the profusion of traditional titles applied to Jesus, the emphasis on his miracles, and the dominant role of the Sermon on the Mount within the structure and theology of Matthew — all are based on Matthew's overriding belief that Jesus is the Messiah and Son of God. It is important to note, however, that the Matthean Jesus redefines and enlarges traditional messianic expectations. For example, the title "Son of God" as applied to Jesus by Matthew, particularly when used in confessional contexts such as 14:33 or 27:54, transcends the bounds of traditional royal messianism. A similar case can be made for Matthew's use of the "Son of David" title which is connected in a particular way to Jesus' mission as healer.[22] Likewise, the notion of the Risen Christ's continuing presence as Emmanuel within the community also pushes beyond the limits of messianism and in the direction of full-blown christology. For Matthew, Davies and Allison assert, christology is more fundamental than messianism (3:719).

The co-authors of this monumental commentary also make another key point: assessing Matthew's christology on the basis of titles alone is inadequate.[23] The healing stories, the use of Moses typology, the profound role given to Jesus as teacher and interpreter of the law, and the defining experience of death and resurrection are essential features of the Gospel in portraying the identity of Jesus. Here again, one senses a maturing of the discussion in the past two decades, leading away from the attempt to feature a single title such as Son of God or Son of Man as the key to Matthew's christology. Instead, one should view the whole narrative and its impact on the reader as the medium for communicating Matthew's theology.[24] Re-

21. Janice Capel Anderson, *Matthew's Narrative Web: Over, and Over, and Over Again*. JSNTSup 91 (Sheffield: JSOT, 1994).

22. See the discussion in Stanton, *A Gospel for a New People*, 180-85; and Donald Senior, *The Gospel of Matthew*. Interpreting Biblical Texts (Nashville: Abingdon, 1997), 56-57.

23. Senior, *The Gospel of Matthew*, 58-62.

24. Kingsbury and Meier had debated whether "Son of God" or "Son of Man" should be seen as the fundamental title for Jesus in Matthew's Gospel. See, e.g., the discussion in Kingsbury, *Matthew*, esp. 40-127; also Jack Dean Kingsbury, *Jesus Christ in Matthew, Mark, and Luke*. Proclamation (Philadelphia: Fortress, 1981), 64-73; John Meier, *The Vision of Matthew: Christ, Church and Morality in the First Gospel*. Theological Inquiries (New York: Paulist, 1979), 210-19.

lated to this has been the fruitful debate triggered by Hans Dieter Betz through his monumental commentary on the Sermon on the Mount.[25] Betz's assertion that the Sermon is not fully digested within the narrative theology of Matthew's Gospel as a whole has, I believe, led to a more thoughtful conversation about the fundamental currents running through Matthew's narrative that link Jesus' role as teacher with the other dimensions of his christology and about how traditional and innovative currents are held together in Matthew's perspective.[26]

Parenthetically, I believe the guild of Matthean scholars also owes a debt of gratitude to the commentary of Davies and Allison — as well as that of Luz and others who do not hesitate to tackle the theological dimensions of the Gospel while giving proper attention to issues of social context and literary character. This is particularly important for the ongoing debate about the identity of the Matthean community, including its relationship to Judaism and the Hellenistic world, as well as attempts to decipher its structure and narrative strategies. Many of these important issues are rooted ultimately in Matthew's christological perspective. Attempting to decipher Matthew's literary and rhetorical strategies without fully engaging the Gospel's theological convictions will lead interpreters in the wrong direction.

Matthew's Place in Early Christianity

The final point in Davies' and Allison's retrospect is most interesting and provides a jump-off point for directions for the future. Matthew, they note, was a "centrist," drawing his theological perspective from both Judaism and the early Christian community. He was not an innovator but a "tradent" or a *tanna*, a "repeater." His urgent pastoral concern was "that the Jewish tradition would be lost in a church inexorably becoming Gentile" (3:722). Much of the characteristic content of Matthew's Gospel is di-

---

25. Hans Dieter Betz, *The Sermon on the Mount*. Hermeneia (Minneapolis: Fortress, 1995).

26. Here too, narrative critical studies can play a substantial and complementary role in how the Sermon on the Mount meshes not only with Matthew's theological perspective but is also integral to the narrative structure of the Gospel as a whole. See, e.g., Janice Capel Anderson, "Matthew: Sermon and Story," in Bauer and Powell, eds., *Treasures New and Old*, 233-50.

rected to this concern: for example, its frequent citation of scripture, including the fulfillment quotations; its evocation of Moses and other typological events from Jewish history; its concern to present Jesus as fulfilling — not destroying — the law, both in his teaching and in his actions. Matthew wanted to preserve his patrimony and to "inextricably (bind) the story of Jesus and therefore all Christians to Judaism" (3:723). This attempt to hold on to the heart of the old while opening the community to the dynamic realities of the new may be reflected in the famous saying of 13:52: the scribe trained for the kingdom of heaven is like "the head of the household who brings out of his treasure what is new and what is old."[27]

If indeed Matthew's ultimate goal was the realization of an ecumenical vision uniting Jewish and Gentile Christians in one community, then he tragically failed. By the turn of the century, Jewish Christian and Gentile Christian communities would be going their separate ways and, ultimately, Christianity would become a Gentile religion. By the time of Ignatius of Antioch, Davies and Allison note, we find an influential Christian writer whose views are far different from Matthew on this score, even though he may be writing for the same region in which Matthew's Gospel was composed. Ignatius thinks of Christianity and Judaism as opposites and hardly alludes to the Old Testament.[28]

The trajectory of Matthew's own brand of Jewish Christianity, Davies and Allison suggest, may have developed into the sect of the Nazoraeans mentioned by Jerome and later by Epiphanius. This Jewish Christian group apparently maintained a high christology and did not demand that Gentile Christians observe all the requirements of the law — qualities not unlike the perspective of Matthew. Perhaps, suggest our commentators, the enigmatic reference to *Nazōraios* in 2:23 may be an indication that the members of Matthew's own community referred to themselves as "Nazoreans," a tradition that would endure in later forms of Jewish Christianity.

Davies' and Allison's final comment on this matter is worth quoting more fully:

27. See the comments of Andries G. van Aarde, *God-With-Us: The Dominant Perspective in Matthew's Story.* Hervormde Teologiese Studies Sup 5 (Pretoria: University of Pretoria Press, 1994), esp. 127-41.

28. See William R. Schoedel, "Ignatius and the Reception of the Gospel of Matthew in Antioch," in Balch, *Social History of the Matthean Community,* 129-77.

. . . the tragedy is that the sort of Christianity, so richly Jewish, that we find in Matthew, and which apparently lived on in the Nazoraeans, did not flourish much past Matthew's time. In the century after Matthew Christianity became a primarily Gentile religion, and Jewish Christians became marginalized. That the Church Fathers are so often confused in their comments about Jewish Christianity shows how far from it most of them were. In one sense, then, our Gospel, as we interpret it, is a monument to a failed hope: its ecumenical goal, the unity of Jewish and Gentile Christian, was not achieved. It is true that in another sense Matthew did not altogether fail, for his Gospel became the favourite among both Jewish- and Gentile-Christian communities. In this circumstance, however, one doubts that the evangelist would have found much consolation. For the Jewish- and Gentile-Christian streams did not long course together: they soon flowed on as divided currents until one of them sadly ceased to be. (3:727)

Davies' and Allison's observations on this score are important for understanding Matthew's Gospel and represent, I believe, an important vantage point for future directions in Matthean scholarship. Matthew's concern about the character of emerging Christianity is another essential dimension of the Gospel alongside its concern for its relationship to formative Judaism. Some time ago Reinhart Hummel described Matthew's Gospel as waging a struggle on "two fronts" — one its relationship to Pharisaic Judaism and the other to antinomian Gentile Christianity.[29] The perspective described by Davies and Allison is an important refinement of Hummel's perspective. Matthew's struggle was not with some kind of antinomian or so-called Pauline Christianity but in a more fundamental way with a form of Christianity that would lose all contact with its Jewish origins and result in Christian communities that were either all Jewish or all Gentile. Matthew's vision was that of an assembly or church in which both Jew and Gentile would flourish together.[30]

This represents a near reversal of perspective for many traditional interpretations of Matthew. The mission thrust of Matthew, for example,

---

29. Reinhart Hummel, *Die Auseinandersetzung zwischen Kirche und Judentum im Matthäusevangelium.* BEvT 33 (Munich: Kaiser, 1963).

30. I have attempted to develop this view of Matthew's Gospel in my 1998 presidential address to the Catholic Biblical Association of America, entitled "Between Two Worlds: Gentiles and Jewish Christians in Matthew's Gospel," *CBQ* 61 (1999): 1-23.

was not that of a definitive rejection of Judaism in favor of a wholehearted Gentile mission — a turn from the lost sheep of the house of Israel to all the nations. Matthew, as some recent interpreters have noted, may have had some ambivalence about the mission to the Gentiles, realizing what the consequences would be if the Jewish roots of Jesus and his teaching were overwhelmed and lost by the success of the mission. Perhaps this is precisely the reluctance on display in Jesus' encounter with the Canaanite woman in 15:21-28 where he rigorously asserts an "Israel first" theology and cedes to the woman's request because of her unrelenting faith.

And even though Matthew's Gospel would ultimately be absorbed by Gentile Christianity and be used as an essential instrument of its teaching, Matthew and his community did not experience themselves as dominant or secure. In fact, Matthew and his community may have viewed themselves as thoroughly marginal — marginal in relationship to the rest of Judaism and marginal in the face of a Church that was becoming increasingly and inevitably Gentile in character.

This underlying "marginal" character of Matthew's Gospel has been observed in a number of ways by some of the most innovative recent studies of the First Gospel, including some by participants at this conference. Dennis Duling has characterized Matthew as a "marginal gospel."[31] Amy-Jill Levine's study of the mission discourse challenged the tendency to view Matthew's perspective on the Gentile mission as an evolutionary movement from unresponsive Jews to responsive Gentiles.[32] Rather, she suggests, the challenge for both Jew and Gentile was to respond to the teaching of Jesus in righteousness, a challenge accepted by the socially marginal — both Jew and Gentile — in contrast to the static elites. Similarly, a series of studies from a feminist perspective by Elaine M. Wainwright and others finds inclusive dynamics deep within the literary and theological currents of Matthew's Gospel.[33] Beginning with a study of discipleship in Matthew, Warren Carter has proposed to study Matthew's entire Gospel precisely under the rubric of marginality, taking his cue from Matthew's enticing concerns with "marginal" characters such as the women of the genealogy,

31. Dennis C. Duling, "Matthew and Marginality," *SBL 1993 Seminar Papers* (Atlanta: Scholars, 1993), 642-71.
32. Amy-Jill Levine, *The Social and Ethnic Dimensions of Matthean Salvation History.* Studies in the Bible and Early Christianity 14 (Lewiston: Edwin Mellen, 1988).
33. See Elaine M. Wainwright, *Shall We Look for Another? A Feminist Rereading of the Matthean Jesus* (Maryknoll: Orbis, 1998).

the Magi, the centurion, the crowds of the sick and disabled, the Canaanite woman, and the least members of the community.[34]

This vantage point, I believe, will prove to be a creative stimulant to future studies of Matthew, whether from a social-cultural, literary, or theological perspective.

Conclusion

The past three decades of Matthean scholarship have been productive and fruitful. There have been important gains in the way the social and religious context of Matthew is understood. The framing of the question about Matthew's relationship to formative Judaism is far more nuanced and informed than it was a generation ago. Similarly, a multitude of excellent studies on particular features of the Gospel have added new depth to the discussion about the literary structure of the Gospel, Matthew's view of salvation history, his incorporation of tradition, and his christology.[35] Finally, the fundamental shift from viewing Matthew as representing the triumph of Gentile Christianity to a community standing precariously astride shifting ground, a community finding itself pushed further to the margin by both formative Judaism and emerging Gentile Christianity, may offer a more profound and provocative perspective for future interpretation of this great Christian text and, indeed, highlight its uncanny relevance for our times.

34. Warren Carter, "Matthew 4:18-22 and Matthean Discipleship: An Audience-Oriented Perspective," *CBQ* 59 (1997): 58-75.

35. Surveys of recent literature can be found in Senior, *What Are They Saying about Matthew?* and Stanton, *A Gospel for a New People*, esp. 1-49.

Matthew's Advice to a Divided Readership

AMY-JILL LEVINE

Interpretation of the Gospel of Matthew has given birth to two sibling schools of interpretation; already having wrestled in the womb of exegetical debate, brother and sister today suffer from lack of communication and misunderstanding. Separated by diverse methods, ideological concerns, and interpretive communities, analyses of the First Gospel are rendered poorer by their respective parochialisms, and each school risks devolving into solipsism and anti-Judaism. The family needs therapeutic intervention.

The older brother, informed by matters historical-critical and adopting an objectivist stance, begins with an emphasis on the *Sitz im Leben* of the text and then draws his various practical, pastoral, or personal conclusions in light of this knowledge. Using source, form, and redaction criticism and occasionally foraying into structuralism and the social sciences (he likes the term "sciences"), he is relatively sure of his data and conclusions. For him, the Gospel is an open book and a gracious guide: any hints of ethnocentrism, sexism, or even conflicting messages — subjects broached by other readers — he deems to be merely misreadings.

The younger sister has only recently found her voice. She understands the Gospel through the filter of her own experiences which, not surprisingly, differ from those of her brother. Whereas the text presents to the brother a benevolent image, the daughter finds something disturbing and oppressive; her conclusions are bolstered when she dons her

22

own interpretive lenses of feminist theory, postcolonial analysis, and post-modernism.

For these siblings, Matt. 15:21-28 is a major site of contention. The brother sees the Canaanite woman's faith and the healing of her child as anticipating and justifying the Church's mission to the Gentiles. The sister sees the depiction of the Canaanite as groveling before her Israelite con-queror as indicative of women's marginalization and Jewish colonialism. No story of redemption, 15:21-28 is for her an elitist, abusive account.

The brother and sister cannot communicate. The brother's histori-cal-critical and social-scientific approaches typically ignore feminist, non-Western, and literary-critical insights, and the sister's politically and ideo-logically aware critiques too often dismiss rather than engage historical-critical research. Even when they do listen to each other, understanding is thwarted. For example, with his typical note of self-confidence, the brother asserts that his sister has approached Matthew's narrative with "inappro-priate questions" and that she has wrongly placed her passage "in the ser-vice of an ideology, as though the Canaanite is an aggressive single parent who here defies cultural taboos and acts to free Jesus from his sexism and racism. . . ."[1] To the contrary, he proclaims, the story is a challenge to all readers to free ourselves of sexism and racism.[2]

The sister, incensed, notes that all texts and interpretations are in ser-vice to an ideology. She asserts that no question is inappropriate. She de-cries the claim that Jesus' "harsh or rude" answer is a "test of faith."[3] She hates even more that the woman's "humility and self-abasement have been hailed as Christian virtues."[4] She notes how "the suppressed voice of the Other strives to be heard in the re-casting of the story from the Canaanite woman's point of view."[5] She even condemns Matthew's construction of

1. M. Eugene Boring's unsubtle summary of Sharon H. Ringe, "A Gentile Woman's Story," in *Feminist Interpretation of the Bible,* ed. Letty M. Russell (Philadelphia: Westminster, 1985), 65-72, in his "The Gospel of Matthew: Introduction, Commentary, and Reflections," *New Interpreter's Bible* 8 (Nashville: Abingdon, 1995): 337.

2. Boring, 338.

3. Kwok Pui-lan, "Overlapping Communities and Multicultural Hermeneutics," in *A Feminist Companion to Reading the Bible: Approaches, Methods and Strategies,* ed. Athalya Brenner and Carole Fontaine (Sheffield: Sheffield Academic, 1997), 209.

4. Kwok, 209.

5. Leticia A. Guardiola-Sáenz, "Borderless Women and Borderless Texts: A Cultural Reading of Matthew 15:21-28," *Semeia* 78 (1997): 69.

the Kingdom, since he, "as a writer from a people that has emerged and grown as a nation with an ideology of chosenness, a common ideology among the imperialist nations, reduces the concept of βασιλεία by filtering it through that oppressive ideology."[6] Only wanly does she wonder "whether these audacious words given to the Canaanite woman . . . capture the perspective of at least some of the more egalitarian Matthean house-churches, in which women were active participants in the community's liturgical and theological life."[7]

In order to bring brother and sister into civil yet honest conversation, a third voice is needed. This is my role. I come as both an historian and as someone who has spent years in Matthean studies, so I have some credibility in the brother's eyes; I also come as feminist practitioner of various literary-critical and social-location based approaches, and as such I share the concerns of the sister. Finally, as a Jew, I come as an outsider to these Christian siblings. It is my religious and ethnic perspective, informed both by historical study and personal experience, that to me indicates one of the greatest dangers of such bifurcated scholarship. When the two schools fail to hear each other and listen only to themselves, one result is anti-Judaism.

My diagnosis is that brother and sister, historian and narratologist, objectivist and experientialist, can learn from each other. Years of work have not brought harmony, but as the following observations show, there are several areas of fruitful dialogue.

The Question of Marginalization

Where the brother concentrates his attention on Jesus, the ultimate insider, in terms of christology, miracle, and approval of the woman's faith, the sister focuses on the woman's ethnicity, gender, and otherness. They would each do well to see through the other's eyes.

---

6. Guardiola-Sáenz, 73 n. 2. The article displays no references to theoretical works on "chosenness," the use of the concept by dispossessed and marginalized, the religious implications of the term, and the particular ways it is adapted by different groups.

7. Elaine M. Wainwright, "The Gospel of Matthew," in *Searching the Scriptures* 2: *A Feminist Commentary,* ed. Elizabeth Schüssler Fiorenza (New York: Crossroad, 1994), 670.

Outcasts and Aliens

The sister highlights the Canaanite woman's "unequal subject position" and her "multiple identities." Contrasting the woman's bowing, begging, and passive witnessing to Jesus' power, she finds this "gentile woman with a daughter with an unspeakable disease" to be "despised by Jews and oppressed as a woman in a patriarchal society."[8] This "social outcast," with no father, husband, brother, or son to protect her, is then seen as subverting convention by appearing in public, speaking with a strange man, and insisting on her own way.[9] Given her distance from male companionship, the Canaanite woman is, finally, seen as "sexually aggressive and hence dangerous."[10]

Focusing on the topic of ethnicity, the sister next insists that the Jewish Jesus and the Jewish Matthew (or, more often, Matthew's "Jewish-Christian" source) have marginalized the Canaanite supplicant. Already in possession of Canaanite land, the Jews — whom Jesus and the disciples at least temporarily represent in the sister's reading — insist on soteriological priority as well. The Canaanite woman is thus "dispossessed"[11] by the colonizing force operating under the ideology of chosenness. Therefore, the sister concludes, Jesus' accession to the Canaanite woman's request shows his willingness to break away from his Zionist (here negatively coded)-intolerant-elitist context.[12]

Such identification necessitates an insistence on Jewish racism and

8. Kwok, 215. Here her reading is based primarily on Mark's version, since the next sentence speaks of this "member of the elite urban class."

9. Ringe, "A Gentile Woman's Story," 70-72; see also discussion in Kwok, 210-11.

10. Elaine M. Wainwright, "A Voice from the Margin: Reading Matthew 15:21-28 in an Australian Feminist Key," in *Reading from this Place*, 2: *Social Location and Biblical Interpretation in Global Perspective*, ed. Fernando F. Segovia and Mary Ann Tolbert (Minneapolis: Fortress, 1995), 144, following Bruce J. Malina, *The New Testament World: Insights from Cultural Anthropology* (Atlanta: John Knox, 1981), 42-47.

11. Guardiola-Sáenz.

12. In an attempt to "take seriously the subjectivity and agency" (111) of the interpretations of women from African Independent Churches in Botswana, Musa W. Dube and her colleagues compromise this subjectivity by asking the loaded question: "Is this story a case of racism between Canaanites and Israelites?" Musa W. Dube, "Readings of *Semoya*: Botswana Women's Interpretation of Matt. 15:21-28," *Semeia* 73 (1996): 119; cf. her comment (124) on their raising the question of "discriminatory nuances. Perhaps because they were unschooled in the western academy, the majority of AIC respondents answered 'no.'"

misogyny. It is from here an easy step to the salvation-historical model which reads Matthew's Gospel as replacing Jews with Gentiles as the new Israel. In this reading, the Jews in Matthew's purview — and all Jews hence — must be xenophobic, elitist, chauvinistic, and misanthropic. Only by following Jesus' acknowledgment of the woman's radical otherness could the Jews find their way to grace.

It is correct that in the context of Matthew's Gospel the Canaanite, as non-Jew and as woman, is an "other" to Jesus and the Twelve. However, this focus on — let alone privileging of — "otherness" has gone too far.

Neither Matthew nor the parallel account in Mark (7:24-30) provides any indication that the woman is outcast, singled out for being unmarried, or a subverter of conventional gender roles. The woman is not depicted as "cast out" (from what or where has she been exiled?). The biblical tradition typically depicts Tyre and Sidon as independent from and, often, in alliance with Israelite and Jewish rulers, rather than as occupied by them. Tyre and Sidon are consequently not "Jewish territory": Jesus, who has restricted his mission to the "lost sheep of the house of Israel" (Matt. 10:6; 15:24), does not step into her territory; she comes out to meet him.[13] If she is "dispossessed," it is by Rome, not by Jews (who are themselves under occupation). There must then be another nuance to her identification as "Canaanite."

If Rabbinic sources could[14] be shown to be applicable to the time of Matthew, the case could be made that the woman was a Canaanite slave. The term *kĕna'ănî* does have this meaning in the Tosefta (*Baba Kamma* 9:10) and the *Mekhilta*. Yet not only are the dates problematic, there is no compelling reason to read the woman as a slave. Indeed, by her forceful manner, she enslaves Jesus, as we shall see. Again, the term "Canaanite" requires another nuance.

Certainly a geographical indicator (cf. Jdt. 5:9, 10; Bar. 3:22; 1 Macc. 9:37),[15] "Canaanite" provides an allusion to the women of the genealogy;[16] it indicates, when combined with the woman's use of Davidic titles for Je-

---

13. Rabbinic sources (*Sotah* 35b) attest the use of "Canaanite" (כנעני) to refer to Canaanites outside of Palestine. So Marcus Jastrow, *A Dictionary of the Targumim, the Talmud Babli and Yerushalmi, and the Midrashic Literature* (Brooklyn: P. Shalom, 1967), 1:650.

14. Jastrow.

15. For discussion and references, see Philip C. Schmitz, "Canaan (Place)," *ABD* 1:828-31. Connection with trade (Job 41:6; Ezek. 16:29; 17:4) appears unlikely.

16. See below.

sus, the role of Israel in the divine plan (i.e., one is not, in this text, saved through the grace of Baal); and it signals the woman's Gentile background. But none of this signals the woman as "outcast."

Although the Gospel does not state explicitly that the woman is single, this is an appropriate conclusion. Problems arise only when "single" is interpreted to mean marginal or outcast. To be single, at least for Matthew, is a state approved rather than disparaged. The Gospel typically depicts characters as detached from biological kinship groups: The woman with the hemorrhage (9:20-22); the anointing woman (26:6-13), and the various women in parables are not attached to families; Peter speaks of leaving all to follow Jesus (19:27); the women who follow Jesus to Golgotha are apart from husbands or fathers (27:55-56).

Nor is there anything subversive to gender codes about a woman's seeking healing for her child: the model is already established by Jeroboam's wife, who approaches Ahijah (1 Kgs. 14:1-14) and the Great Woman of Shunem, who approaches Elisha (2 Kgs. 4:18-37). These allusions, especially coupled with the Canaanite woman's identification as "mother" and her complete focus on her daughter's healing, also mitigate any hypothetical sexual coding.[17]

Moreover, the narrative does not display, as the sister sometimes asserts, Jesus as moving "to the periphery where he can . . . cut through those [ethnic and gender] boundaries."[18] Matthew has not firmly articulated gender boundaries; Jesus heals both men and women, and both men and women appear among both his followers and his detractors. Nor do ethnic barriers break down at this point of the story. Jesus' mission does not extend to the Gentiles in Tyre and Sidon; it is the Canaanite who breaks whatever hypothetical boundary exists by her "coming out" *(exelthousa)* to Jesus. Moreover, the Canaanite woman does not follow him, and her lack of doing so is highlighted by a comparison of her to the Jewish blind men of 20:29-34. Like the woman, the men address Jesus as "son of David" and "Lord," ask for "mercy," are initially restrained by Jesus' disciples, and have to make clear, in response to Jesus' question, what they want. Yet when they

17. The lack of such coding is also attested by patristic sources which read the woman in light of 1 Kgs. 17:8-24 and regard her as a widow. Cf. Ps.-Clementine Homilies 2.19; some mss. of Mark; see discussion in W. D. Davies and Dale C. Allison, Jr., *A Critical and Exegetical Commentary on the Gospel According to Saint Matthew* 2. ICC (Edinburgh: T. & T. Clark, 1991), 545.

18. Wainwright, "A Voice from the Margin," 142.

regain their sight, they, unlike the woman, "followed him." A broken boundary would require a Gentile mission; prior to the resurrection, Matthew's Gospel does not provide this scene.

The Dangers of the Purity System

Why the Canaanite woman remains an exception — she is initially refused a healing and she does not become a follower of Jesus — is another question, and one that relates directly to a new interpretation promulgated by the sister: the claim that Jesus' reluctance is premised on Jewish purity codes. Ironically, this is her one move which her historical-critical brother heartily approves. More ironically, it is one based on unsupported historical claims and unthinking Christian supersessionism. The more healthy reading would be for sister and brother, together, to abandon the position.

The sister proposes to read Matthew 15 in terms of what is inadequately labeled "purity legislation," and to insist that purity concerns undergird the "gentiles' ambiguous, marginal position in relation to Jesus (and in relation to the Matthean group as well)."[19] According to this theory, when Jesus yields to the woman's plea, "significant contact is made . . . the boundaries that purity rules define and defend have been breached, even though no law has been broken."[20] The thesis is not entirely arbitrary: the Canaanite woman appears directly after Jesus' assertion that "to eat with unwashed hands does not defile" (15:20). Moreover, Jesus does not, *contra* Mark's parallel account, enter the woman's house; one could conclude that Matthew sought to protect Jesus from contact with Gentile impurity.

The brother agrees: this reading strategy is not based on gender, or experience, or rhetoric, or any other method he would be inclined to label as subjectivist (always negative, in his eyes) or ahistorical. It is, rather, a hallmark of "social scientific criticism."

Good will between brother objectivist and sister postmodernist cannot be achieved through the importing of a discipline alien to both interests and approaches. To apply to the Gospel a category, purity, that the nar-

19. Anthony J. Saldarini, *Matthew's Christian-Jewish Community* (Chicago: University of Chicago Press, 1994), 70.
20. Saldarini, 141.

rative does not itself introduce is the initial problem; a second concern is Matthew's own interest in preserving purity legislation (albeit as unrelated to Jewish/Gentile distinctions); and a third is the ultimately ahistorical, Pauline supported application of purity concerns to the Gospel. One might have thought that the sister, so sensitive to experience and so striving for universalism and ecumenism in her readings, might have noticed a problem with the condemnation of purity legislation: her naive view castigates Judaism, and any other tradition (Muslim, Hindu, etc.) in which purity is practiced.

There is, first, no *compelling* reason to interpret the story in terms of purity. With no law broken, with a healing apparently from a distance — at the least, we are given no indication that Jesus touches the child; like the centurion's son of Matthew 8, the girl may not be present — where is the breach? Although unclear from arguments proffered by both sister and brother, Matthew does not describe the woman as "ritually impure"[21] or "ritually unclean";[22] rather, the First Gospel removes language suggestive of purity concerns. While Mark 7:25 speaks of the child's *unclean (akatharton)* spirit, Matt. 15:22 mentions only "demon possession" *(kakōs daimonizetai)*. While Mark precedes the account of the Syro-Phoenician woman with the notice that Jesus "declared all foods clean" (7:19), Matthew makes no such claim.

My case is enhanced by the brother and sister's failure to attach the label of impurity to the centurion of 8:5-13, whose story parallels that of the Canaanite woman. Both healings depict Gentiles petitioning on behalf of absent weaker figures (a slave or son; a daughter), depict the Gentile's subordination to Jesus, reflect Jesus' reluctance to perform the miracle, comment on the faith of the petitioner, and positively contrast that faith with the lack displayed by insiders.[23]

The point of Matthew's Gospel is less that women and Gentiles are marginalized than that Jews, both men and women, have priority in Jesus' mission.[24] The model of "chosenness" — a term Matthew does not use — is then extended by the Great Commission to include all who conform to

21. Saldarini, 140, applies this label to her.
22. Wainwright, "The Gospel of Matthew," 651.
23. E.g., 8:11-12; see Peter's "little faith" of 14:31.
24. The priority is not, however, designed ultimately to condemn the Jews; the mission to Israel is never abrogated but is, rather, at the Great Commission extended to include "all the Gentiles" (28:19).

Jesus' teaching. While the notion of chosenness can and has been corrupted, to see it *only* as an imperialistic tool and to tar Matthew, the Jew, with this entirely negative label is bad history and naive realpolitik. It overlooks the value of the ideology during times of oppression, it ignores the positive definitions which Jews have attached to the term (e.g., chosen to follow the commandments, chosen to be a blessing to others), and it ignores the fact that the Gospel is, finally, a Christian, not a Jewish, text. At worst, it reinscribes Christian anti-Judaism.

The Rejections

Xenophobia and Ethnocentrism

When first approached by the Canaanite woman who cried out to him, "Have mercy on me, Lord, Son of David; my daughter is tormented by a demon," Jesus "did not answer her a word" (15:21-22). For the sister, this silence "functions rhetorically . . . as the encoding of a very strong objection to the possibilities . . . that would allow the participation of women and Gentiles in the liturgical and theological life of the community."[25] Ostensibly supporting this subordination of women's ministry is the observation that, to this point in the narrative, women's voices have not been recorded.[26] More, the sister claims that the woman, by raising her voice "in public in the presence of males," challenges Jesus to break down gender barriers.[27]

The feminist instincts of this sister are sharp, but they clash with the rest of the Gospel. Jesus' rebuff is consistent with other Gentile contacts. To the centurion's parallel request in ch. 8, Jesus asks, "Shall I come and heal him?" That is, do you really expect me, Jesus, to aid you, a Roman officer? Reading 8:7 as a question not only foreshadows the conversation with the Canaanite, it also provides the motive for the centurion's protestations in 8:8-9.

To make the case that the woman is defying convention, the sister

25. Wainwright, "The Gospel of Matthew," 671; see also "A Voice from the Margin," 139.

26. Unless we accept Rachel's lament [2:18] and appeals to Wisdom [11:9] as representatives of female voice.

27. Wainwright, "A Voice from the Margin," 139.

must first demonstrate that it was anomalous for women to speak in public. This cultural convention was likely typical for upper-class women, but it is countered by the equally conventional scene of a parent — frequently a woman — asking a sage or miracle worker for help with an ailing child. In addition to the biblical parallels noted above, other examples include Apollonius of Tyana's encounter with "a little woman pleading for her boy . . . who had been possessed by a demon for the past two years" (Philostratus *Life of Apollonius* 3.38). Finally, there is no indication from the hand of the Evangelist that the woman's request, or even her public appearance, is odd. Thus, claims of the woman's transgressing gender boundaries rest on a very questionable reconstruction.

Moreover, because Gentiles (such as the centurion at the cross) and women (such as those at the tomb) have positive, vocal roles elsewhere in the Gospel, it is difficult to read the Canaanite woman as a cipher for all, or even any, women and Gentiles in Matthew's community, let alone women and Gentiles facing marginalization from androcentric, ethnocentric Jews or Christians. For this Gospel, there is neither a quintessential woman nor a quintessential Gentile. The female, Gentile petitioner in Matthew 15 is rebuffed because Jesus' mission is, as he stated in 10:5-6 and reiterates after her second request, to the "lost sheep of the house of Israel" (15:24). The point is not that Matthew is anti-Gentile or anti-woman. It is also not that Jesus is testing the woman's faith. It is that Jesus went first to his own. However, an explanation is still needed for Jesus' comment in 15:26, for he seems here to move from an internal focus to an external insult.

When the woman a third time asks "Lord, help me," Jesus responds, "It is not fair to take the children's food and throw it to the dogs" (15:26). The woman retorts, "Yes, Lord *(kyrios)*, yet even the dogs eat the crumbs that fall from their masters' table" (15:27). None of the brother's explanations for this harsh saying — which range from romantic eisegesis to historical invention — satisfies. The sister is correct: The "parable which, totally devoid of conciliatory overtones, almost inevitably strikes the modern Christian [and the Jew as well, I might add] as too off-putting, even cruel, as designed to wound a human heart."[28] But her own interpretation threatens to inscribe new but equally oppressive readings.

For the brother, the label "dogs" is really a gentle reference to household puppies, since unlike Mark's *kiōn*, Matthew uses the diminutive

---

28. Davies and Allison, 2:552.

kynarion. Moreover, Jesus was "undoubtedly speaking in a half-humorous tenderness of manner," with "teasing challenge," and with a "twinkle in the eye."[29] Consequently, "we can be quite sure that the smile on Jesus' face and the compassion in his eyes robbed the words of all insult and bitterness."[30] This argument is hardly credible. The Matthean Jesus is a complex figure, but he is not twinkly, and a cajoling response to an individual in desperate circumstances is not humane. Nor is the brother's romantic apologetic consistently applied. I doubt he would regard Jesus' excoriations against the Scribes and Pharisees as punctuated with twinkles. Nor again does the diminutive "puppy" help; as feminists frequently remark, being called "little bitch" is no improvement to being called "bitch."

The brother's second apologetic is that Jesus is using conventional language, that "*dog* was a common Jewish term for Gentiles based on their making no distinction between clean and unclean foods. It is not necessarily a derogatory term."[31] Even if this view were plausible in the abstract — which I doubt — it does not hold for the Gospel. Matt. 7:6, in which Jesus warns his disciples not to give "to dogs what is holy or to throw pearls before swine," makes it clear that dogs, like swine, are at best undeserving. For 7:6, "dog" is an insult, applicable to Jew or Gentile. Debatable also is whether the expression is a "common term for Gentiles." There are no clear Jewish sources that support the claim of conventionality.[32] Although a term of disapprobation in Hebrew (1 Sam. 17:43; Ps. 22:16; Prov. 26:11; Isa. 56:10-11) as well as Greek (e.g., "Cynic") thought, "dog" is not tied in either case to ethnic identity. Therefore, the interpreter must find a better understanding of Jesus' harsh response.

The third explanation, relying on source-criticism, claims that Matthew was constrained to repeat material from Mark. Then, Mark's version

---

29. The first citation is from A. H. McNeile, *The Gospel According to Saint Matthew* (London: Macmillan, 1915; repr. 1961), 231; the second and third from R. T. France, *Matthew.* Tyndale New Testament Commentaries (Grand Rapids: Wm. B. Eerdmans, 1987), 247. Both are cited, with appropriate critique, by Boring, 336 n. 343.

30. William Barclay, *The Gospel of Matthew*, rev. ed. (Philadelphia: Westminster, 1995), 2:122; cited, approvingly, by Robert H. Mounce, *Matthew.* New International Biblical Commentary (Peabody: Hendrickson, 1995), 153.

31. Mounce, 154.

32. See discussion and sources in Amy-Jill Levine, *The Social and Ethnic Dimensions of Matthean Salvation History.* Studies in the Bible and Early Christianity 14 (Lewiston: Edwin Mellen, 1988), 147-50.

receives a political explanation: viewing Mark's "a Greek, Syro-Phoenician by birth" (7:26) as indicating upper-class status, and positing that the woman is part of the Gentile urban population of Tyre and Sidon whose economically expansive activities were putting pressure on Galilean Jewish peasants, Gerd Theissen locates Jesus' response in the context of material need: rich Gentiles should not expect to take the food from the poor Jewish children.[33] Correct or not, this thesis is not applicable to Matthew. Matthew's petitioner is not Greek and a "Syro-Phoenician" but Canaanite, and there is no indication of her class status one way or the other.

The fourth explanation proposes that Matthew has retrojected into the time of Jesus debates about the Gentile mission within the early Jewish-Christian church. This reading exonerates both Jesus and Matthew from the insult: it stems rather from those hypothetical xenophobic, ethnocentric *Jewish* believers within Matthew's church. In this construct, Matthew the Evangelist then corrects this negative view by emphasizing the woman's faith in spite of Jesus' (Jewish) concerns. This explanation of a retrojected missionary discussion is at best inconclusive and, more likely, another example of anti-Jewish apologetic. Finally, it is not warranted by the narrative: the woman does not follow Jesus; his healing of her daughter is exceptional and only undertaken after her refusal to leave; the story does not provide a model for Gentiles to enter the community. At best, the pericope suggests that the church members should be gracious to their non-Christian neighbors but not necessarily invite them to dinner and not necessarily expect that these Gentiles will want to join the fold.

We have, then, an insult preserved by a Christian Evangelist in a Christian Gospel. The sister eloquently speaks of being "brought up short by [the woman's] humiliation. No one, regardless of other attributes of their lives, deserves such treatment."[34] She asserts that Jesus' comment represents the "worst form of chauvinism"; it is a "violent rebuff" that reveals "incredible insolence."[35] To this point, I am in sympathy with her.

---

33. Gerd Theissen, *The Gospels in Context: Social and Political History in the Synoptic Tradition* (Minneapolis: Fortress, 1991), 61-80; see also the discussion of this reading in Kwok, 209-10.

34. Sharon H. Ringe, "A Gentile Woman's Story, Revisited," in *A Feminist Companion to Mark and Matthew*, ed. Amy-Jill Levine (Sheffield: Sheffield Academic Press, 1999), ms. 21. I thank Professor Ringe for allowing me to cite from her manuscript.

35. F. W. Beare, *The Gospel According to Matthew* (San Francisco: Harper and Row, 1981), 342; cited by Davies and Allison, 2:552 n. 41, and by Mounce, 153.

Then, she goes on: "Look," she says, "at Isa. 56:10." There "dog" refers to those who are "blind and without knowledge." "Knowledge in this case is inclusive of Torah knowledge. . . . The woman is not eligible to receive the bread of the insider not only because of her Gentile status but also because of her lack of access to Torah because of being a woman."[36] Albeit well motivated, the sister goes too far. Jewish women, especially those of the upper classes, had access to education; in synagogues they heard expositions of Torah; they may also have had access to education in the home. In the Canaanite woman's case, there is no reason for her to be schooled in Torah; the sister has introduced a category irrelevant to the pericope. Furthermore, Jewish women were not called "dogs," so again the connection to Isa. 56:10 fails. Nor is the Canaanite, as Isaiah begins, a "sentinel of Israel." The expression is harsh, but there is no reason to drag in some invented Jewish misogyny to enhance its bite.

Why then the insult? Matthew has already provided an answer: Israel has priority in Jesus' mission; the time for the Canaanites has not yet come. Here, perhaps, we have some indication of the nuance of her ethnic label: unlike the Canaanite Rahab, who according to Matthew's genealogy (1:5) made an alliance with Israel, this woman has affiliated with Tyre and Sidon. Thus Jesus insists on Israel's soteriological priority in his mission, and he waits for her to acknowledge that priority. Each is waiting for the other to yield. Were I the Canaanite mother, I may well have done the same. But ignoring one of Matthew's major thematics will not do. The Canaanite is indeed "the Other with a culture and identity of her own . . . who should be respected for who she is."[37] But this is a modern perception, and not Matthew's. Matthew has not written a multicultural Gospel; Matthew has written a narrative of promises to Israel.

Of course, the sister will now accuse me of being complicit in the androcentric and elitist interests of the Gospel. She will state that my reading, like "the vast majority [of interpretations of this pericope, is] performed in complicity with patriarchy and imperialism."[38] My response: the story Matthew tells is, finally, androcentric, or better, christocentric; it is the story of Jesus. We can always tell the story of the Canaanite woman, as we can of the centurion or of Pilate. But, in fairness to the brother, and

36. Wainwright, "The Gospel of Matthew," 672.
37. Guardiola-Sáenz, 70.
38. Guardiola-Sáenz, 70.

to the Gospel, we might also note that Matthew chose to tell the story of Jesus. To fault those interpreters who recognize Matthew's interests of patriarchal complicity, while often a legitimate claim, threatens on occasion to replace close reading and analysis with *ad hominem* claims if not defamation of character.

Before both brother and sister bond only in their dislike of me, I must turn to some attempts at reconstruction or, better, therapy.

Therapeutic Session 1: Genealogy

Brother and sister have come to agreement that Jesus' comment is not palatable, and they even agree on how it might be contextualized in terms of Matthew's soteriological program. But the brother is not yet convinced that the Canaanite has a valid subject position, and the sister worries that any recuperation of the Canaanite's subservience will ultimately serve patriarchy.

Given this ongoing distrust, I decided to employ a well-known and frequently successful technique of family therapy and pastoral care: I looked to Matthew's genogram, the family tree. There, in the genealogy, appear figures who would support both historical-critical and feminist-liberationist aims.

Matthew 15, it turns out, is not the first reference to Canaanite women. At least two other Canaanite mothers, Tamar and Rahab, appear in the genealogy (1:3, 5). This intertextual identification provides partial support for several of the theories adduced already. The genealogy bolsters the reading of Matthew 15 as foreshadowing the extension of the gospel to the Gentiles, as well as the role of women in this expansion.

In turn, the foremothers' presence compromises the claims of those who would have the Canaanite woman reject Israel's election. The "Gentile" identities of Tamar and Rahab are subordinated to Matthew's Jewish interests. Tamar insists on her position in Judah's family by seducing the patriarch. Rahab explicitly cites Israel's status in salvation history, and she betrays her own people in order to preserve her family and herself. Matthew in turn merges these Gentile women into the account of Jesus, the "son of Abraham, the son of David."

For both Tamar and Rahab, the future lies not with other Canaanites but in the house of Israel. Similarly, the Canaanite woman knows that what she needs belongs not to her own people, but to the Jews and, especially, to Jesus. She is willing to acknowledge Jesus' lordship (three times) and to subordinate her ethnic claims by making reference to Jesus as "Son of David" (a title which does not appear on the lips of Mark's Syro-Phoenician). Whether her statements are signs of conversionary faith (so the brother) or sarcastic protests to the dominator (so the sister),[39] or a bit of both, Matthew does not say.

For some postcolonial perspectives, this reading would be an affront, for it presents all three Canaanite women as collaborationists at worst and, at best, as assimilationists. Then again, what choice had they? Tamar was already legally enmeshed in Judah's family; Rahab either knew that Jericho was doomed (the surface reading of her response to the king in Joshua 2) or she was hedging her bets (the subtext); Matthew's Canaanite woman recognized that her needs could only be met by an outside source. She acts in service for her daughter, and so indicates that — at least for her — the personal and familial outweigh the ethnic and political. Her alternative was to hold her ground, insist on her own ethnic identity and self-determination, and allow her child to die. Neither choice is without merit; neither is ideal.

Like the women in the genealogy, the Canaanite takes action which appears at first as scandalous. Tamar has sexual intercourse with her father-in-law when her levirate rights are not honored; Rahab the prostitute protects the spies; Ruth the Moabite places Boaz in a compromising position on the threshing floor; the "wife of Uriah" is brought by David into an adulterous act. In each case, the women act when the men with whom they are paired fail. Even Bathsheba's identification as "she of Uriah" shows the fidelity of the ethnic other — Uriah the Hittite — when David, rather than going to war, goes to bed.

So too the Canaanite woman acts righteously when the man with whom she is paired, Jesus, fails to respond. Jesus is thus in the role of Judah, the Israelite spies, Boaz, and David: he remains consistent in his role of patriarch. By "kneeling before him" (*proskynei autō*), she does not, necessarily, worship him, as the brother insists; rather, she stops his movement. He can either walk around her, as she literally holds her ground, or

---

39. Guardiola-Sáenz, *passim;* cf. Ringe, for whom "faith consists of the woman's willingness to engage both risk and trust; it is not a Christian confession" ("A Gentile Woman's Story," 71; see also Kwok, 213).

he can respond. In turn, his insult is in part a commentary on her physical position: kneeling or heeling — begging like a dog — is not the proper position for someone about to receive the master's food.

Therapeutic Session 2: Comparative Case Studies

As Wendy Cotter observes in her fascinating study of petitions made to heroes in Greek sources, the refusal-redress mode serves to show the character of the protagonist,[40] even as it highlights the righteousness of the petitioner. In each case, the elite character yields to the importunings of his subordinate and, by so doing, shows his willingness to cede, momentarily, his position of authority; in each case, he performs a service for a weaker member of his constituency. Thus, to read Matthew's account as simply an indication of Jewish xenophobia or Zionist elitism yanks the pericope out of cultural context.

For example, Macrobius records:

> An old soldier who found himself in danger of losing an action at law in which he was the defendant accosted the Emperor in a public place with a request that he would appear for him in court. Augustus at once chose one of his suite to act as counsel and introduced the litigant to him. But the soldier, stripping his sleeve and showing his scars, shouted at the top of his voice, 'When you were in danger at Actium, I didn't look for a substitute but I fought for you in person.' The Emperor blushed, and fearing to be thought both haughty and ungrateful, appeared in court on the man's behalf. (*Saturnalia* 2.4.27)[41]

A second example, from Dio Cassius's *Roman History* (69.6.3), offers a female protagonist: "At any rate, once, when a woman made a request of him [Hadrian] as he passed by on a journey, he at first said to her, 'I haven't time,' but afterwards, when she cried out, 'Cease, then, being the Emperor,' he turned about and granted her a hearing." Dio explains, then, why he tells such stories about Hadrian: "This is a kind of preface, of a summary nature, that I have been giving in regard to his character"

---

40. Wendy Cotter, *The Christ of Miracles: Portrait Through Encounter* (forthcoming); my thanks to Prof. Cotter for sharing her research.

41. Translation by Wendy Cotter (personal letter, 16 July 1998).

(69.8.1).[42] Similarly, Matthew reveals something of Jesus' character: he yields when pressed by his subordinates, and this is a positive sign of his character.

The same model appears in Rabbinic midrash; the connections in imagery (namely, importuners, a rebuff, a dialogue, food, dogs, elites and marginals, and a change of mind) are startling:

> During years of scarcity, Rabbi opened his storehouse of victuals, proclaiming, Let those who are masters of Scripture, masters of Mishnah, masters of Gemara, masters of *Halakhah,* or masters of *Aggada* enter, but those who are unlearned may not. R. Jonathan ben Amram pushed his way in and said to Rabbi, "Master, give me food." Rabbi asked him, "My son, have you studied Scripture?" He replied, "No." "Have you studied Mishnah?" "No." "If so, how can I give you food?" R. Jonathan: "Give me food, for even a dog and a raven are given food." So he gave him some food. After he went away, Rabbi's conscience troubled him, and he said, "Woe is me that I have given my bread to a man without learning!" R. Simeon bar Rabbi ventured to say to him, "Perhaps it is your disciple Jonathan ben Amram, who all his life has refused to derive any perquisite from honor paid to the Torah." Upon inquiry, it was found to be so. As a result, Rabbi said, "All may enter." (*b. Baba Batra* 8a).[43]

Rabbi, like Matthew's Jesus, is an honored and well-respected teacher; both learn a lesson about worth, charity, and inclusivity taught to them by subordinates. In each case as well, the subordinates make their case on the basis of rhetoric: each appropriates a term of personal insult in order to obtain the desired gift, but neither is, at the end, left shamed.

Intertextual connections to the woman's language reveal something of her character as well. Her parlaying of the epithet "dog" recollects the verbal sparring of her genealogical sisters. Ruth uses the words of Boaz to her own advantage. Boaz wishes for Ruth that she find refuge "under the wings" *(hypo tas pterygas autou)* of Israel's G-d (Ruth 2:12), and Ruth, in turn, urges Boaz to "Spread your cloak *(peribaleis to pterygion sou)* over your servant" (3:9). Similarly the Canaanite woman takes Jesus' proclama-

42. Cotter, personal letter.
43. From *The Book of Legends: Sefer Ha-Aggadah,* ed. H.'im N. Bialik and Yeoshua H. Ravnitzky, trans. W. G. Braude (New York: Schocken, 1992), 265.

tion of her inferiority and turns it to her own advantage.[44] This is the role of the trickster, the person without power, the colonized subject. This is the role of the Cynic, the social critic who calls householders to accountability. Cynics take their name from the Greek for "dog"; that the woman's retort also plays on the aural connection between "Canaanite" *(Kananaia)* and "dogs" *(kynaria)* may be more than happy accident.[45]

By stopping Jesus, by turning his words back at him, by tenaciously seeking her will not by strength but by wit, the Canaanite woman conforms to the trickster roles of her foremothers Rahab and Tamar, and she need not be seen by the sister as powerless, groveling, or coopted. By recognizing the harshness of Jesus' rebuff, the son need not view the pericope as simplistic or unproblematic.

Therapeutic Session 3: The Politics of Readings

An emphasis on the woman as an ethnic outsider, especially a "despised" one (typically, the specifics on who is doing the despising are assumed but not argued; typically, it is the "Jews" who are assumed to despise Canaanites), tends to overlook the political situation of Matthew's story world and historical context. In both settings, the real power is neither Israel nor Canaan. For the story world, the real power is that of the Church; for the historical setting, the real power is Rome. Delimiting discussion to Jews and Canaanites, commentators release from culpability the true power brokers. Those divided readers of Matthew, so obsessed with gendered ethnocentricity, see only a partial picture. Once Rome and the Church enter the discussion, the screen changes.

First, the anti-Jewish readings of the pericope — those that highlight Jewish ethnocentrism, exclusivity, clannishness, etc. — appear for what they really are: products of the Church. Matthew is not a text written for or preserved by the Synagogue. While emerging out of a Jewish matrix, and while still hopeful of Jewish baptism, its focus has shifted to the Gentile world. Even if the pericope is to be cited as a form of temporarily limited Jewish ethnic superiority, this superiority is proclaimed not by the Synagogue, but by the Church.

44. Ringe, "A Gentile Woman's Story, Revisited," ms. 13.
45. Davies and Allison, 2:547; see also Levine, *Social and Ethnic Dimensions*, 151.

Second, by concentrating on Jewish ethnic interests, readers risk eliminating the real source of supersessionist oppression in the 1st century: Rome. It is Rome that occupies the land held by the Canaanites; the Jews are under the same political domination as their Canaanite neighbors. This historical reality to some extent mitigates against the claims either group would make for dominance.

Once we recognize these two elements with power, we can read Matthew's account as indicating resistance to it. By emphasizing Jesus' mission to the "lost sheep of the house of Israel," Matthew preserves a focus on ethnic Judaism within a Church turning toward the Gentile world. By labeling the woman a Canaanite, Matthew refuses to dismiss the non-Jewish population of the land. Both Jew and Canaanite thereby disrupt the increasing hegemony and homogeneity of church and state. And, with the woman's notice that both "masters" and "dogs" eat the same food, she provides a major means by which social hierarchies can, finally, be broken down.

Doctor's Notes

The brothers and sisters who derive identity in dialogue and debate with Matthew's Gospel may eventually realize that they will accomplish much more by working together rather than by working apart. Historians and social scientists can learn from literary critics, feminists, and postcolonial readers that their arguments are necessarily subjective and incomplete; they are no less motivated by subjective positions or conditioned by ideological presuppositions. More, they need to recognize that they bear a responsibility to those whose lives are, by choice or not, ruled by particular interpretations of the Gospel, and that what is liberating for some may be oppressive for others. The sister has recognized elements in the text which the brother has dismissed or overlooked; by bringing the marginal into the center, her readings enrich us all.

The sister may in turn learn from those textually oriented older brothers: Attention to the entire Gospel text, and to the nuances of the Greek, serves to prevent solipsism; history can contravene the tendency to categorize all women's experience as the same.

Once both come to terms with the problems posed not just by their own ideological blinders but, especially, with the problems posed by Matthew's text, healing can begin. Once both can recognize the anti-Jewish readings created by social-location based criticism done apart from historical rigor, and by an objectivist historical approach apart from consideration of diversity and competing values, the family of Matthean scholarship may make a change for the better, not only in relation to textual interpretation, but for Shalom.

The Early Reception of Matthew's Gospel: New Evidence from Papyri?

GRAHAM N. STANTON

What happened to Matthew's Gospel in the first decades after it was written? How was it used, and where? Who were the first Christian writers to quote or allude to this Gospel? Did the Evangelist Matthew write for one Christian community or for all Christians everywhere? Scholars who have participated in recent discussion concerning the early reception of Matthew's Gospel would readily agree that we have more questions than answers.

I shall not attempt here to offer bold new solutions to long-standing puzzles. My aim is modest: I hope to show that recently published papyri fragments of Matthew's Gospel are relevant to discussion concerning its early reception. Before I turn to the new evidence, I shall sketch briefly some of the issues that have been prominent in recent discussion.

If we accept that the Evangelist Luke has used Matthew's Gospel in the composition of his Gospel (whether or not he also used Mark), we not only deem Q to be an aberration in modern Gospel criticism, but we have also found important evidence for the early reception of Matthew. On this view the Evangelist Luke was so unimpressed by Matthew that he vandalized this carefully crafted Gospel and reshaped many of its traditions. This very early negative reception of Matthew would be in stark contrast with its almost universal popularity in later decades and centuries. Along with most scholars, I do not accept that Luke dismantled Matthew, but dissenting voices are still heard.[1]

---

1. See esp. Allan J. McNicol, ed., *Beyond the Q Impasse: Luke's Use of Matthew* (Valley

If, as a minority of scholars believes, either the Fourth Evangelist or earlier editors of Johannine traditions had a copy of Matthew to hand, then it would not be so much a case of vandalism as of benign neglect. Nonetheless, this would be an interesting example of the early reception of Matthew. In my view Matthew and John share some emphases, and have a similar social setting, but are independent of one another.

The possibility that I Peter knew and used Matthew has been canvassed again recently.[2] However, in the two passages that are most often referred to, the evidence is hardly overwhelming. I Pet. 3:14 and 4:14 seem to echo Matt. 5:10, but there are only three Greek words in common. Matt. 5:16 and I Pet. 2:12 are strikingly similar in content, but they have only four Greek words in common. Did the author of I Peter have a copy of Matthew to hand, or did he know some Matthean traditions by heart? A decision is difficult, and there is a third option which is made a little more likely by some considerations advanced in the final section of this paper: the author of I Peter may have possessed a notebook with a collection of Matthean verses in it.

These questions have also been asked with reference to the Apostolic Fathers. Scholarly opinion has keenly divided for several decades. In 1950 Edouard Massaux detected the use of Matthew's Gospel in many early Christian writings outside the New Testament; some 40 years later his huge study was translated into English and published in three volumes with some additional material.[3] In his 1954 thesis which became influential in its published version,[4] Helmut Koester defended a minimalist position, but without discussing Massaux's work. Koester claimed that most of the apparent references in the Apostolic Fathers to the Synoptic Gospels (and to Matthew in particular) were best explained by the survival of oral tradi-

---

Forge: Trinity, 1996). See also Mark S. Goodacre, *Goulder and the Gospels: An Examination of a New Paradigm.* JSNTSup 133 (Sheffield: Sheffield Academic, 1996), for a judicious discussion of Michael D. Goulder's views concerning Luke's use of Matthew.

2. Cf. Ulrich Luz, *Matthew 1–7* (Minneapolis: Augsburg, 1989), 93: "I believe one must seriously consider the possibility that I Peter presupposes Matthew." Rainer Metzner, *Die Rezeption des Matthäusevangeliums im 1. Petrusbrief.* WUNT 74 (Tübingen: Mohr, 1995), claims that I Peter is the first witness to Matthew's Gospel.

3. Edouard Massaux, *The Influence of the Gospel of Saint Matthew on Christian Literature before Saint Irenaeus,* ed. Arthur J. Bellinzoni (Macon: Mercer University Press, 1993).

4. Helmut Koester, *Synoptische Überlieferung bei den apostolischen Vätern.* TU 65 (Berlin: Akademie, 1957).

tion. Wolf-Dietrich Köhler's 1987 monograph on the same topic reaches conclusions which are closer to Massaux's than to Koester's.[5] Stalemate seems to have been reached.

More recently the early reception of the Gospels has been tackled from a fresh perspective in a symposium edited by Richard J. Bauckham.[6] For decades now most writers on the Gospels have accepted as axiomatic that the four Evangelists all wrote for their own particular Christian communities. Writers on Matthew have assumed that on the basis of the text of this Gospel (and especially the Evangelist's redaction of Mark), it is possible to reconstruct the make-up, tensions, and concerns of "the Matthean community." The essays edited by Bauckham offer a "new paradigm": the Evangelists did not write for one Christian community, or even for a cluster of Christian communities, but for all Christians everywhere.

I welcome many of the essayists' concerns. In recent years I have become increasingly uneasy about the constructs, "the Q community," "the Matthean community," "the Johannine community," and so on.[7] However, firm new evidence for the actual circulation of the first copies of the Gospels is not set out in any of the essays edited by Bauckham. The essayists focus on the intentions of the Evangelists and have little to say about the evidence for the early reception of the Gospels.

Conspicuous by its absence from all the above discussions of the early reception of Matthew is the evidence of the earliest surviving copies of this Gospel. Similarly, in the recently published major commentaries on Matthew, as well as in the continuing flood of monographs, next to nothing is said about the evidence for the early circulation and reception of Matthew which is provided by the earliest surviving papyri.

So in the first part of this paper I shall discuss the earliest papyri fragments of Matthew, with special reference to the Oxyrhynchus papyri published in 1997 and 1998.[8] These papyri force us to reconsider the

5. Wolf-Dietrich Köhler, *Die Rezeption des Mattäusevangeliums in der Zeit vor Irenäus.* WUNT 2/24 (Tübingen: Mohr, 1987).

6. Richard J. Bauckham, ed., *The Gospels for All Christians: Rethinking the Gospel Audiences* (Grand Rapids: Wm. B. Eerdmans, 1998). See also Philip F. Esler, "Community and Gospel in Early Christianity: A Response to Richard Bauckham's *Gospels for All Christians*," *SJT* (1998): 235-48; and Bauckham's reply (249-53).

7. See Graham N. Stanton, "Revisiting Matthew's Communities," *1994 SBL Seminar Papers.* SBLASP 33 (Atlanta: Scholars, 1994), 9-23.

8. E. W. Handley et al., eds., *The Oxyrhynchus Papyri* 64 (London: Egypt Exploration

widely held view that in contrast to the carefully produced contemporary copies of Graeco-Jewish writings, early copies of the Gospels were the "workaday," "utilitarian," handbooks of an inward-looking sect.

The recently published early papyri of Matthew (and of John's Gospel) are all in the codex format, rather than the roll. This comes as no surprise, for very nearly all the earliest surviving copies of New Testament writings are in this format. Nonetheless, these papyri fragments from codices force us to return to two basic questions which I shall discuss in the second part of this paper. Why did Christian scribes become obsessed with the codex in the 2nd and 3rd centuries at a time when the roll was the norm in non-Christian circles? What light does use of the codex format shed on the early reception of the Gospels?

Early Papyri of Matthew's Gospel

Several Greek paleographers have been more astute than Matthean scholars in their use of the evidence of the earliest copies of the Gospels for their early reception. In his important Schweich lectures, *Manuscript, Society and Belief in Early Christian Egypt,* Colin H. Roberts broke new ground.[9] As his title implies, Roberts shows how early Christian manuscripts shed light on the social and religious setting of early Christianity in Egypt. I am convinced that Roberts was asking the right questions, but the recently published papyri force us to modify several of his conclusions — conclusions which have influenced a number of New Testament scholars.

First I must sketch the consensus view, of which the paleographers Roberts and Sir Eric G. Turner[10] are the most distinguished proponents. In their view, manuscripts written in Greek in the early centuries of the Christian era can be divided into two groups: "bookhands" and "docu-

---

Society, 1997); M. W. Haslam et al., eds., *The Oxyrhynchus Papyri* 65 (London: Egypt Exploration Society, 1998). For discussion of the textual evidence of these papyri, see J. K. Elliott, *NovT,* forthcoming.

9. Colin H. Roberts, *Manuscript, Society and Belief in Early Christian Egypt* (London: Oxford University Press, 1979).

10. Eric G. Turner, *The Typology of the Early Codex* (Philadelphia: University of Pennsylvania Press, 1977). See also Gugliano Cavallo and Hernig Maehler, *Greek Bookhands of the Early Byzantine Period, A.D. 300-800. BulletinSup* 47 (London: University of London Institute of Classical Studies, 1987).

mentary hands." Bookhands were used for literary works; they were carefully written by very skilled scribes, often by slaves. Bookhands use upright, independent letters, often with serifs. They are usually bilinear; i.e., individual letters rarely protrude beyond two imaginary horizontal lines on the papyrus or parchment. Manuscripts prepared carefully in this way were more expensive; they were used by the more educated elite. The "classic" examples of Christian manuscripts from the 4th century in this style are Codex Sinaiticus, a "pulpit edition" of the whole Greek Bible, and Codex Vaticanus, a "pulpit edition" of the Gospels, Acts, and most of the Pauline corpus.[11]

Documentary hands were used for workaday documents of all kinds. They were written rapidly, usually with long lines, and with little concern for bilinearity. Ligatures were often used (i.e., some individual letters were joined together. Manuscripts written in this way were often used in a business setting or for private use. In comparison with "bookhands," they were "down-market."

However, it is important to note that documentary hands were sometimes used for literary works. For example, a copy of Aristotle's *Politeia Athenon* on a roll from the end of the 1st century has obviously been written very quickly, with little regard for the appearance of the text.[12] Presumably this was a private rather than a library copy.

In his 1977 Schweich lectures Roberts contrasted sharply the "hieratic elegance of the Graeco-Jewish rolls of the Law" with the "workaday appearance of the first Christian codices (whether of Old Testament or of Christian writings) . . ." (pp. 19-20). With a few exceptions, Christian manuscripts are "based. . . on the model of the documents, not on that of Greek classical manuscripts nor on that of the Greco-Jewish tradition" (p. 20). Roberts concluded that if Christian communities are faintly mirrored in their books, they would seem "to have been composed not so much of the intellectuals or the wealthy as of ordinary men of the middle or lower middle classes" (p. 25).

In the same year Turner made similar observations in his now classic study of papyrus codices of the 2nd or 3rd centuries. He noted that it is not

11. For an important fresh discussion of the origin of Sinaiticus and Vaticanus, see T. H. Skeat, "The Codex Sinaiticus, the Codex Vaticanus, and Constantine," *JTS* 50 (1999): 583-625.

12. Eric G. Turner, *Greek Manuscripts of the Ancient World*, 2nd ed. (Oxford: Oxford University Press, 1983).

easy to find examples of calligraphy among papyrus codices of that time: "Their handwriting is in fact often of an informal and workaday type, fairly quickly written, serviceable rather than beautiful, of value to a man interested in the content of what he is reading rather than its presentation." Turner then lists some examples, including the majority of the Chester Beatty codices: "These give the impression of being 'utility' books; margins are small, lines usually long"; their status is second-class in comparison with contemporary papyrus roll.[13]

The views of these two giants among paleographers have been echoed by several New Testament scholars. In his impressive 1997 study, Harry Y. Gamble notes that a bookhand is rarely found in Christian texts before the 4th century; with Sinaiticus and Vaticanus "a barrier was broken": "never before had Christian books been so fine."[14] Up until this time, Christians had little aesthetic regard for their literature; neither do they seem to have had a cultic attitude towards their books. In contrast, Jewish Greek manuscripts are better written: they "usually display an even, formal script with tendencies not only toward a bookhand but toward a somewhat decorated style with footed and serified letters."[15] Similar comments have been made recently by Loveday Alexander[16] and Bart D. Ehrman.[17] Hence it is not an exaggeration to claim that the Roberts-Turner view has become the consensus among New Testament scholars.

The Oxyrhynchus papyri published in 1997 and 1998 force us to modify the consensus view. I shall set out below what are almost certainly the seven earliest surviving papyri of Matthew's Gospel. There is general agreement that these seven papyri are all from no later than the middle of the 3rd century, though papyrologists are always rightly wary about dating precisely what are often very fragmentary writings. I shall set out the papyri according to their 𝔓 number (as used in modern editions of the Greek

---

13. Turner, *The Typology of the Early Codex*, 37.

14. Harry Y. Gamble, *Books and Readers in the Early Church: A History of Early Christian Texts* (New Haven: Yale University Press, 1995), 80.

15. Gamble, 79.

16. Loveday Alexander, "Ancient Book Production and the Circulation of the Gospels," in Bauckham, *The Gospels for All Christians*, 71-111.

17. Bart D. Ehrman, "The Text as Window: New Testament Manuscripts and the Social History of Early Christianity," in *The Text of the New Testament in Contemporary Research*, ed. Ehrman and Michael W. Holmes, Studies and Documents 46 (Grand Rapids: Wm. B. Eerdmans, 1995), 372-75.

text); this corresponds closely to the order in which the papyri were first published.[18]

I. 𝔓1 (= P. Oxy. 2). This small fragment of Matthew's genealogy (1:1-9, 14-20) is usually dated to the early 3rd century. The hand is generally bilinear, with only a few ligatures. It is perhaps halfway between a bookhand and a documentary hand. When this fragment was first published in 1898, it was considered to be "the oldest known manuscript of any part of the New Testament."[19]

II. 𝔓45 (= P. Chester Beatty I). This codex, which is usually dated to the first half of the 3rd century, contains parts of the final chapters of Matthew (20:24-32; 21:13-19; 25:41–26:39), as well as parts of Mark, Luke, John, and Acts. The first editor noted that the codex is written by a competent scribe, but without calligraphic pretensions, in a small and very clear hand; the letters have a decided slope to the right, as opposed to the uprightness generally found in Roman hands of the first two centuries.[20] T. C. Skeat, the doyen of contemporary papyrologists, has recently observed that in contrast to 𝔓64+𝔓67+𝔓4 (Number IV below in this list of early Matthean papyri), 𝔓45 was "not intended for liturgical use."[21]

III. 𝔓53 (Ann Arbor, University of Michigan, Inv. 6652). This small fragment of 26:29-35 published in 1937 may date from the middle of the 3rd century. The hand is described as "semi-uncial," with upright symmetrical letters.[22]

IV. 𝔓64 (Magdalen College, Oxford, Gr. 18, 1957) + 𝔓67 (P. Barcelona I, 1961). These fragments of Matthew 3, 5, and 26 are from the same codex as the more extensive fragments of Luke 1, 3, and 5 known as

18. For fuller details of Numbers I to V in my list, see Kurt Aland, *Repertorium der griechischen christlichen Papyri* (Berlin: de Gruyter, 1976).

19. Bernard P. Grenfell and Arthur S. Hunt, eds., *The Oxyrhynchus Papyri* Part 1 (London: Egypt Exploration Fund, 1898), 4. There is a good reproduction of this fragment as the Frontispiece to this edition.

20. Frederick G. Kenyon, ed., *The Chester Beatty Biblical Papyri II* (London: Emery Walker, 1933), viii-ix.

21. T. C. Skeat, "The Oldest Manuscript of the Four Gospels?" *NTS* 43 (1997): 1-34, cited in Stanton, "The Fourfold Gospel," *NTS* 43 (1997): 328 n. 36.

22. See Aland. A separate sheet, probably not from the same codex, contains Acts 9:33–10:1.

𝔓4 (Paris, Bibliothèque Nationale, Suppl. Gr. 1120, 1892). 𝔓64 was considered by its first editor, C. H. Roberts, to date from the end of the 2nd century. In spite of the attempt of Carsten Peter Thiede to date 𝔓64 and 𝔓67 to the 1st century, Roberts's dating is still generally accepted.[23] Skeat's theory that 𝔓64 + 𝔓67 + 𝔓4 are from the same four-Gospel codex is winning wide support.[24]

Roberts recognized that 𝔓64 was an early example of a biblical uncial hand: "a thoroughgoing literary production," i.e., a predecessor of Codex Sinaiticus and Codex Vaticanus.[25]

V. 𝔓77 (= P. Oxy. XXIV 2683, 1968). Another fragment from the same page of Matthew 23 has recently been published (P. Oxy. LXIV 4405, 1997). The first editor of P. Oxy. 2683, Peter J. Parsons, noted that 𝔓77 is "delicately executed with a fine pen," to be dated to the late 2nd century, and hence among the oldest New Testament texts.[26] Roberts noted its elegant hand, and its use of "what was or became a standard system of chapter division as well as punctuation and breathings."[27]

VI. 𝔓103 (= P. Oxy. 4403, 1997). This small fragment of Matthew 13 and 14 is dated by its recent editor, J. David Thomas, to the late 2nd or the early 3rd century.[28] In Thomas's opinion "the hand is quite elegant, with noticeable hooks at the top of most hastas and occasional serifs elsewhere." The hand is so similar to P. Oxy. 4405 = 𝔓77 (V above) that Thomas allows the possibility that they may be from the same codex, though he concludes that it is "safest to treat the papyri as from two different codices."

---

23. For full discussion and references, see Graham N. Stanton, *Gospel Truth? New Light on Jesus and the Gospels* (Valley Forge: Trinity, 1997), 1-10; the 1997 paperback edition includes an Afterword with further references. See also Harald Vocke, "Papyrus Magdalen 17 — Weitere Argumente gegen die Frühdatierung des angeblichen Jesus-Papyrus," *ZPE* 113 (1996): 153-57.

24. Skeat, *NTS* 43 (1997): 1-34.

25. Roberts, *Manuscript, Society and Belief,* 13. Skeat noted that in this codex "organised text-division is now carried back well into the second century"; *NTS* 43 (1997): 7. I have commented on the significance of the two columns in this codex; see Graham N. Stanton, *NTS* 43 (1997): 317-46, esp. 327-28. In a letter to me dated 30 March 1996, Skeat notes that the hand of 𝔓64 + 𝔓67 + 𝔓4 is quite clearly a literary one.

26. Peter J. Parsons, in *The Oxyrhynchus Papyri* 34 (London: Egypt Exploration Society, 1968).

27. Roberts, *Manuscript, Society and Belief,* 23.

28. J. D. Thomas, in Handley et al., *The Oxyrhynchus Papyri* 64, 5-6.

VII. 𝔓104 (= P. Oxy. 4404, 1997). Thomas considers that this fragment of Matthew 21 may be assigned "with some confidence to the second half of the second century, while not wishing to exclude altogether a slightly earlier or a slightly later date."[29] Thomas notes that the hand is very carefully written, with extensive use of serifs; bilinearity is strictly observed. Once again Thomas refers to the hand as "elegant."

In formulating what I have dubbed above "the consensus view," Roberts drew on a list of what he considered in 1977 to be the 10 earliest Christian biblical papyri and the four earliest Christian nonbiblical papyri.[30] Roberts emphasized that, with three exceptions, "there is no calligraphic hand in the group."[31] In 10 cases out of 14, Roberts detected "basically a documentary hand"; these earliest papyri might be described as "reformed documentary."[32] The three exceptions were Numbers IV and V in my list above, along with P. Oxy. I, 1, one of the three Greek fragments of the Gospel of Thomas.

In the list above of the seven earliest papyri of Matthew's Gospel, Numbers IV and V are not, as Roberts supposed, exceptions to the general pattern of "reformed documentary" hands; they are the rule! The recent publication of Numbers VI and VII has altered the picture very considerably: four of the earliest seven papyri of Matthew are at least as close to "bookhands" as they are to "reformed documentary" hands. It is worth noting that even though dating papyri is a skilled art rather than a science, the more literary hands among the seven (my Numbers IV, V, VI, and VII) have the strongest claims to be the earliest of the group.

The fact that four of the seven earliest surviving papyri of Matthew are carefully written in an elegant hand is significant, but it is of course possible that future publication of further papyri may spring further surprises. My main point is that the consensus view now needs to be modified: the earliest surviving copies of the Gospels present a much more diverse picture than recent scholarship has allowed. The seven earliest papyri of Matthew suggest that this Gospel was used both in private and in public

---

29. Thomas, 8.
30. C. H. Roberts, "Books in the Graeco-Roman World and in the New Testament," in *The Cambridge History of the Bible*, ed. Peter R. Ackroyd and Christopher F. Evans, 1 (Cambridge: Cambridge University Press, 1970): 48-66.
31. Roberts, *Manuscript, Society and Belief*, 12-13.
32. Roberts, *Manuscript, Society and Belief*, 14.

settings; it was not considered by some of those who copied it and used it in the second half of the 2nd century to be of "second-class" status, quite without literary pretensions.

My insistence that the consensus view needs to be modified is supported by several recently published papyri of John's Gospel. (i) 𝔓90 (= P. Oxy. 3523), fragments of John 18 and 19 first published in 1983, is dated confidently to the end of the 2nd century.[33] Its decorated style with small serifs is considered to be similar to 𝔓104, Number VII above, described as an "elegant" hand.[34] (ii) 𝔓95 (= Florence, P. Laur. Inv. II/31), an early 3rd-century fragment of John 5 first published in 1985, is in the biblical uncial or majuscule style, i.e., not unlike IV in my list above.[35]

Two of the four codex papyri fragments of John's Gospel published in 1998 provide further confirmation of a greater degree of diversity among early copies of Christian writings than has usually been accepted. (iii) 𝔓108 (= P. Oxy. 4447) is in a "handsome, medium-size, upright capital hand," "firmly bilinear." (iv) 𝔓109 (= P. Oxy. 4448) is "a very plain, upright, unligatured round hand": an "inept one of literary pretensions fashioned with a blunt pen."[36]

Several further points need to be noted. By the latter half of the 2nd century, many copies of Matthew and John were made with great skill and at some expense. The communities for which they were made must have been reasonably wealthy, perhaps with a higher degree of literacy than has usually been supposed.[37] The carefully made copies, some with signs of punctuation, strongly suggest that they were used for public rather than

---

33. See W. J. Elliott and D. C. Parker, eds., *The New Testament in Greek*, 4: *The Gospel According to St John*, 1: *The Papyri* (Leiden: Brill, 1995), for details and plates (47a and b). T. C. Skeat, in *The Oxyrhynchus Papyri* 50, ed. A. K. Bowman et al. (London: Egypt Exploration Society, 1983), 3-8, notes that the codex may possibly have contained two Gospels.

34. Thomas, 8.

35. S. R. Pickering, *Recently Published New Testament Papyri: P89–P95*. Papyrology and Historical Perspectives 2 (Sydney: Ancient History Documentary Research Centre, Macquarie University, 1991), 49. See Elliott and Parker for details and plates (48b and c).

36. P. Oxy. 4447 and 4448 are edited by W. E. H. Cockle in Haslam et al., *The Oxyrhynchus Papyri* 65:16-20.

37. Eldon Jay Epp, "The Codex and Literacy in Early Christianity and at Oxyrhynchus: Issues Raised by Harry Y. Gamble's *Books and Readers in the Early Church*," *Critical Review of Books in Religion* 10 (1997): 29-32, suggests that the papyri from Oxyrhynchus encourage at least a questioning of the 10 to 20 percent average literacy for the entire Graeco-Roman world proposed by W. Harris.

private reading. They confirm Justin Martyr's comment from the middle of the 2nd century that "the memoirs of the apostles," i.e. the Gospels, were read in the context of worship "as long as time permits" (1 Apol 67).

There is no reason to doubt that the Gospels were often also used as "workaday," "utilitarian" handbooks, or even as "school handbooks" or "manuals of the teaching traditions of this pragmatically oriented group."[38] But the recently published papyri suggest that by the second half of the 2nd century, much earlier than has usually been assumed, their literary qualities and their authoritative status for the life and faith of the Church were widely recognized.

I noted above that Roberts and Gamble have both drawn a sharp contrast between the "hieratic elegance" of Graeco-Jewish writings with their "even, formal script with tendencies not only toward a bookhand but toward a somewhat decorated style with footed and serifed letters" and the "workaday appearance" of first Christian codices.[39] The recently published evidence suggests that Roberts and Gamble were incorrect to differentiate Christian and Jewish attitudes to authoritative texts on the basis of the handwriting styles used. The most striking difference is the marked preference of early Christian scribes for the codex format and their use of *nomina sacra.*[40]

This observation is confirmed by two of the papyri published in 1998 in volume 65 of the *Oxyrhynchus Papyri.* P. Oxy. 4442 is a fragment of an early 3rd-century codex of a Septuagintal text of Exodus 20; it has a "good-sized formal majuscule, upright and basically bilinear."[41] It is broadly comparable with 𝔓64 + 𝔓67 (Matthew) and 𝔓4 (Luke), Number IV above, and therefore closer to a bookhand than to a documentary hand.

On the other hand, P. Oxy. 4443 is a late 1st- or early 2nd-century roll with a Septuagintal text of Esther. K. L. Luchner, its editor, notes that it is "fluent and broadly bilinear, but with its frequent ligatures, cursive forms, enlarged initial letters and tall risers/deep descenders . . . it perhaps owes more to official documentary styles than to bookhands." Its roll rather

---

38. Alexander, 105.

39. Roberts, *Manuscript, Society and Belief,* 19-20; Gamble, 79.

40. On the latter, see esp. Larry W. Hurtado, "The Origin of the *Nomina Sacra:* A Proposal," *JBL* 117 (1998): 655-73.

41. D. Colomo, the editor of P. Oxy. 4442, in Haslam et al., *The Oxyrhynchus Papyri* 65.

than codex format strongly suggests that it is Jewish rather than Christian. I shall turn to early Christian adoption of the codex format shortly.

The recently published early papyri fragments of Matthew and John confirm that these Gospels were particularly popular in the town of Oxyrhynchus. This is no surprise, for Matthew and John were the two favorite Gospels in the early centuries, no doubt partly because they were both considered to have been written by apostles. Not all the Oxryhynchus papyri were written in Egypt, so some of these papyri codices of Matthew and John may have been written elsewhere. Some are in Latin, which would have been known by few in Oxyrhynchus where the papyri were discovered. P. Oxy. 30, the codex in Latin now usually entitled *De Bellis Macedonicis*, probably originated in Rome.[42] A fragment of Irenaeus, P. Oxy. 405 (a roll), travelled all the way from Lyon to Oxyrhynchus within 20 years of its production, "not long after the ink was dry on the author's manuscript," to quote Roberts's memorable comment.[43] Although our knowledge of the social setting of early Christianity in Oxyrhynchus is still limited, there is no reason to suppose that the evidence of the Christian papyri discovered there is unrepresentative.[44]

The Origins of the Codex Format

All the early copies of the Gospels (and nearly all early copies of Christian writings) use the codex format (the forerunner of the modern book) rather than the roll, which remained preponderant outside Christian circles until the beginning of the 4th century. As expected, the recently published papyri of Matthew and John are all in the codex format. This further evidence for early Christian preference for the codex over the roll forces us to consider once again the reasons for early Christian obsession with the codex.

The codex was a development of the earlier use of wooden tablets,

42. Joseph van Haelst, "Les Origines du Codex," in *Les Débuts du Codex*, ed. Alain Blanchard (Turnhout: Brepols, 1989), 27.

43. Roberts, *Manuscript, Society and Belief*, 53.

44. See esp. Eldon Jay Epp, "The New Testament Papyri at Oxyrhynchus in Their Social and Intellectual Context," in *Sayings of Jesus: Canonical and Non-canonical*, ed. William L. Petersen, Johan S. Vos, and Henk J. De Jonge. NovTSup 89 (Leiden: Brill, 1997), 47-68.

several of which could be held together by a cord which passed through holes in the tablets. *Codex* was the Latin word for a set of tablets held together in this way. Tablets were covered in wax which was incised with a stylus and used for notes of various kinds, including school exercises; they could be readily reused. We now have a number of surviving examples of such stylus tablets from the 1st and later centuries.[45]

Until recently it was generally assumed that stylus tablets were the standard writing material for letters and documents in those parts of the Roman Empire where papyrus was not readily available. However, the publication in 1983 and 1994 of the very large number of writing tablets from Vindolanda (Northumberland, England) which date from ca. A.D. 100 necessitates a reappraisal of this view. The Vindolanda discoveries have not yet received the attention from New Testament scholars which they deserve. They came too late for discussion in Roberts's volume, and unfortunately they receive no more than passing mention in van Haelst's major study[46] and in Gamble's fine survey.[47]

The Vindolanda tablets are "thin slivers of smooth wood which are written with pen and ink," and may conveniently be referred to as "leaf tablets."[48] Most were used for official documents, as well as for letters and drafts of letters. However, at least one of the Vindolanda tablets contains a literary text, a line of Virgil; three others may be literary or semi-literary.[49] In the light of their publication, it is probable that some of the many literary references in 1st- and 2nd-century writings to notebooks *(pugillaria)* may be to leaf tablets rather than to stylus tablets.[50]

In 1983, the editors of the Vindolanda tablets accepted that for two reasons the tablets could not be described as a primitive codex: the "concertina" format of many of the tablets, and the fact that with only a couple

45. For full details and references, see Alan K. Bowman and J. David Thomas, *Vindolanda: The Latin Writing-Tablets*. Britannia Monograph Series 4 (London: Society for the Promotion of Roman Studies, 1983), 33-35.

46. Van Haelst, 15-16. Van Haelst underestimates the importance of the Vindolanda tablets for the origin of the codex on the basis of the "concertina" format and the absence of writing on both sides (15 n. 5). However, as I have noted above, there is now further evidence of diversity in format.

47. Gamble, 268 n. 35.

48. Bowman and Thomas, *Vindolanda*, 32.

49. Alan K. Bowman, *Life and Letters on the Roman Frontier: Vindolanda and Its People* (New York: Routledge, 1998), 18.

50. Bowman and Thomas, *Vindolanda*, 43.

of partial exceptions they were not written on both sides of the leaf. However, they also noted that the existence of this wooden notebook in this format at a period which was clearly an important one for the development of the codex is significant.[51]

In 1994 the tablets were re-edited, together with the considerable finds from the 1985-89 excavations. The editors note that there was no standard format for documents, though a diptych format, with the address written on the back of the right-hand half of the diptych, is the norm for letters.[52] Somewhat surprisingly, the editors do not comment further on the relationship of the leaf tablets to the origins of the codex. But there can now be little doubt that with the very thin Vindolanda leaf tablets from ca. A.D. 100, inscribed with pen and ink, we have extant examples of notebooks which were the forerunners of the codex.[53] They are a more direct antecedent than reusable stylus tablets covered in wax, even though we have more extant examples of the latter.

It has been generally accepted for some time now that parchment or papyrus notebooks (*membranae, membranai*) were also the forerunners of the codex,[54] even though the earliest *extant* examples are from the end of the 2nd or the 3rd century A.D. There is plenty of literary evidence which confirms that they were well known and widely used much earlier.[55] Quintilian's comments from ca. A.D. 90 are particularly important: "It is best to write on wax owing to the facility which it offers for erasure, though weak sight may make it desirable to employ parchment by preference. . . . But whichever we employ, we must leave blank pages that we may be free to make additions when we will" (*Inst. or.* 10.3.31-32). The reference here to wax tablets and to pages on the left side being left blank confirms that Quintilian is aware of the advantages of the notebook.

---

51. Bowman and Thomas, *Vindolanda,* 40-44.

52. Alan K. Bowman and J. David Thomas, *The Vindolanda Writing-tablets: Tabulae Vindolandenses II* (London: British Museum, 1994), 40-46.

53. Bowman, *Life and Letters on the Roman Frontier,* 10, notes that with writing-tablets still coming out of the ground in the 1990s, conclusions can only be tentative and provisional.

54. Cf. van Haelst, 20: "Le carnet de parchemin est une étape intermédiaire indispensable entre la tablette de cire et le codex. Ce sont ses feuillets qui, multipliés selon les besoins, pourront éventuellement contenir une oeuvre littéraire de quelque étendue."

55. See C. H. Roberts and T. C. Skeat, *The Birth of the Codex* (London: Oxford University Press, 1983), 15-23; and van Haelst, 18, for details and bibliography.

Perhaps it is not surprising that examples of parchment or papyrus notebooks from an earlier period have not survived, and that only recently have excavations at Vindolanda and a few other sites brought to light wooden leaf tablets. These notebooks were used for letters, and for ephemeral notes and documents of various kinds, but not for writings which might be treasured by a later generation. For my present purpose, the literary evidence for the widespread use of different types of notebooks together with the extant examples from the end of the 1st century confirm that for some people in the Graeco-Roman world notebooks were part of everyday life.

We are still unable to reconstruct with confidence how, why, and when the more substantial papyrus and parchment codex evolved out of the wooden, parchment, or papyrus notebook.[56] But literary evidence confirms that by the end of the 1st century the codex was being used by a small number of non-Christian writers for more substantial writings than notes, documents, drafts, and letters. As we shall see below, some of these writings were literary: it is a mistake to assume from the origins of the codex that this format was reserved solely for utilitarian writings or handbooks.[57]

At present there are two rivals for the accolade of the earliest *extant* codex: P. Oxy. 30, a parchment codex in Latin from ca. A.D. 100 which is usually known as *De Bellis Macedonicis*, and 𝔓52, the well-known papyrus fragment of John 18 which probably dates from ca. A.D. 125. Although P. Oxy. 30 is fragmentary, it is clearly a historical writing, and not an ephemeral set of notes.

Was the codex format a Christian invention? The earliest extant examples just noted do not settle the question. Their paleographical dating is not certain, and in any case there is literary evidence for earlier non-Christian use of the codex which must be weighed carefully.

Writing between A.D. 84 and 86, the Roman poet Martial refers to the availability of parchment codices for travellers: pocket editions of Homer, Virgil, Cicero, Livy, and Ovid which are referred with the words *in membranis* or *in pugillaribus membraneis* (*Ep.* 1.2, and 14.184-92). Al-

---

56. Roberts and Skeat, 10, correctly note that the transition from papyrus to parchment was of an entirely different character from, and quite unconnected with, the transition from roll to codex. They allow the possibility that the papyrus codex and the parchment codex may have developed in parallel (29). See also Turner, *The Typology of the Early Codex*, ch. 3.

57. Roberts and Skeat, 5 n. 1, note that it is quite wrong to describe the papyrus codex as a "Bastardform."

though Roberts and Skeat claimed in their influential *The Birth of the Codex,* that Martial's "experiment was still-born,"[58] their arguments have not carried the day.

We do have a sprinkling of codices of non-Christian writings from the 2nd century. Although they make up only 2 percent of the total (the remainder are on rolls), they cannot be dismissed as insignificant. One is a parchment in Latin (P. Oxy. 30, noted above). Three are parchment codices in Greek; 14 are papyrus codices in Greek. Many are literary writings.[59]

The evidence of P. Petaeus 30 (first published in 1969) is particularly important. This letter in Greek, which can be dated confidently to the 2nd century, but not more precisely, refers to eight parchment codices *(membranai)* which were purchased and six more which were not. P. Petaeus 30 "implies a touring book-seller offering literary *membranae* in the second century."[60] The social setting is important: these codices were part of a *mobile* bookshop. Martial, it will be recalled, refers to pocket editions of literary codices *(membranae)* which *travellers* would find useful. The earliest non-Christian codices seem to have been used for a variety of writings, including literary writings in the "classical canon" of the day. As far as we can judge, they first became popular with travellers.[61]

Is it more likely that non-Christian scribes were influenced by Christian scribes in the initial development of the codex, or vice versa? Neither the earliest extant codices nor the literary evidence is absolutely decisive.[62] However, in my view the literary evidence from Martial and the evidence of P. Petaeus 30 strongly suggest that codices were not unknown in non-Christian circles in the latter half of the 1st century, i.e., at the time of the composition of the NT writings. At this time it is most unlikely that inven-

58. Roberts and Skeat, 29.

59. See the slightly different lists with full details in Roberts and Skeat, 71; and van Haelst, 23-25.

60. Eric G. Turner, *Greek Papyri,* 2nd ed. (Oxford: Clarendon, 1980), 204.

61. Michael McCormick, "Typology, Codicology and Papyrology," *Scriptorium* 35 (1981): 331-34, suggests that the literary as well as the grammatical fragments may have been used by travelling teachers.

62. Several more recent writers have been reluctant to accept the view of Roberts and Skeat that Christians invented the codex. See, e.g., van Haelst, 13-35; Robin Lane Fox, "Literacy and Power in Early Christianity," in *Literacy and Power in the Ancient World,* ed. Alan K. Bowman and Greg Woolf (Cambridge: Cambridge University Press, 1994), 140; also Epp, *Critical Review* 10 (1997): 15-16, who is now more hesitant than in some of his earlier publications.

tion of the codex format by Christian scribes would have been imitated and developed by non-Christian scribes, albeit in a limited way. So in all probability the roll was used for the original copies of the New Testament writings. Luke-Acts offers some support: like many writers of his day, Luke designed his two volumes to fit onto a standard sized roll apiece. Within a couple of generations of their composition, the earliest Christian writings began to circulate in codices.

If Christian scribes did not invent the codex, why did it become the almost universally accepted format for Christian writings, perhaps from ca. A.D. 100? In a recent publication I discussed the various explanations which have been offered and then set out my own:

> Early codices, whether Roman or Christian, were quite small in size and therefore much more portable than rolls. Christian scribes preparing writings to be carried by missionaries, messengers, and travellers over long distances would have readily appreciated the advantages of the codex.[63] Their general counter-cultural stance would have made them more willing than their non-Christian counterparts to break with the almost unanimous preference for the roll and experiment with the unfashionable codex.[64]

I also noted that copying and using the Old Testament scriptures and their foundation writings in a new format was one of the ways Christians expressed their sense of "newness." Once the new format began to be adopted, its usefulness for collections of writings such as the four Gospels and the Pauline corpus would have enhanced its value.

Eldon Jay Epp has recently added a further important consideration. The likely content of the codices carried by early Christian missionaries and teachers (whether Mark, Old Testament *testimonia*, the Pauline corpus, the four-Gospel codex) is less important than the mere presence and use of the codex "in the highly charged setting of evangelism and edification in pristine Christianity — especially when a respected visitor is present with this new mark (i.e., a codex) of his/her calling."[65]

All these factors were instrumental in encouraging Christian scribes

---

63. See esp. Michael McCormick, "The Birth of the Codex and the Apostolic Life-style," *Scriptorium* 39 (1985): 150-58.

64. Stanton, *NTS* 43 (1997): 338-39.

65. Epp, *Critical Review* 10 (1997): 21.

to use the new codex format. But they all relate to what I would now call stage two: the rapid acceptance of the new format. How are we to explain stage one: the initial use of the codex format by Christian scribes at a time when in all probability rolls of Christian writings were in existence, and when the roll was the norm in society at large?

I am now convinced that use of papyri codices for Gospels, for Pauline Epistles, and for Christian copies of the Septuagint was preceded by Christian use of parchment or papyrus notebooks. As we have seen above, several types of notebooks were widely used in the Graeco-Roman world in the 1st century. The first followers of Jesus (pre-Easter, as well as post-Easter) will have been familiar with them.[66] So it is natural to suppose that notebooks will have been used for collections of scriptural passages, for collections of sayings of Jesus, and for drafts of letters.[67] It would not have been easy for Christian missionaries or teachers to carry a handful of rolls of favorite Christian scriptures such as the Psalms and Isaiah on their often arduous journeys. So we can readily understand why notebooks may have been used.

In words attributed to Paul, 2 Tim. 4:13 provides important support for this suggestion: "When you come, bring the (traveller's) cloak I left with Carpus at Troas, and the books (in roll format), particularly my notebooks *(malista tas membranas)*" (or possibly, "my books in codex form").[68] What were the contents of the notebooks *(tas membranas)* which a writer of a later generation associated with Paul the traveller? Perhaps a collection of "faithful sayings," or favorite Old Testament passages, or even Jesus traditions!

I do not think that any of the "big bang" theories which have been advanced for the adoption of the codex by Christian scribes is convincing.[69] Once they discovered how useful the codex format was, it very

---

66. Luz, 46-47, suggests that Q traditions may have been collected in a rather large notebook "bound together with strings on the margin. It permitted an insertion of new leaves at any time." See also Migaku Sato, *Q und Prophetie: Studien zur Gattungs- und Traditionsgeschichte der Quelle Q.* WUNT 2/29 (Tübingen: Mohr, 1988). Alan R. Millard, *Discoveries from the Time of Jesus* (Oxford: Lion, 1990), 167-69, draws attention to archaeological evidence for the amount of writing being done in 1st-century Palestine and suggests that reports of Jesus' sayings and actions may have been recorded in notebooks.

67. E. Randolph Richards, *The Secretary in the Letters of Paul.* WUNT 2/42 (Tübingen: Mohr, 1991), 164-65 and 191, suggests that Paul kept notes for his letters in notebooks.

68. See McCormick, *Scriptorium* 35 (1981): 331-34.

69. See Stanton, *NTS* 43 (1997): 336-39, for details.

quickly became the norm for copies of the Gospels, of Paul's letters, and for Christian copies of the scriptures. I have set out above the reasons why I think this happened.

The speed with which the new format was adopted universally within early Christianity is astonishing, as is the rapid deployment and development of *nomina sacra*. Both factors are directly relevant to any inquiry into the early reception of the Gospels. At first sight they seem to offer support for the claim that the Gospels were written for all Christians, rather than for a set of individual Christian communities.[70] However, in my judgment the codex became the norm for copies of the Gospels only a couple of generations after they were first written.

There is a further consideration which has an even more direct bearing on the early reception of the Gospels, and of Matthew in particular. We need not suppose that once the codex began to be used, notebooks with Jesus traditions (or of favorite passages of scripture) immediately ceased to be used. Quintilian speaks of seeing Cicero's own notes for some of his speeches, which were still in circulation more than a century after the author's death![71] So why should we not suppose that notebooks with Jesus traditions, some in their Matthean form, continued to be used even after copies of Matthew's Gospel began to circulate? Christian communities which did not have a copy of a full Gospel may have had to make do with parchment or papyrus notebooks for some time.

This suggestion takes us back to the opening paragraphs of this paper: the stalemate reached in discussions of the early reception of Matthew's Gospel. As I noted, some scholars consider that the evidence points unequivocally to the use of oral traditions, while others appeal to use of a written copy of Matthew's Gospel. However, the evidence needs to be scrutinized afresh. If Christian missionaries and teachers continued to use papyrus or parchment notebooks with Jesus traditions (and Old Testament passages) *alongside* copies of the Gospels and oral traditions, we should not be surprised at the varied ways Matthean traditions are cited or alluded to in the Apostolic Fathers and in Justin Martyr.

The recently published papyri encourage us to reconsider several other widely accepted views. The often-repeated claim that the Gospels were considered at first to be utilitarian handbooks written, by and large, in a "re-

70. Bauckham, *The Gospels for All Christians*.
71. Quintilian *Inst. Or.* 10.7.30-31. I owe this reference to Alexander, 93.

formed documentary" style needs to be modified. I have emphasized that the customary division of scribal hands into "bookhands" and "documentary hands" is an oversimplification as far as the earliest papyri of the Gospels are concerned. Some of the papyri of the Gospels are carefully written in hands which are closer to the literary than to the documentary end of what should be considered as a spectrum of styles of handwriting.

Many of the earliest papyri of the Gospels do not, as has been claimed, differ markedly from the Graeco-Jewish writings of the period, though Christian preference for the codex and use of *nomina sacra* do set them apart. By the latter half of the 2nd century, if not even earlier, some (but by no means all) *codex* copies of the Gospels were prepared as carefully as were some *rolls* of Graeco-Jewish writings. In both cases the care lavished on their preparation reflects their authoritative status for the life and worship of the communities in which they were treasured.

Early Christian obsession with the codex does not call these conclusions into question. As we have seen, the codex was a natural development from the widespread use of wooden, papyrus, and parchment notebooks. But we should not suppose that the *contents* of the codex were necessarily considered to be "second class." Martial confirms that towards the end of the 1st century the codex was used by travellers for literary writings; our earliest extant non-Christian papyrus codex is a historical work, and we do have a handful of 2nd-century codices with literary texts.

Christians had their own good reasons for preferring the codex to the roll. What continues to surprise is the rapid and almost universal adoption of this format by Christian scribes, as well as their use of *nomina sacra*. That both "fashions" caught on so quickly and so universally suggests that Christian communities were in much closer touch with one another than we have usually supposed. Students of Matthew's Gospel, and indeed of all the NT writings, would do well to ponder anew the implications of this phenomenon.

Matthew's Gospel:
Pastoral Problems and Possibilities

DANIEL J. HARRINGTON, S.J.

Whenever I teach a course about Matthew's Gospel or preach a series of homilies on Matthean texts, I think of Bill Thompson. I first met Bill in Chicago in 1971 during my first full year of teaching. It was also the first time that I taught a course on Matthew. Bill gave me personal encouragement and practical suggestions. But what Bill communicated most of all to me was his passionate commitment to both the text of Matthew's Gospel and its significance for people today. Bill could never be satisfied with treating Matthew merely as a literary work or as ancient history. He was also concerned — even obsessed — with its meaning here and now. He regarded Matthew the Evangelist as a pastoral theologian, and in his efforts at communicating this insight Bill himself became a pastoral theologian.

To biblical specialists, Bill Thompson is best known for his redaction-critical (or more accurately, composition-critical) analysis of Matthew's fourth discourse (17:22–18:35). He entitled this massively detailed study *Matthew's Advice to a Divided Community: Mt 17,22–18,35* (1970), thus evoking the pastoral significance of Matthew even in his doctoral dissertation. He regarded the discourse as Matthew's composition but based on traditional sources. He described its content as advice or instruction rather than law or prescription. And he viewed the instruction as addressing the tensions and scandals troubling Matthew's own community. From this careful literary analysis Matthew emerged as a pastoral theologian, one who found in the Jewish and early Christian theological tradition the resources for dealing with the concerns of a faith-community in the present.

In a popular exposition published almost 20 years later and entitled *Matthew's Story: Good News for Uncertain Times* (1989), one can see even more directly Bill Thompson the pastoral theologian at work. On the one hand, he used the literary method of narrative analysis and tried to take seriously the origin of Matthew's Gospel in the historical crisis that confronted all Jews (including Jewish Christians) with the destruction of the Jerusalem temple in A.D. 70 ("uncertain times"). On the other hand, he drew parallels between Matthew's uncertain times and our own, outlined methods for focusing on Matthew's Gospel in prayer, and proposed questions for reflection and discussion. This little book is a gem — an excellent example of pastoral theology, and a model of integrating biblical scholarship and pastoral concern.

In memory of the friend and fellow Jesuit who taught me so much about Matthew's Gospel and about the relation between biblical exegesis and pastoral theology, I would like to discuss three topics that bring together these two disciplines in the light of some developments in Matthean scholarship over the past decade. These discussions will show, I hope, that Bill Thompson was on the right track in his insistence on the pastoral significance of serious biblical scholarship.

The three topics I have chosen are the interpretation and actualization of scripture, Christian-Jewish relations, and Christian life. These topics interested Bill Thompson, and they interest me. In recent years they have been treated by Matthean scholars from various perspectives, and they are important for pastoral theology. I will address them both as a bibliographer (I have been general editor of *New Testament Abstracts* since 1972) and as a pastoral theologian (which I try to be in my teaching and preaching). I am concerned with the links between developments in the recent academic study of Matthew's Gospel and pastoral theology.

The Interpretation and Actualization of Matthew's Gospel

Biblical interpretation involves the explication of texts. The dominant model of textual explication that has evolved in modern biblical studies is the historical-critical method. This approach examines Matthew's Gospel in its 1st-century setting. It operates on the literary, historical, and theological levels.

The value of applying the historical-critical method to Matthew's Gospel is well illustrated by the recently completed three-volume commentary by W. D. Davies and Dale C. Allison, *A Critical and Exegetical Commentary on the Gospel According to Saint Matthew*.[1] The two authors set out to write a historical-critical commentary, with particular attention to ancient Jewish sources and parallels (including Rabbinic literature), as a way of understanding the "plain sense" of Matthew's Gospel. In dealing with each passage they treat questions of literary form and structure, consider source-critical issues, provide a substantial phrase-by-phrase exegesis (philological notes, word statistics, various parallels, reflections on historical value, etc.), summarize the results and relate them to Matthean theology as a whole, and list selected bibliography. In three volumes and more than 2400 pages, Davies and Allison provide a rich and respectful reading of Matthew's Gospel in its most likely historical setting — the crisis facing all Jews (including Christian Jews) after the A.D. 70 destruction of the Jerusalem temple.

In recent years the historical-critical method of biblical interpretation has been criticized and challenged. I believe, however, that works such as those of Davies and Allison brilliantly vindicate the positive values of historical criticism. But it is not the only method. In the past few years new literary and hermeneutical methods have been developed and applied to Matthew's Gospel as well as to other biblical texts.

Here I will cite only three examples. Daniel Patte's *The Gospel According to Matthew: A Structural Commentary on Matthew's Faith*[2] seeks to show what conviction the Evangelist conveyed to his readers in each passage by giving special attention to the narrative oppositions and thematic features. In *Towards a Feminist Critical Reading of the Gospel according to Matthew*,[3] Elaine Wainwright presents a narrative analysis, with particular attention to issues of gender. After focusing on episodes in which women are prominent (1:1-25; 8:14-15; 9:18-26; 15:21-28) and placing them in their wider Matthean context, she concludes that the Matthean vision of *ekklesia* was inclusive and allowed for women's participation in a way that

---

1. 3 vols. (Edinburgh: T. & T. Clark, 1988-1997).
2. (1987; repr. Valley Forge: Trinity, 1996).
3. BZNW 60 (Berlin: de Gruyter, 1991).

64

was not always possible in the prevailing patriarchal culture. In a narrative-critical study entitled *Matthew's Narrative Web: Over, and Over, and Over Again,*[4] Janice Capel Anderson examines Matthew's narrative rhetoric, characterization, plot, and structure, and concludes that Matthew's Gospel consists of a series of interlocking echoes that run through the narrative and draw the reader into a narrative web spun with the threads of verbal repetition ("over, and over, and over again").

Structural analysis, feminist analysis, and narrative criticism are now part of biblical interpretation — as are social science methods, canonical criticism, semiotics, semantic analysis, and many other approaches. Moreover, reflection on the process of hermeneutics has highlighted the social location of the interpreter and inspired liberationist, feminist and womanist, deconstructionist, and other kinds of readings.

What is the pastoral significance of this proliferation of new methods of biblical interpretation? Should religious educators, preachers, and all concerned with what scripture means now care about these developments in the academic study of Matthew's Gospel? Some initial reactions might be fear or despair or (better) humility. Yet exposure to some of these new approaches can have positive significance for pastoral ministers. The biblical text is so rich that no one method or way of reading can exhaust its meaning and significance. Indeed, the biblical text needs and deserves many perspectives and approaches. Moreover, these new methods make us aware of the complexity and multiple layers involved in the interpretive process, and set us free to explore the various facets of a text and to keep coming back to find new and fresh aspects.

I remain convinced of the value of the historical-critical method of biblical interpretation. And I remain convinced that its disciplined approach to studying biblical texts is fundamental to their theological and pastoral appropriation and actualization. And I am also pleased that in recent years the process of biblical interpretation has been expanded and enriched by these new methods.

Perhaps even more important for pastoral ministers has been the increased attention in recent years to the appropriation and actualization of the biblical text. Here our friend Bill Thompson was ahead of his time. In his little book, *Matthew's Story: Good News for Uncertain Times,* he encouraged the practice of *lectio divina* (the ancient monastic practice

4. JSNTSup 91 (Sheffield: JSOT, 1994).

of spiritual reading applied to scripture). He showed how it can be done with regard to Matthew's Gospel. There are four simple steps: *lectio* (What does the text say?), *meditatio* (What does it say to me?), *oratio* (What do I want to say to God on the basis of this text?), and *contemplatio* and/or *actio* (What difference might this text make in my life?). This tested method of appropriation can be used and adapted by any reader of Matthew's Gospel.

Another tested method of appropriation is Ignatian contemplation. Developed by St. Ignatius Loyola, the founder of the Society of Jesus and the patron saint of this university, this approach features the use of the imagination and the application of the senses. It challenges us to place ourselves inside a Gospel scene, to reflect on what we might see and hear (or even taste, smell, and touch), and to identify with the various characters in the episode. Ignatian contemplation builds on the close reading of a biblical text *(lectio)*, fits most obviously in *meditatio*, and is intended to stimulate *oratio* and *contemplatio* and/or *actio*.

These approaches to the appropriation of biblical texts can structure and enrich the process of actualization — making the texts come alive in the pastoral practice of the Church, whether it be religious education, Bible study, preaching, or liturgy. Appropriation and actualization are legitimate steps in the process of biblical interpretation.

Recent Matthew research has helped us all to recognize the positive value and the limitations of the historical-critical method. Matthew's Gospel has also been a fruitful proving ground for the application of "new" methods. And for those who exercise pastoral ministry, Matthew's Gospel provides a wonderful opportunity for appropriation and actualization.

Christian-Jewish Relations

I want to approach the issue of Matthew's Gospel and Christian-Jewish relations from two perspectives: the academic and the pastoral. As a biblical scholar trained in early Judaism I have had a special interest in Matthew for 30 years. As a Roman Catholic priest I preach every Sunday in two churches in the Boston area. Every third year the Sunday Gospel texts are taken from Matthew. As a seminary professor I try to help students for the Christian ministry to prepare for a lifetime of preaching and teaching Matthew's Gospel among other texts. Thus for me the academic and pastoral aspects of the issue of Matthew and Judaism come together. I want to reflect on possibilities and problems on both levels.

As a NT specialist I embrace the hypothesis that Matthew's Gospel should be read not only as a Christian Gospel but also as a Jewish book. I suppose that it was composed for a largely Jewish-Christian community in a city with a large Greek-speaking Jewish population ca. A.D. 85 or 90. I see it as one response among several to the crisis facing all Jews in the late 1st century. Without the Jerusalem temple, and with even less control over the land of Israel, how could the people of God continue? The apocalyptists represented in 4 Ezra and 2 Baruch counseled patient waiting until God's promises might be fulfilled. The revolutionaries sought to regroup their forces for what was to be the Bar Kokhba revolt of A.D. 132-35. Those engaged in the movement that we now call "formative Judaism" gathered traditions from various sources and promoted a more exact observance of the Torah. And Jewish Christians like Matthew pointed to Jesus of Nazareth as the fulfillment of God's promises to Israel and as the authoritative interpreter of the Torah.

In its historical setting — the crisis facing all Jews in the late 1st century — Matthew's Gospel was a Jewish book. In its content it is also a Jewish book. The use of a Gospel synopsis will show that in editing Mark's Gospel Matthew has Jesus take Jewish-Christian positions on issues that were especially controversial in the late 1st century. For a community of Sabbath observers (see 24:20), Matthew in 12:1-14 (cf. Mark 2:23–3:6) strengthens the argumentation and places Jesus' position more fully within the context of Jewish debate. With regard to ritual purity and other traditions, Matthew in 15:1-20 has Jesus stop short of declaring all foods clean (cf. Mark 7:19). With the exceptive clauses in 5:31-32 and 19:9 Matthew appears to align Jesus' attitudes toward divorce with those of Shammai.

The hypothesis that Matthew is a Jewish book of the late 1st century also helps to explain those elements that are sometimes called "anti-Jewish." The most obvious examples are the heated denunciations of the scribes and Pharisees in ch. 23, as well as the sneering references to "their synagogues," and the people's self-curse, "His blood be on us and on our children" (27:25). This is the kind of polemical language that one might expect in a 1st-century family quarrel. For those engaged in the struggle over Jewish identity after the temple's destruction, the stakes were high, and the modes of expression did not follow the canons of modern academic politeness (as Matthew 23 shows so clearly). One can find good parallels in the Qumran scrolls and indeed in texts from all over the Greco-Roman world.

Again three books will have to suffice to illustrate an important trend in recent Matthean research. In *Matthew's Gospel and Formative Judaism: The Social World of the Matthean Community*,[5] J. Andrew Overman contends that Matthew's Gospel should be read as reflecting the experience of a Jewish-Christian community in competition and conflict with formative Judaism after the destruction of the Jerusalem temple in A.D. 70. Anthony J. Saldarini in *Matthew's Christian-Jewish Community*[6] argues that the Matthean group and its spokesperson, the author of Matthew's Gospel, were Jews who believed in Jesus as the Messiah and Son of God, still thought of themselves as Jews, and were still identified with the Jewish community by others. In *A Rabbi Talks with Jesus*,[7] Jacob Neusner, a famous Jewish scholar of Rabbinic Judaism, explains why, if he had been in the land of Israel during the 1st century A.D., he would not have joined the circle of Jesus' disciples. In doing so he takes up specific teachings of Matthew's Jesus on fulfillment of the Law, parents and family, sabbath observance, holiness and perfection, tithing, and other issues.

I have referred to the idea of Matthew as a late 1st-century Jewish book as a hypothesis. There will always remain some uncertainty about any historical hypothesis. But this seems to me to be a very good historical hypothesis. It is historically plausible. It explains the textual evidence very well. And it is superior to other hypotheses about Matthew's Gospel (e.g., that it conveys eyewitness testimony to Jesus, or that the Evangelist and/or his community were Gentiles, or that it was written without any relation to historical events).

The problem came (and still comes) when Matthew's Gospel was no longer read as a Jewish book and when the readers were primarily Gentiles. Then Matthew had the potential to be become an anti-Jewish book. And indeed, that potential has all too often been actualized throughout history.

Matthew's Gospel is a perfect example of the need for biblical scholars to proceed on both the literary and the historical levels. Those who

5. (Minneapolis: Fortress, 1990).
6. (Chicago: University of Chicago Press, 1994).
7. (New York: Doubleday, 1993).

proceed only on the literary level make a Jewish book into an anti-Jewish one by taking it out of its historical context, and thus distort the book.

What might all this mean for pastoral practitioners? The sociological studies of anti-Judaism from the last generation showed that Christian preachers and religious educators played a pivotal role (whether consciously or not) in promoting anti-Judaism. In that process Matthew's Gospel (and especially ch. 23) has surely been a major element in shaping negative Christian stereotypes of Jews. More recent sociological studies have shown that significant progress has been made in educating Christian preachers and teachers about anti-Judaism, and in helping them to present a more accurate picture of Jews and Judaism.

On the pastoral level, the first step must be that pastors and teachers (Jewish and Christian alike) need to recognize the power of the offices that they hold, and the responsibility that they have in carrying them out. For us as biblical scholars to ignore the needs and concerns of pastors and religious educators is foolish and irresponsible. They constitute a large portion of the public for whom we write and to whom we speak — either directly or through our students.

A second step on the pastoral level is to help God's people — Jews and Christians both — to become aware of the historical dynamics surrounding the emergence of both early Christianity and Rabbinic Judaism. Matthew 23 — at least according to the "Matthew as a Jewish book" hypothesis — provides a snapshot of that relationship in the late 1st century. It allows both Jews and Christians today to look at a decisive moment in their early histories. It helps them to develop a historical consciousness about their faith traditions. It also encourages them to realize that both groups are not obligated to continue to relate in exactly the same ways as their religious ancestors did in the late 1st century. Perhaps we can reverse an old dictum: Those who read history are not doomed to repeat it.

A third pastoral suggestion: To study Matthew's Gospel in a mixed group of Jews and Christians is perhaps the most effective tool in helping both groups to appreciate what they have in common and where they differ. Christians will experience what Jews find painful, offensive, and dangerous about their sacred texts. Jews will come to see what Christians take from Jewish traditions and what they change in the light of their convictions about Jesus. Both Jews and Christians will come away sobered and more sensitive. Thus the goal of mutual understanding will be fostered.

Christian Life

One can argue strongly that Matthew's Gospel has been the most influential book in the Bible for Christian life. Under the term "Christian life" I include spirituality (how one stands before God and relates to others in light of that relationship), ethics or moral theology (the principles and precepts that structure Christian life), and community (the nature of the Church, its structures, and its hopes). As a revised and expanded edition of Mark's Gospel, Matthew's Gospel added greatly to the content of Jesus' teaching by including material from the Sayings Source Q and special Matthean traditions. The most obvious structural feature of Matthew's Gospel is, of course, the five great discourses: the Sermon on the Mount (chs. 5–7), the Missionary Discourse (ch. 10), the Parables of God's Kingdom (ch. 13), the Advice to a Divided Community (ch. 18), and the Eschatological Discourse (chs. 24–25). There is plenty of instructional material in Matthew about Christian life.

Moreover, the way in which Matthew portrays Jesus highlights his role as a teacher. Indeed Jesus is *the* teacher: "You have one instructor, the Messiah" (23:10). This quotation can serve as an occasion to call attention to some recent books on Matthew's contribution to shaping Christian life. Samuel Byrskog in *Jesus the Only Teacher: Didactic Authority and Transmission in Ancient Israel, Ancient Judaism and the Matthean Community*[8] investigates the relation between the understanding of Jesus as the only teacher and the transmission of the Jesus tradition in the Matthean community. He concludes that the conception of Jesus as the only teacher defined the setting of transmission as the school of Jesus, and that the transmitters (including Matthew in particular) regarded themselves as pupils of no one else but Jesus. The topic of Jesus the teacher has been treated by Celia M. Deutsch from a different angle in her *Lady Wisdom, Jesus, and the Sages: Metaphor and Social Context in Matthew's Gospel.*[9] As her title indicates, Deutsch links the figure of Lady Wisdom, the teaching of Jesus, and the teachers in the Matthean community ("the sages"), and argues that Matthew identified Jesus with Wisdom in order to understand who Jesus is and to establish the superiority of Matthew's teaching class.

The content of Jesus' teaching according to Matthew has been illu-

8. ConBNT 24 (Stockholm: Almqvist & Wiksell, 1994).
9. (Valley Forge: Trinity, 1996).

mined greatly by several studies. In his monumental commentary, *The Sermon on the Mount*,[10] Hans Dieter Betz views Matt. 5–7 as an epitome of Jesus' wisdom created by the early Jesus movement to instruct converts from Judaism. Betz's encyclopedic treatment of the ancient literary parallels and of the history of scholarship makes his book a valuable reference tool regarding what is probably the most significant and certainly the most influential ethical instruction in the New Testament. Another important block of Matthean ethical material is treated by Warren Carter in *Households and Discipleship: A Study of Matthew 19–20*.[11] Carter argues that Matthew 19–20 proposes an alternative household pattern (on matters such as marriage and divorce, children, wealth, etc.) that contrasted with the conventional hierarchical household patterns of 1st-century Antiochene society and that forms an integral part of the understanding of discipleship gained through hearing the Matthean narrative.

Bill Thompson correctly identified Matthew as a pastoral theologian. This insight has been well developed by Mark Allan Powell in *God With Us: A Pastoral Theology of Matthew's Gospel*,[12] who suggests that Matthew's theology is better approached through the categories of pastoral theology (mission, worship, teaching, stewardship, and social justice) than the categories of systematic theology (christology, ecclesiology, eschatology, etc.). And in the retrospect to their massive historical-critical commentary, Davies and Allison characterize Matthew as "a pastoral theologian" and his Gospel as "pastoral theology . . . primarily concerned to guide a community."[13]

Matthew's vision of Christian life was well summarized by Thompson in *Matthew's Story:* "He [Matthew] encourages us with the following invitations: Recall your roots! Delay gratification! Deepen faith! Grow in love! Wait with patience! Become like children! Lament your losses! Lead by serving! Go out to the nations! Choose life!" He went on to say why Matthew emphasized these themes and to express their significance for readers today: "Matthew highlights these themes, because he wants his story to show how Christians are to recover their past, face the reality of their present uncertain times, and move with conviction into the future."[14]

With their descriptions of content and goal, Thompson's two state-

---

10. Hermeneia (Minneapolis: Fortress, 1995).
11. JSNTSup 103 (Sheffield: JSOT, 1994).
12. (Minneapolis: Fortress, 1995).
13. Davies and Allison, 3 (1997): 703, 705.
14. *Matthew's Story,* 147.

ments help to define Matthew as a pastoral theologian. At this point, having surveyed some recent scholarly contributions regarding Matthew and Christian life and having sketched what I mean by pastoral theology, I want to reflect on Matthew's possible contributions to shaping Christian life in three areas that are obviously part of pastoral theology: spirituality, ethics, and Church.

I understand spirituality as how one stands before God and relates to others in the light of this relationship. The spirituality promoted by Matthew's Gospel is focused on God's kingdom ("strive first for the kingdom of God and his righteousness"; 6:33) and expressed in a willingness to follow Jesus along the way of discipleship ("follow me"; 4:19; 9:9). It is rooted in God's choice of and love for Israel (1:1-17) and at the same time animated by the new action of God in Jesus the Messiah ("new wine"; 9:17). Matthean spirituality respects the religious practices and traditions of Israel ("do whatever they teach you"; 23:3), while insisting on the individual's purity of intention ("beware of practicing your piety before others"; 6:1) and willingness to regard Jesus as the authoritative interpreter of the biblical tradition ("I say to you"; 5:22, etc.). It is oriented toward both community life ("where two or there are gathered in my name, I am there among them"; 18:20) and mission ("make disciples of all the nations"; 28:19). Matthean spirituality insists on the close relation between knowing and doing in the present ("you will know them by their fruits"; 7:20), and hopes for the Lord's parousia ("what will be the sign of your coming and of the end of the age?" 24:3) and lives in watchful anticipation of it ("Keep awake therefore, for you know neither the day nor the hour"; 25:13).

Matthew's Gospel in general and the Sermon on the Mount in particular have long been key texts for Christian ethics and moral theology. Against the horizon of the kingdom of heaven and discipleship, Matthew's Gospel presents the double love-command (love of God and neighbor) as Jesus' summary of the Torah (22:34-40), challenges Jesus' disciples to love their enemies (5:38-48), and teaches the Golden Rule ("do to others as you would have them do to you"; 7:12). It provides radical teachings about marriage and divorce (19:1-12), while showing pastoral sensitivity in allowing an exception to Jesus' prohibition of divorce (5:32; 19:9). It warns against excessive concern about property, money, and other material goods (6:25-34; 19:16-30), while promising abundant rewards to those who faithfully follow Jesus (19:27-30). It shows respect for the Torah of Israel (5:17-20), while viewing it through the lens of Jesus as the "one teacher" (23:8) and the changed circumstances of the Jewish people (including Christian Jews) after A.D. 70.

Moral theologians today such as Joseph J. Kotva in *The Christian Case for Virtue Ethics*[15] discern an affinity or close fit between Matthew's ethical teachings and Christian virtue ethics in the following areas: fullness of life in God's kingdom as the *telos,* emphasis on internal dispositions, character traits that contribute to the common good, perfection as a goal, a balance between law and love, the need for a teacher and for formation, and so forth. At least, the virtue ethics approach is superior to characterizations of the Sermon on the Mount as the new law, an impossible ethic, an interim ethic, or "evangelical counsels" for a select few.

Matthew is aptly called the "Gospel of the Church." This is so because it contains many passages that concern the Christian community and because through the centuries the Church (especially the Catholic Church) has taken it as one of its most authoritative texts. Among the four Gospels, only Matthew uses the work *ekklēsia* (16:18; 18:17). Only Matthew gives the promise to Peter as the rock on which the Church is to be built (16:17-19). Only Matthew provides the promise of the risen Christ to be with the Christian community "always, to the end of the age" (28:20). At the same time, Matthew reckons with scandals within the community, spiritual tepidity, and apostasy (18:1-35; 24:10-11). He also outlines pastoral procedures for reconciling those who stray or sin (18:12-20). Even Peter, however prominent he may be, is also the exemplar of "little faith" (14:28-31) and needs forgiveness for having denied Jesus three times during the Passion narrative (26:69-75).

Matthew the Evangelist is well described as a pastoral theologian. His Gospel provides the elements of a rich spirituality, wise and practical instructions for living as a Christian, and a reverent and realistic vision of the Church. The biblical scholar whose memory we honor at this colloquium had a rare vision of and a passion for pastoral theology — for appropriating and actualizing the text of Matthew's Gospel, for recognizing the significance of the past for the present and future, and for showing how the biblical text can influence various aspects of Christian life today. His example teaches us that biblical scholars must attend to the needs of God's people and share their learning with a Church and a world living in "uncertain times." This, after all, is precisely what Matthew the Evangelist did.

15. (Washington: Georgetown University Press, 1996).

The Matthean Jesus and the Healing of Women

ELAINE WAINWRIGHT, R.S.M.

*"What is needed is to study Matthew in terms of Matthew. . . . Conse-
quently I wish to by-pass synoptic comparison and exegetical detail . . .
and concentrate on Matthew's composition."*[1]

As early as 1971, William G. Thompson undertook a study of Matt. 8:1–
9:34, the major collection of healing stories in that Gospel, from the point
of view of the composition of the Gospel rather than a study of sources.[2]
This was at a time when redaction criticism was firmly established as the
dominant methodology in the study of the Synoptic Gospels and was set
to remain so for at least the next 10 to 15 years. In his undertaking,
Thompson was therefore a pathfinder, and it is a privilege to participate in
this colloquium and to honor him by seeking new ways of interpreting the
Matthean text, as he did, for both an academic and an ecclesial readership.

Twenty-seven years on from his pathfinding article, with many studies of Matt. 8–9 in the interim, I wish in this paper to seek for a new path in
the interpretation of these chapters by bringing new questions to the text
and combining some of the contemporary methodologies of biblical stud-

1. William G. Thompson, "Reflections on the Composition of Mt 8:1–9:34," *CBQ* 33
(1971): 366.
2. This is also the methodology Thompson used in his study of Matt. 18, *Matthew's
Advice to a Divided Community (Mt 17,22–18,35).* AnBib 44 (Rome: Pontifical Biblical Institute, 1970).

ies in a way that will enable me to address these questions. As the title of the paper suggests, the healings of women within the narratives of Matt. 8–9 will be brought into focus, first in their own right, but then as a lens for interpreting the Matthean Jesus within the context of the reign-of-God movement which is characterized by healing as a key feature. In keeping with Thompson's composition criticism of 1971, it will be a "study of Matthew in terms of Matthew" but in the light of contemporary literary and rhetorical methodologies combined with a socio-cultural perspective that takes particular account of the insights of medical anthropology.

Scholarship without Women and the Difference Difference Makes

When one focuses attention on the healing of women within the context of the healings of Matt. 8–9, one becomes aware that the significant body of scholarship concentrated on these chapters which spanned the 1970s, and of which Thompson's article is a part, was indeed scholarship which was gender blind. The scholars themselves were male and, while the healings of women were not ignored, they were subsumed under general categories. I do not wish here to simply revisit or summarize that scholarship, as that has already been done most recently by Alistair Stewart-Sykes[3] and W. D. Davies and Dale C. Allison.[4] Rather, I will use it as a point of dialogue in the establishing of the approach particular to this study.

A brief glance over the titles of the six studies which I have chosen as representative of contemporary foundational studies of Matt. 8–9 reveals that, in most of them, healing has been subsumed under the generic category "miracle." Rather than being seen and interpreted specifically as healing stories and in the context of the socio-cultural and religious meaning of the prevailing system of health care, they are placed in the context of the miraculous which is interpreted to serve particular thematic perspectives in the Gospel narrative.[5] Insufficient account is taken of the difference that

3. Alistair Stewart-Sykes, "Matthew's 'Miracle Chapters': From Composition to Narrative and Back Again," *Scripture Bulletin* 25/2 (1995): 55-65.
4. W. D. Davies and Dale C. Allison, *A Critical and Exegetical Commentary on the Gospel According to Saint Matthew* 2 (Edinburgh: T. & T. Clark, 1991): 1-5.
5. Since the word "miracle" does not appear in the Gospel text, E. van Eck and A. G. van Aarde, "Sickness and Healing in Mark: A Social Scientific Interpretation," *Neotesta-*

attention to the different types of miracle stories makes. And so Heinz-Joachim Held, whose work "Matthew as Interpreter of the Miracle Stories" is foundational to the studies of the 1970s (even though it first appeared in German in 1960), points out that "no importance is attached to the details" of what he calls "the healing miracles."[6] Rather, they serve a "particular theological theme" which Held identified as threefold: christology, faith, and discipleship. These he attached to a threefold division of Matt. 8–9.[7] Healing as such was obscured in favor of theological themes which were valorized.

Thompson's article, "Reflections on the Composition of Matt 8:1–9:34," published in 1971, relies not only on Held's division of the chapters but also his dominant themes. Thompson is concerned, however, to demonstrate the literary interconnections within the chapters which point to the artistry of the author. In this his summary is most revealing — "we find the Evangelist an intelligent man who not only reacted to the material inherited from his sources, but also created a new interpretation of the Gospel tradition for the community he served."[8] His emphasis was composition rather than a study of healing as central to these chapters.

Although Christoph Burger in his study, "Jesu Taten nach Matthäus 8 und 9," proposes a fourfold division, introducing the theme of the community's separating itself from Judaism,[9] he too concluded that the chapters were thematic, providing a foundational story or legend (Gründungslegende) for the Christian Church.[10] Jack Dean Kingsbury takes up Burger's division in his "Observations on the 'Miracle Chapters' of Matthew 8–9,"[11] and while he disagrees with Burger's emphasis on the Church, he simply transfers it to an emphasis on christology, in particular seeking to establish "Son of God" as the central christological metaphor. Healing is

---

mentica 27 (1993): 27-54, note that this is an "etic" category, i.e., an analytic construct of scholars rather than the vocabulary and construct of the 1st century.

6. Heinz-Joachim Held, "Matthew as Interpreter of the Miracle Stories," in Tradition and Interpretation in Matthew, ed. Günther Bornkamm, Gerhard Barth, and Held, 2nd ed. (London: SCM, 1982), 210.

7. Held, 246-53 in particular but passim. Held himself also sought to emphasize that these themes cannot be confined rigidly to a particular story or group of stories but that they overlap throughout the chapters. See in particular, 169.

8. Thompson, CBQ 33 (1971): 388.

9. Burger, ZTK 70 (1973): 272-87.

10. Burger, 287.

11. CBQ 40 (1978): 559-73.

obscured in the service of a title of Jesus which appears only once (8:29) in the entire two chapters. Kingsbury's concluding sentence is demonstrative of this:

> Paraenetically, they [chs. 8 and 9] invite these Christians, as persons of faith, to approach the exalted Son of God, under whose lordship and in whose presence they live, and to offer to him their petitions for help in the sure knowledge that he desires to hear them and will employ his divine power to aid them in time of trial and need.[12]

Birger Gerhardsson in *The Mighty Acts of Jesus according to Matthew*[13] and John Paul Heil, "Significant Aspects of the Healing Miracles in Matthew,"[14] both give particular attention to healing as a specific within the Matthean Gospel. Gerhardsson distinguishes the therapeutic from the nontherapeutic miracles and draws the conclusion from his study of the former that the focus is not on sick people and healing but on *Jesus* healing, with the emphasis on Jesus, and how he does it. He goes on, however, to indicate that the Matthean author "has *put the relationship between Jesus and the supplicants* under the magnifying glass."[15] Gerhardsson's approach is literary, as is that of Heil, whose title is the only one which contains the word "healing." While Gerhardsson's conclusions focus attention on the relationship between Jesus and the supplicants *in* the text, Heil, who interprets the miracles as ushering in the reign-of-God as "saving experiences in themselves,"[16] turns his final attention to the readers *of* the text. He asks in conclusion:

1. What do Jesus' healings mean for the "charismatic" activity of the members of Matthew's community as *doers* of healings and exorcisms?
2. What do Jesus' healings mean for the members of Matthew's community as *recipients* of the gifts of the salvation brought by Jesus?[17]

---

12. Kingsbury, 573.
13. (Lund: CWK Gleerup, 1979).
14. *CBQ* 41 (1979): 274-87.
15. Gerhardsson, 45.
16. Heil, 281.
17. Heil, 285.

I began this brief survey with a recognition that, in the studies included,[18] there is little specific attention given to healing stories in the light of healing itself. No account is taken of the difference that specific attention to healing might make to interpretation. In this study, therefore, I wish to consider healing in its own right rather than as a subset of miracles. In reviewing the works above, it became clear to me, in a way that I found surprising, that the studies are almost exclusively literary and take little or no account of healing activity in the Greco-Roman world apart from literary accounts of it in the Gospel narratives.[19] This lacuna opens the way for situating this study within a broader socio-cultural context of 1st-century healing through the lens of cultural anthropology, a difference in the central methodological approach which may allow different interpretations to emerge. This may also further highlight the relationship between Jesus and those coming for healing to which Gerhardsson has drawn attention but in the context of a broader system. Such a study, with its initial focus on the healing of women, is an engaged study, one which recognizes that the study itself is informed by questions about the effect of our interpretations of the healing stories today. This realization has also drawn my attention to the fact that none of the earlier studies take account of their engaged academic or ecclesial social locations, the presuppositions of the scholars, or the ethical effect of their interpretations.[20] Women are subsumed under the marginal or the supplicants; and the possibility of

18. I am aware that I have not included in this study K. Gatzweiler, "Les récits de miracles dans l'Evangile selon saint Matthieu," in *L'Évangile selon Matthieu: Rédaction et théologie*, ed. M. Didier. BETL 29 (Gembloux: Duculot, 1972), 209-20. For Gatzweiler also, the stories are considered "miracles." There is no specific attention given to the difference between healing stories and other stories which are arrayed under the title "miracle."

19. It should be noted that this is not the case in the latter part of the work of Gerd Theissen, *Miracle Stories of the Early Christian Tradition* (Edinburgh: T. & T. Clark, 1983). This work was first published in German in 1974 — *Urchristliche Wundergeschichten* (Gütersloh: Gerd Mohn) — and it influenced the Matthean studies of Matt. 8–9 in the latter part of the 1970s.

20. I find this particularly so in Kingsbury's conclusion about the centrality of the "son of God" title; see 562-66. It is also of significance to note here the critique made by Stevan L. Davies, *Jesus the Healer: Possession, Trance, and the Origins of Christianity* (New York: Continuum, 1995), of the extraordinary emphasis among scholars on Jesus the teacher and the almost universal neglect of healing in the search for the historical Jesus. He says rather tellingly (10): "Every scholar engaged in Jesus research is by profession a teacher and so every construction of Jesus the Teacher is formulated by a teacher. These teachers, professors by trade, should wonder if there is not a bit of a Jesus-Like-Us in their constructions."

multiple meanings emerging from differences in the Matthean audience is obscured by the search for *the* meaning of the text as intended by the author.[21] This study begins therefore with the question whether specific attention given to healing, and particularly the healing of women in the context of Matt. 8–9 and interpreted within the complexity of a diverse Matthean audience,[22] may enable new ethical interpretations of this text to speak to the diversity of theological approaches and concerns at the end of the 20th century and into the 21st.

Difference Included

While both the general and the specific Matthean studies of the 1970s focused on "miracles" as an etic category that obscured difference, both the literary and social scientific studies that have emerged in the late 1980s into the 1990s have taken much more account of healing in its own right and in its broader socio-cultural and religious context. They begin, therefore, to prepare the way for this study in its particularity.

As far as I can determine, the only new literary or narrative study of Matt. 8–9 in particular to appear since the 1970s is the 1995 *Scripture Bulletin* article of Stewart-Sykes, "Matthew's 'Miracle Chapters': From Composition to Narrative and Back Again." It is disappointing in that it purports to be a narrative study but is much more concerned with sources and authorial intention.[23] It has also reverted to the earlier focus on miracle rather than healing. Other full-length studies of Matthew that have appeared in the last decade or so have, however, either adopted a narrative approach or been influenced by the new literary criticism. Both Kingsbury and Thompson belong to the former, in that they have undertaken studies — *Matthew as Story* and *Matthew's Story: Good News for Uncertain Times* — which give particular attention to the characteristics of the narrative. For Kingsbury this has led to a recognition that *therapeuein* is significant in the narrative, in particular in the summary passages of 4:23 and 9:35,

21. Even Heil's questions regarding Matthew's readers (285-87) are discussed in terms of authorial intention.

22. This approach to the Matthean audience has been developed in my recent study, *Shall We Look for Another? A Feminist Rereading of the Matthean Jesus* (Maryknoll: Orbis, 1998), 35-49.

23. Stewart-Sykes, 61-62.

and hence it establishes healing as constitutive of Jesus' ministry.[24] He devotes a small section of his text to "The Healing of Jesus."[25] Thompson, on the other hand, refers to healing specifically in his chapter heading — "Jesus Preaches, Teaches, and Heals in Galilee" — but reverts to the etic category of "miracle" in his analysis of the story elements — circumstances, miracle, and aftermath.[26] There is ambivalence, therefore, around his interpretation of Jesus' healing activity.

Daniel J. Harrington, David E. Garland, J. Andrew Overman, and Donald Senior have each undertaken a study of the Matthean Gospel within the 1990s. While none of these purport to be a new literary critical study of the Gospel *per se,* they do take account of literary aspects of the text in light of these new approaches. For each, healing emerges as a significant emic category and Jesus is interpreted as healer.[27] There is in these studies, however, little attention given to healing within the broader health care system, and hence the dominant focus is on the identity of Jesus and his power and authority to heal.

Parallel to these studies, however, another body of literature was emerging, namely the socio-historical and social-scientific approaches to biblical studies; and, in particular, the medical anthropological study of biblical healing.[28] Its first application to the Matthean healing stories was John J. Pilch's article, "The Health Care System in Matthew: A Social Science Analysis."[29] Key elements emerge from Pilch's study, namely, the understanding of illness as a social rather than biomedical reality, focus on the health care system as a whole rather than just on the healer or even the

24. Jack Dean Kingsbury, *Matthew as Story* (Philadelphia: Fortress, 1986). I make reference here to the first edition of Kingsbury's book in order to locate it chronologically. A second edition was published in 1988.

25. Kingsbury, *Matthew as Story,* 70-72.

26. *Matthew's Story,* 74-79, in particular 74.

27. Daniel J. Harrington, *The Gospel of Matthew.* Sacra Pagina 1 (Collegeville: Liturgical, 1991); David E. Garland, *Reading Matthew: A Literary and Theological Commentary on the First Gospel* (New York: Crossroad, 1993); J. Andrew Overman, *Church and Community in Crisis: The Gospel According to Matthew* (Valley Forge: Trinity, 1996); and Donald Senior, *The Gospel of Matthew* (Nashville: Abingdon, 1997).

28. In this regard, note the general studies by Larry P. Hogan, *Healing in the Second Tempel [sic] Period.* NTOA 21 (Göttingen: Vandenhoeck & Ruprecht, 1992); and Hector Avalos, *Illness and Health Care in the Ancient Near East: The Role of the Temple in Greece, Mesopotamia, and Israel.* HSM 54 (Atlanta: Scholars, 1995).

29. *BTB* 16 (1986): 102-6.

healer and recipient apart from the social and hermeneutical system, and the relationship between healing and social boundaries. Pilch does take account of the difference between the healings of women and men,[30] an area which I am suggesting requires more detailed study. In a later article, "Reading Matthew Anthropologically: Healing in Cultural Perspective," Pilch draws particular attention to the 1st-century Mediterranean preference for "being" as a mode of activity rather than "doing," which characterizes 20th-century Western societies.[31] Attention to difference — difference in methodology, in gender perspective, in the particularities of the deeds of Jesus — is beginning to provide and will open up further potential for uncovering various possibilities in the interpretations of the healing activity in the Matthean Gospel. From this standpoint, therefore, it is now possible to give particular attention to the healing of women from both a literary and medical anthropological perspective.

Women in the Health Care System: A Matthean Perspective

That Matt. 8–9 is explicitly concerned with healing within the context of the threefold ministry of Jesus as teaching, preaching, and healing is made clear by the framing statements of 4:23 and 9:35:

> And Jesus went about all Galilee [the cities and villages], teaching in their synagogues and proclaiming the good news of the kingdom, and curing every disease and every infirmity among the people.

In my 1991 narrative study of the female characters of the Matthean Gospel, I established a three-part structure for the healings and other "miracle" stories of Matt. 8–9 broken by two buffer pericopes which continue the narrative movement of the Gospel. In this way the two chapters reflect the frame, emphasizing both Jesus' healing and his preaching and teaching. Given the strategic placement of the three healing stories of women immediately before the first buffer pericope and immediately after the second, I concluded that the reader's understanding and interpretation of these healings "is influenced not only by the group to which each belongs but also by the 'buffer' pericope alongside which it has been

30. *BTB* 16 (1986): 103, 104.
31. *Listening* 24 (1989): 278-89.

Diagram 1: Narrative Structure of Matthew 8–9

Individuals	Character Group	Response	Respondent
Crowds follow Jesus (8:1)			
Leper (8:1-4)	Leper — Unclean (male)	Say nothing to anyone Go — show yourself to the priest	Jesus
Centurion's servant (8:5-13)	Gentile/servant (male)	As you believed — Let it be done to you	Jesus
Peter's mother-in-law (8:14-15)	Woman — ill (female)	Rose and served him	Woman

Healing of many (8:16-17)

    [Buffer Pericope A]

Following Jesus (8:18-22)

Individuals	Character Group	Response	Respondent
Calming of storm (8:23-27)	Disciples (male)	Men of little faith What sort of man is this?	Jesus Disciples
Gadarene demoniacs (8:28-34)	Gentile — possessed (male)	Go away!	All the city
Paralytic (9:1-8)	Sick (male)	Afraid/glorified God Blaspheme	Crowd Scribes

Matthew — called and follows (9:9-13)

    [Buffer Pericope B]

Fasting/new wine — old skins (9:14-17)

Individuals	Character Group	Response	Respondent
Ruler's daughter + Woman with hemorrhage (9:18-26)	Young girl/dead Woman/unclean (female)	Fame spread Your faith has made you well	Jesus
Blind men (9:27-31)	Sick (male)	See no one knows it Spread his fame	Jesus Men
Dumb demoniac (9:32-34)	Demon-possessed (male)	Marvel Murmur	Crowd Pharisees

Compassion on the crowds (9:35-36; v. 36 as transition)

placed."[32] I then demonstrated that inclusion and liberation were significant themes of the buffer pericopes and may, therefore, have shaped the interpretation of the healing stories of the three female characters.[33]

The communities of reception of these healing stories, and those of Matt. 8–9 generally, participated in and shared the perspectives on healing and women's healing power which characterized the 1st-century Greco-Roman and Jewish worlds. In the Greco-Roman world, there appears to have been a tension surrounding the incorporation of women healers into the professional sector of the health care system that extends as far back as the 4th century B.C.E. It is captured in the story of Agnodike, who had to disguise her "true sex" in order to study and practice medicine among women.[34] It is glimpsed in the passing references to women healers in the Hippocratic corpus.[35] By the 1st century of the Common Era, however, public inscriptions from Rome which commemorate female physicians and midwives[36] point toward a more significant incorporation of women into the professional sector of the health care system. While this is muted, there is no doubt that they continued to function more predominantly in the secular folk sector.

In Greco-Roman Palestine of the 1st century, influenced as it has been by the biblical tradition in which healing was depicted as the exclusive work of Israel's God, physicians and their healing power were constructed within the symbolic universe of what Klaus Seybold and Ulrich B. Mueller call "Yahweh's healing monopoly."[37] It should be noted in this regard that there is no indication of the gender of recognized physicians but that the metaphoric world of the divine healer is male. Another element in

---

32. Elaine Mary Wainwright, *Towards a Feminist Critical Reading of the Gospel according to Matthew.* BZNW 60 (Berlin: de Gruyter, 1991), 82.

33. In light of my more recent work which suggests diverse communities of interpretation within the Matthean context, see *Shall We Look for Another?* I would want to add a rider to this last statement, namely, at least among some of the households of reception of the text.

34. Hyginus *Fabula* 274.10-13, translated in Helen King, "Agnodike and the Profession of Medicine," *Proceedings of the Cambridge Philological Society* N.S. 32 (1986): 53-77.

35. Hippocrates *Fleshes* 19; *Diseases of Women* 1.68.

36. Mary R. Lefkowitz and Maureen B. Fant, *Women's Life in Greece and Rome: A Source Book in Translation,* 2nd ed. (Baltimore: Johns Hopkins University Press, 1992), 264-65, §§369-72 and 267, §377.

37. Klaus Seybold and Ulrich B. Mueller, *Sickness and Healing* (Nashville: Abingdon, 1981), 105. See also the references to physicians in T. Job 38; Sir. 38:1-15.

Israel's health care system is glimpsed in Exod. 1:8-21, namely midwives. They are rarely mentioned in the biblical text, whose authors were male and whose concerns were not women's care of women, but they may have been as natural in Israel's health care system as was divine healing power. Tal Ilan includes this profession of midwife among the occupations available to the women of Palestine in the Greco-Roman period, noting that it must have been limited to women since only feminine forms are used in the Rabbinic literature.[38] She conjectures from this that women may have gone on to supplement the knowledge gained in midwifery to enable them to also work as physicians. Data in this regard is so scarce, though, that one is left with the image of women's healing in Greco-Roman Palestine functioning almost invisibly in the socio-cultural construction of healing and especially within its semantic and symbolic universes. Would it have been surprising, therefore, especially among the more egalitarian households of the Matthean community that there was no explicit reference to women as midwives or physicians or their being commissioned to exercise any of the healing arts in the entire Matthean narrative?[39]

Healing as constructed within the Matthean narrative belongs more to the magico-religious folk sector of the health care system than to the professional sector.[40] Within this sector in the Greco-Roman world generally, women tend to be clients rather than healers, and as medical anthropologist Arthur Kleinman concludes, "Most clients in folk practice are females."[41] A study of dedicatory inscriptions from the Athenian Asklepieion and stelae from the Epidaurian Asklepieion reveals, however, a significant trend. The inscriptions record simply the gift and the name of the giver, and for all the inventories 51.39 percent of the dedicants are women and 48.52 percent are men.[42] When one examines the accounts of healing on the Epidaurian stelae, accounts redacted by the priests of the temple, it is astounding that on stela A

38. Tal Ilan, *Jewish Women in Greco-Roman Palestine* (Peabody: Hendrickson, 1996), 189.

39. Even more so, would it have been surprising that there is no such reference within the entire corpus of the Christian scriptures?

40. This is also the conclusion of Pilch, *BTB* 16 (1986): 105.

41. Arthur Kleinman, *Patients and Healers in the Context of Culture: An Exploration of the Borderland between Anthropology, Medicine, and Psychiatry* (Berkeley: University of California Press, 1980), 206.

42. Sara B. Aleshire, *The Athenian Asklepieion: The People, Their Dedications, and the Inventories* (Amsterdam: Gieben, 1989), 45.

only 15 percent of the accounts are of women healed and on stela B, 32.8 percent. Very similar percentages occur within the Matthean Gospel narrative, where the healing narratives of women account for three out of nine, or 33.3 percent, within the collection of healings in Matt. 8–9. With the increasing power and centrality of the divine Asklepios within the folk sector of the Greco-Roman health care system and the gradual diminishment of the power of his daughters, Hygieia and Panacea, as female divine healers, divine healing power both in Israel and other sections of the Greco-Roman world was engendered male. Women were clients of the male divine healer, but accounts of male healings were valorized over those of women in the emerging narratives. It is this world which constitutes the backdrop to the healing of women in the Matthean Gospel.[43]

For this analysis, I will use explicitly Kleinman's five categories of criteria for cross-cultural examination of the therapeutic relationship — institutional setting, characteristics of the interpersonal interaction, idiom of communication, clinical reality, and therapeutic stages and mechanisms[44] — allowing them to overlap somewhat as the analysis unfolds.

The *settings* for the healings of Peter's mother-in-law, the ruler's daughter, and the woman with the hemorrhage are all noninstitutional, as they are for all the healings of Matt. 8–9. Two take place in a house: the first in the house of Peter (8:14),[45] and the second in the ruler's house (9:23). The hemorrhaging woman is healed along the way to the ruler's house (9:19). The events are episodic in nature, as are all the Matthean healings, and are performed for individuals even though, like the other healings, they are illness- rather than disease-oriented with the social and cultural implications of illness either explicit or implicit in the healing account.[46] In two of the accounts, those located within a house, the women are clearly embedded within a familial context. One is named mother-in-law of the

---

43. For a more extensive exploration of this world, see my article "'Your Faith Has Made You Well': Jesus, Women and Healing in the Gospel of Matthew," in *Transformative Encounters: Jesus and Women Re-viewed,* ed. Ingrid Rosa Kitzberger (Leiden: E. J. Brill, 2000). The following analysis of women's healing in Matt. 8–9 is similar to the analysis found in that article.

44. Kleinman, 207-8.

45. For a much more extensive analysis of the possible symbolism of this location, see Wainwright, *Towards a Feminist Critical Reading,* 184-85.

46. Pilch, *BTB* 16 (1986): 102, defines "illness" as "a socially disvalued state in which many others besides the stricken individual are involved."

owner of the house, Peter, who is a key character in the Matthean narrative. The other is daughter of the ruler, who is active in seeking her healing. The hemorrhaging woman stands alone in the narrative, even though her condition implies significant social effects. She alone initiates her own healing and, except for this small fissure in the text, the narratives construct women as passive and in need of male healing power, as in the dominant narrative of the Hippocratic treatises as well as in the Epidaurian inscriptions. The world of women healers is all but obscured. Only the initiative of the hemorrhaging woman and her undertaking of an action which she believed would bring her healing constructs woman in an active mode in the healing process. Like the Epidaurian texts, these Gospel narratives participate in and hence maintain the ideology of healing and its genderization current in 1st-century Palestine and in Jewish communities beyond its borders.[47]

In none of the Matthean accounts, or elsewhere in the Gospel, is Jesus named as a physician and hence belonging to the professional sector of the health care system.[48] He would likely have been located by the majority of the Matthean communities or households of reception within the world of the holy ones of charismatic Judaism — those who drew their healing power from God.[49] This would place Jesus within the folk sector as Pilch has suggested.[50] Pilch goes on then to define the folk-healer as "real and effective but . . . not accepted by everyone as legitimate," a description which well fits the reaction of the Pharisees to Jesus at the close of the healing accounts (9:34; cf. also 12:14, 24).[51] The type of healing being predicated of Jesus in this early stage of analysis locates him firmly within Israel's health care system as mediator of divine healing.

The quality of the relationship between healer and healed within the

47. Pilch (*BTB* 16 [1986]: 103) notes that "women in Matthew appear to be afflicted with illnesses that affect the domestic setting which in the Middle East is a sphere proper to women." It is of note in this regard that the only other account in Matt. 8–9 which makes reference to the household is that of the centurion's servant, but while the servant is lying sick in the house, the healing is undertaken by Jesus at a distance and not in the setting of the house.

48. The only time the word *iatros* is used in the Gospel is in the parabolic saying of Jesus in 9:12: "Those who are well have no need of a physician, but those who are sick."

49. Géza Vermès, *Jesus the Jew: A Historian's Reading of the Gospels* (London: Collins, 1973), 65-80.

50. Pilch, *BTB* 16 (1986): 105.

51. Pilch, *BTB* 16 (1986): 105.

context of *the interpersonal interaction* being developed by these Matthean healing accounts is an intimate one and like the Asklepian healings constructs a world of divine compassion similar to the world they construct.[52] The person needing healing does not have to make a pilgrimage to a distant shrine, but rather the healing power of Jesus is integrated into the normal activities of both the healer and the healed. Jesus enters Peter's house for a purpose that is unstated in the narrative, healing Peter's mother-in-law when he sees her lying sick with a fever (8:14). It is while he is in a discussion with his disciples that the ruler approaches him to bring his daughter back to life (9:18), and on the way to the ruler's house a woman touches his garment for healing (9:20). The use of some form of the verb of movement *erchomai* (*elthōn* in 8:14 and 9:18; and *proselthousa* in 9:20) conveys this sense of the integration of Jesus' healing into ordinary everyday activities.

In each of the accounts *the idiom of communication* of healing within the context of the relationship is by way of touch. Jesus touches the hand of Peter's mother-in-law (8:15), the woman with the hemorrhage touches Jesus' garment (9:20), and Jesus takes the young woman's hand (9:25). This constructs the healing conveyed by Jesus in each of these accounts within an intimate encounter, as the encounter through sleep, dream, or vision in the Asklepian temple may have been.

The *attitudes* of the participants in the healing interaction are significant toward the development of the semantic and symbolic world of healing. There is an apparent silence in this regard in the account of Jesus' healing of Peter's mother-in-law. We learn nothing of her attitude to Jesus as healer. The immediate reaction of Jesus upon seeing her lying sick with a fever may have been understood to imply his desire that healing and wholeness be extended to those whose world was shattered, broken, or controlled by forces that debilitated or destroyed body or spirit.[53] This is reiterated by the narrator's evocation of the intertext: He took our infirmities and bore our diseases (8:17; cf. Isa. 53:4).

The listener to the tales does, on the other hand, encounter the atti-

52. Note here also the interconnectedness with the buffer pericope — "I desire mercy, not sacrifice" (9:13) — and with the narration of Jesus' compassion (9:36).

53. See Wainwright, *Towards a Feminist Critical Reading*, 180-82, for a more lengthy discussion of the significance of the verb "to see" in 8:14 as indicative of the construction and reception of this story as not only an account of healing but also a narrative of call or vocation.

tude of the hemorrhaging woman. She expresses, albeit to herself, the profound conviction that if she but touch the hem of the garment of the charismatic holy one, she would be made well. Her use of the verb *sōzō* constructs the semantic world of healing in terms of freedom from disease but also situates that healing within a broader religious framework, given that the verb carries with it connotations of divine salvation or preservation from eternal death.[54] Within the Matthean narrative, it is in fact the verb used to designate Jesus' future role at the time of his conception — he will save his people from their sins (1:21). As indicator of a desire for transformative or restorative intervention similar to that of the hemorrhaging woman, it is the cry for help on the lips of the disciples during the storm on the lake (8:25). At a number of other points in the narrative it carries stronger connotations of final transformation or restoration (10:22; 16:25; 19:25; 24:13, 22). Only as an ironic challenge to Jesus, healer by divine power but dying on the cross, does the meaning revert to that of the more immediate — "save yourself" (27:40, 42, 49).

Jesus' desire to restore life and wholeness is further emphasized by his immediate response to the ruler's request to come and heal his daughter who, in the words of the narrative, "has just died" (9:18). In the language of the father's request — "come and lay your hand on her, and she will live" — the semantic world of healing is extended to very explicitly include the restoration of life which was symbolically included in the verb *sōzō* in the enclosed narrative of 9:20-22. Within the Matthean Gospel the verb "to live" (*zaō*) of 9:18 is most predominantly used as descriptive of God who is called the Living God or God of the Living [16:16; 22:32] and therefore intimately associates restoration to life with divine power. Thus, this brief analysis of the attitudes of both healer and healed within the healing encounter has enabled us to uncover elements of the belief system among 1st-century Jewish Christians who constructed healing as a transformative and restorative encounter with divine power, mediated through the one commissioned with this healing or restoration. These narratives of women's healings in their turn functioned rhetorically to shape a belief in Jesus as the one so commissioned and in divine power for healing accessible in the ordinariness of everyday life and in the intimacy

54. See Walter Bauer, William F. Arndt, and F. Wilbur Gingrich, *A Greek-English Lexicon of the New Testament and Other Early Christian Literature,* 2nd ed. (Chicago: University of Chicago Press, 1979), 798, for these possibilities within the semantic range of the verb.

of human touch, accessible to women as well as men in the reign-of-God movement which is at hand (4:17).

Turning to the *clinical reality,* it appears from the above analysis that the efficacy of these healing encounters between Jesus and the three women is derived from their sacred quality as conveyed by the language of the encounter, even though the setting is secular. It could be suggested, however, that by the end of the 1st century the *oikos* setting of two of the miracles was already a liminal term between the secular and sacred and that the language of "hemorrhage" shares a similar liminal realm because of the religious laws which governed bodily discharges in 1st-century Palestine. Kleinman, while recognizing the therapeutic strengths of the sacred aspect of the system of healing, also acknowledges that therein lies one of its limitations, in that the very sacred nature of the encounter "limits the extent to which it can be 'rationalised' as part of a secular organization of health care."[55] In terms of our study, this may be one of the characteristics of the system which has virtually displaced women healers from the symbolic universe of early Christianity in the Greco-Roman world, especially in light of the fact that in the Matthean narrative, immediately following the construction of this sacred aspect of healing in Matt. 8–9, 12 male disciples are singled out to be commissioned to heal as Jesus healed (10:1, 8), sharing the sacred power. There is no explicit account of women being commissioned to share that same power.

Attention to the language which describes both the clinical reality as well as *the therapeutic stages and mechanisms* reveals layers of the semantic and symbolic world of healing within the Matthean narrative. In each case, the problem is *named* or given a *cultural label*[56] in terms of a very concrete disease: one woman is "lying sick with a fever" *(beblēmenēn kai pyressousan);* another has "suffered from a hemorrhage for twelve years *(haimorroousa dōdeka etē);* and the young girl has "just died" *(arti eteleutēsen).* Those descriptions would have evoked varieties of meaning intertextually within a Matthean Jewish Christian audience in the Greco-Roman world. For some fever may have been commonly associated with malaria,[57] while

55. Kleinman, 241.

56. See Kleinman, 243, for the *three states* through which healing passes: a culturally legitimated name; the manipulation of the cultural label as "a symbolic form external to the patient"; and finally a new label sanctioned.

57. Colin J. Hemer, "Medicine in the New Testament World," in *Medicine and the Bible,* ed. Bernard Palmer (Exeter: Paternoster, 1986), 70.

the professional sector had constructed it multivalently requiring a variety of cures.[58] It was a disease, often serious to fatal, which needed to be cured. Given the construction of women as suffering predominantly from gynecologically related diseases within the professional sector and perhaps too in the folk sector, the general reference to a woman suffering with a hemorrhage for 12 years may have evoked the construction of this female hemorrhage as uterine.[59] The Levitical laws within Judaism and their interpretation during the 1st century may have likewise contributed to such an understanding.[60] Within the Hippocratic corpus, a significant section deals with hemorrhages, but it seems that generally when the sick one is not specifically gendered, they can refer to nasal hemorrhages.[61] Whatever its origin, the length of the woman's suffering would have rendered her physically vulnerable. That a young girl had just died and healing was requested for her by her father would have recalled for the hearers the social, familial, and personal precariousness of the time of transition from young girl to nubile maiden.[62] From this it is clear that one layer within the health care system of early Christianity is that of actual diseases or even physical death as needing therapeutic attention. As such, according to Kleinman, these conditions are given a culturally legitimated name or label within the health care system.[63]

In two of the three accounts of women's healing, the cultural label was manipulated by Jesus as healer by way of the instrument of touch. In the third, it is the hemorrhaging woman whose action is instrumental in her healing. That which was culturally sanctioned as dangerous to touch was manipulated by that very touch. As a result, a new label was sanc-

58. See Hippocrates *Affections* 1.10-15 by way of example.

59. See Soranus *Gynecology* §3.10.

60. For a detailed study of this see Shaye J. D. Cohen, "Menstruants and the Sacred in Judaism and Christianity," in *Women's History and Ancient History*, ed. Sarah B. Pomeroy (Chapel Hill: University of North Carolina Press, 1991), 273-99.

61. Hippocrates *Prorrhetic* 1.132-50. See also Amy-Jill Levine, "Discharging Responsibility: Matthean Jesus, Biblical Law, and Hemorrhaging Woman," in *Treasures New and Old: Recent Contributions to Matthean Studies*, ed. David R. Bauer and Mark Allan Powell (Atlanta: Scholars, 1996), 379-97, who warns against too ready an assumption that the hemorrhage is uterine.

62. Antoinette Wire, "Ancient Miracle Stories and Women's Social World," *Forum* 2 (1986): 77-78; and Nancy Demand, *Birth, Death, and Motherhood in Classical Greece* (Baltimore: Johns Hopkins University Press, 1994), 11.

63. Kleinman, 243.

tioned. It is these which are of interest in terms of both the semantic and symbolic nature of healing and gender, especially its Christian construction. The woman of 9:20-22 can no longer be described in terms of her illness, but she has been made well or saved *(esōthē)*, participant therefore in the fullness of what that word entails within the symbolic universe of the Matthean narrative as described above. Both Peter's mother-in-law and the young girl are labelled anew as having been lifted or raised up *(ēgerthē)*. While this new description of the two women can be understood simply on a clinical level, it must be remembered that it also shares in the new interpretive lens through which the emerging Christian community understood that the most destructive of forces, namely death, could be overcome [see in particular 28:6 in relation to Jesus]. Peter's mother-in-law is not only raised but she also ministers to Jesus *(diēkonei autōi)*. Pilch understands this as restoration to a "desirable state of being," but he considers that for women in Mediterranean culture the state more proper to women rather than men is that of "doing" rather than "being" and the sphere for that is the home.[64] Examination of the semantic value of *diakoneō* within the narrative world of the Matthean text and the call or vocation element in the story type[65] leads to a recognition that the healing accounts function to not only construct healing as transformative of somatic aspects of women's lives but also of their socio-cultural and religious lives as well. Each woman is named as participant in the transformative universe associated with Jesus — that of service (20:28), of saving (1:21), and of being raised to new life (28:6).

In the healing accounts of women in Matt. 8–9, women's bodies are the site of the most significant transformative powers associated with Jesus — service, saving, and resurrection.[66] Certainly, they are not the healers in these transformative encounters but the healed, and neither are they given a commission to heal as are the 12 male apostles (10:1, 8). Women's bodies, however, configure the divine healing power, mediated through Jesus. One could imagine how such an insight could have been subsumed under a focus upon the identity of Jesus as divinely authorized healer who commissions male co-workers within a scribal reception of the Matthean Gospel.

64. Pilch, *Listening* 24 (1989): 286.
65. Wainwright, *Towards a Feminist Critical Reading,* 85-86, 186-87.
66. As well as drawing this conclusion from the study undertaken herein, I have also been informed in this insight by Levine, 396-97.

Within a more egalitarian household of reception, however, it may have been possible that the new culturally sanctioned labels given to three women by way of these healing stories could have created two possible worlds of meaning. First, the new labels incorporate these women into the healing and transformative symbolic universe associated with both Jesus and also the God of Jesus who raises from death. As such these stories may have functioned to authorize those women of the Matthean community engaged in healing and transformative work within the community and even beyond its boundaries in the secular folk sector of the Gospel provenance's health care system. Second, the labelling of women healed in the same way that Jesus is labelled constructs a view of the reign-of-God movement, through the lens of its health care system, in which women participate in the reign-of-God movement with Jesus as transformative healers rather than simply being recipients of Jesus' benevolent healing power. It is not just a relationship between Jesus and supplicant which always places Jesus in the superior position as Gerhardsson and others propose. Rather, the narrative could have constructed, for at least some households of reception, a more multivalent understanding of healing within the reign-of-God movement which authorized movement between doing and receiving healing, and this movement was symbolized for the community by women as well as men.[67]

Just as Mary Rose D'Angelo suggests that we "re-member" Jesus "as prophet *within* a prophetic movement,"[68] this paper is suggesting that we re-member Jesus as healer *within* a movement which has healing as a core characteristic, a healing movement. She suggests that the community of women and men shared a common spirit of prophecy. This can be amplified by a recognition of their sharing of a common spirit of healing. One of

67. This is not the one-dimensional intention of the author for the readers which Heil's article suggests [see note 21 above], but recognizes different modes of reception within the Matthean community.

68. Mary Rose D'Angelo, "Re-membering Jesus: Women, Prophecy and Resistance in the Memory of the Early Churches," *Horizons* 19 (1992): 202. D'Angelo says of her use of the hyphenated word "re-member" that it "comes from a feminist context; it conveys together the ideas of bringing what has been hidden out of the shadows of history, of putting together what has been dismembered and of making someone a member of oneself/of the community in a new way." She goes on to say that "[t]his constellation of meanings is particularly appropriate not only as a description of what feminists must do to recover the history of women from the gospels and the Christian tradition, but also as a description of any twentieth century and scholarly approach to Jesus in the gospels."

the significant aspects of this understanding to this point is that it invites the community into this world of shared healing by way of stories of the healing of women so that, just as the stories of male characters were intended to function symbolically for the entire community, so too, it can be claimed, can the stories of female characters so function. Before developing such implications, I would like to turn, in conclusion, to a brief survey of the healing of men in Matt. 8–9 in light of the above analysis.

Men in the Health Care System: A Matthean Perspective

This discussion will obviously not be able to be undertaken with the same degree of detail as in the previous section. It is significant, however, to highlight some aspects particular to men in the Matthean health care system.

It has already been pointed out that the healings of men as well as women are episodic in the Gospel, and we have also noted that the settings for the male healings are noninstitutional, in that they take place out of doors as far as one can discern from the narrative. Jesus encounters the person desiring healing in the context of his own ordinary everyday movements around the Galilean area. While these male healings like those of women are integrated into this everydayness, they also have a more formal characteristic in that two men kneel to Jesus (the leper and the father requesting the healing of his daughter) and three use formal titles for Jesus (*Kyrie* is used by the leper [8:2], the centurion [8:6, 8], and the two blind men [9:28]; *hyie tou theou* by the Gadarene demoniacs [8:29]; and *hios Dauid* by the two blind men [9:27]).

When one turns to examine the three stages within the *therapeutic stages and mechanisms,* the result is not as focused as with the healing of women. I will not examine the cultural label for the disease or illness, but simply note one of the significant differences in the mode of manipulation of that label and the new sanctioned label given to the recipients of healing. It is of interest to begin with the paralytic, whose new status is that of being raised (9:7) as it was for Peter's mother-in-law and for the ruler's daughter. He too carries in his body the configuration predicated of Jesus later in the Gospel (28:6). It seems, however, as though his new status is truncated in that he simply returns to his house *(egertheis apēlthen eis ton oikon autou),* whereas Peter's mother-in-law takes up her role of *diakonia* (8:15) and the young woman's future is left open-ended (9:25). The mode of manipulation in this healing as in many other male healings is by Jesus' word (according to the narrator or the actual words of Jesus being narrated). The man's status is changed from paralytic lying on his bed to the raised one who can go to his home. The words of Jesus which bring about the transformation are twofold in this narrative. Initially Jesus invites the paralytic to "Take heart" and then proclaims transformation — "your sins are forgiven" (9:2). When Jesus' claiming of this healing authority is challenged by the scribes, he uses the more traditional healing formula — "Rise, take up your bed and go home" (9:6). Within the symbolic universe of the narrative, illness and the effect of sin are intimately connected, and so to be forgiven or to be raised up are synonymous new cultural labels. The forgiven one, the raised one, configures in his body released from its infirmity a significant aspect of the ministry of Jesus, although it should be noted that it is only in this story that Jesus, under the title of the Human One *(huios tou anthrōpou)*, is characterized as having authority to forgive sins (9:6). As we saw earlier, in 1:21, he is characterized as the one who will save people from sin, the verb *sōzō* being used instead of *aphiēmi.* The story of the healing of the paralytic functions, therefore, as do the stories of the healing of women.

A number of the other new labels are simply descriptive — the leper's leprosy is cleansed (8:3), the eyes of the blind are opened (9:30), the dumb man speaks [9:33], the demons perish in the waters (8:32), and the centurion's servant is made well (8:13). They speak of the transformative, the liberating, and the inclusive nature of the healing reign-of-God but do not narrate the same configuration of aspects of Jesus' reign-of-God ministry in the bodies of those healed. The configuration does occur, however, in the bodies of women and men. It incorporates both women and men into both the doing and the receiving of healing within the movement characterized by its healing. It incorporates into the narrative another aspect of healing other than that noted above, namely Jesus as the authorized healer and the male apostles as the ones authorized by him to heal. This is to read the narrative from one perspective, but this study has demonstrated that different reading positions enable different readings to emerge.

Conclusion

As these stories are appropriated beyond the constructions of healing and gender in the Greco-Roman world, the transformative healing of Jesus may be configured in the bodies of women and men: their paralysis, their bleeding, their dying, and their rising. Participation in the transformative power of healing as constructed by the Gospel narrative for both women and men outside the officially sanctioned and commissioned group of males is not simply to be recipients but, sanctioned by the initiative of the hemorrhaging woman and the new labels given to marginal women and men, to take up their new task of healing. This is to make a deep connection between our world and that of the Matthean recipients of the Gospel, to recognize our own authority to heal the brokenness and the sin of our world, our universe. This is to read the Gospel narrative symbolically and rhetorically for today's world. Women and men as active participants in their own healing, in the healing of human relationships and human brokenness, and in the healing of the universe may be transformed by their faith to be healers as well as healed in the interplay of movement toward transformation. In this they continue the healing and being healed configured in the body of the Matthean Jesus who died and was raised up by divine power and authority given until the close of the age.

Matthew and Community Formation

RICHARD S. ASCOUGH

Introduction

Dennis C. Duling has recently argued that "[t]he Matthean *ekklesia* can be described as a fictive kinship group or fictive brotherhood association"; that is, it is a type of voluntary association.[1] He warns that although the associa-

1. Dennis C. Duling, "The Matthean Brotherhood and Marginal Scribal Leadership,"

I did not have the opportunity to meet Bill Thompson, and this I regret. However, it has become increasingly clear to me that Bill Thompson's presence still very much pervades the corridors and the ethos of Institute of Pastoral Studies at Loyola University Chicago — a presence that has been pointed out to me on many occasions. His contributions to biblical scholarship have been significant, and his continued input will be missed. His concern for the pastoral application of biblical texts was well received by many who might otherwise have failed to grasp the implications of academic scholarship for pastoral ministry. (See William G. Thompson, *Matthew's Advice to a Divided Community (Mt. 17,22–18,35); Matthew's Story: Good News for Uncertain Times;* Eugene A. LaVerdiere and Thompson, "New Testament Communities in Transition: A Study of Matthew and Luke," *TS* 37 [1976]: 593-97.) I feel it a great honor to participate in this symposium in memory of Bill Thompson, and to have been asked to contribute on a topic which launched Prof. Thompson's academic career — community in Matthew. (*Matthew's Advice to a Divided Community,* Thompson's doctoral dissertation, examines the composition of Matt. 17:22–18:35, texts which have enjoyed privileged status among those examining Matthew's ecclesiology.)

tions do not explain every aspect of the Matthean group, "they explain some of its features."[2] In essence, I think this evaluation is correct. However, the case needs to be argued and illustrated, two tasks which Duling only partially fulfills.[3] In fact, despite his description of voluntary associations, ultimately Duling finds the Jewish background and the LXX more informative for understanding the Matthean community.[4] While it is true that Duling gives a brief description of Jewish groups as voluntary associations in order to justify his use of the category of "association," ultimately he has not really employed the non-Jewish material in understanding the Matthean material.[5] In stating this, I would by no means deny the connection of the Matthean com-

---

in *Modelling Early Christianity: Social-Scientific Studies of the New Testament in Its Context,* ed. Philip F. Esler (London: Routledge, 1995), 178, 163; cf. Bruce J. Malina, "Early Christian Groups: Using small group formation theory to explain Christian organizations," in Esler, 107, 108; Duling, "Social-Scientific Small Group Research and Second Testament Study," *BTB* 25 (1995): 188.

2. Duling, "Matthean Brotherhood," 159.

3. Duling cites, but does not quote, only *IG* II[2] 1368 and *CIL* 2112. Since the presentation of this paper, Duling has developed part of his argument in detail by showing how the group process of conflict resolution reflected in Matt. 18:15-17 has parallels in, among other things, the process in the association of the Iobacchi (*IG* II[2] 1368); Dennis C. Duling, "Matthew 18:15-17: Conflict, Confrontation, and Conflict Resolution in a 'Fictive Kin' Association," *SBL 1998 Seminar Papers.* SBLASP 37 (Atlanta: Scholars, 1998), 1:253-95.

4. In fact, despite suggesting that Jewish groups are voluntary associations Duling still seems tied to the idea that Judaism itself was a closed system when he argues that Matthew's scribes are "marginal scribes" and that the group would be viewed as "marginal" ("Matthean Brotherhood," 178-80). Although he attempts to be more broadly based, all of his examples and arguments are grounded in the Jewish world view. The "marginality" of the group is lessened when one sees the Matthean group as yet another variation of the voluntary associations of antiquity, no more or less marginal than the others but at the same time understanding themselves as somehow "better" and set apart from other groups. Even this sense of being "better" than another group can be seen in voluntary associations — the Iobacchi of Athens proclaim, "now we are the best of all" (*IG* II[2] 1368). Even in his later paper ("Conflict Resolution") Duling emphasizes the group at Qumran, albeit following Moshe Weinfeld (*The Organizational Pattern and the Penal Code of the Qumran Sect: A Comparison with Guilds and Religious Associations of the Hellenistic Period.* NTOA 2 [Göttingen: Vandenhoeck & Ruprecht, 1986]) in understanding the Qumran group as a voluntary association.

5. See Duling, "Matthean Brotherhood," 163-64. E.g., Duling's discussion of the leadership designation of "scribe" *(grammateus)* in Matthew sees their background only in Judaism (172-80). However, one can also note that scribes were common in non-Jewish associations; see *IG* II[2] 1317, 1328, 1390; LSAM 3; *SIG*[3] 1012; *P.Mich.* 246, 248. This same limitation is true of his discussion of "brotherhood" where all of his examples come from the synagogues (166-70). Non-Jewish groups are only mentioned in passing.

munity with Judaism. In this way the work of Duling is not only interesting but also compelling. However, his thesis that the Matthean community can be understood as a voluntary association can be strengthened when one takes account of a broader database of material from the associations.[6]

Duling is not the only one to understand the Matthean community as a voluntary association. This is also the assessment of Anthony J. Saldarini, who states that "within Greco-Roman society, Matthew's group would have been understood as a private, voluntary association" and it is within this social context that it must be understood.[7] He understands the Matthean group to be a "deviant association," i.e., an association that has been formed by those who have been rejected by the dominant forces in society and are attempting to defend and restore "respectability to their 'deviant' behavior."[8] He goes on to suggest that

> Matthew's community engages in many of the functions of a deviant association. It recruits members, develops a coherent world view and belief system, articulates an ideology and rhetoric to sustain its behavior, and attacks competing social institutions and groups. The formation of such a voluntary association requires adjustment to a new situation, the need to assign new community functions and status rankings, and the creation of new community goals. All of these activities are carried out in the narrative through the sermons and teachings of Jesus.[9]

Yet in his comparison of voluntary associations and the Matthean group Saldarini fails to note significant differences along with the similarities.

6. Cf. Duling's own invitation ("Matthean Brotherhood," 159) for further study: "This hypothesis will have to be eventually tested with other variables in the Gospel." Cf. Duling, "Matthew 18:15-17."

7. Anthony J. Saldarini, *Matthew's Christian-Jewish Community* (Chicago: University of Chicago Press, 1994), 197; cf. 120.

8. Saldarini, *Matthew's Christian-Jewish Community,* 111; cf. "The Gospel of Matthew and Jewish-Christian Conflict," in *Social History of the Matthean Community: Cross-Disciplinary Approaches,* ed. David L. Balch (Minneapolis: Fortress, 1991), 54.

9. Saldarini, *Matthew's Christian-Jewish Community,* 112; cf. "Jewish-Christian Conflict," 55. It is unclear whether Saldarini means to indicate that all voluntary associations in antiquity were deviant associations or whether this is a sub-type of associations. If the former, then this can be called into question. If the latter, he needs to show examples of such from antiquity and how they are defined as "deviant" against their wider Greco-Roman context.

For example, he suggests that active membership in an association "depends on feelings of solidarity with other members of the group"[10] and suggests that disputes among members would break down relationships and threaten the survival of the group. Yet, as we shall show below, the inscriptional record reveals that association members were highly agonistic and competition among members was often encouraged in group legislation, a marked difference from the Matthean group.

A third voice which may be added to this understanding is that of Michael H. Crosby, who argues that household-based, nonhierarchical voluntary associations are reflected in the house church envisioned by Matthew.[11] Crosby provides the most information about how Matthew's group could be understood as a voluntary association although, like Duling and Saldarini, he relies primarily upon secondary works rather than illustrating his points from primary data. Furthermore, he emphasizes the egalitarian nature of the associations and suggests that the Matthean community builds upon this "potential threat to the status quo of patriarchy" by being even more inclusive.[12] While I would affirm the sense that the Matthean community is striving to be more egalitarian in outlook,[13] I would question Crosby's initial assumption about the egalitarian nature of the associations.[14] In fact, with a predominant emphasis on their own leadership structure, associations seem to have reflected *both* egalitarianism and hierarchy at the same time.

Bruce J. Malina has shown that the first three stages of community growth can be designated as community formation, community cohesion, and community regulations — what he calls "forming," "storming," and "norming."[15] Only after these stages have been completed is the group in a position to enter the "performing" stage, when group members work co-

---

10. Saldarini, *Matthew's Christian-Jewish Community*, 103.

11. Michael H. Crosby, *House of Disciples: Church, Economics, and Justice in Matthew* (Maryknoll: Orbis, 1988), 104-10; cf. 29-31.

12. Crosby, 106; cf. 108.

13. Cf. Crosby, 110.

14. Crosby's only evidence for this "threat to patriarchy" is his citation of John E. Stambaugh and David L. Balch (*The New Testament in Its Social Environment,* Library of Early Christianity 2 [Philadelphia: Westminster, 1986], 125), which, in my reading, does not frame the issue of egalitarianism in the associations in this way.

15. Malina, 103-5, drawing on B. W. Tuckman, "Development Sequence in Small Groups," *Psychological Bulletin* 63 (1965): 384-99.

operatively towards a particular goal.[16] By using this model as a framework,[17] and supplementing the work of Duling, Saldarini, and Crosby with my own work with voluntary association inscriptions, I intend to illustrate where Matthew reflects typical features of voluntary associations and where there are notable differences. Viewing the Matthean community against a wide background of associations may help us understand more clearly the dynamics of social interaction reflected in the Gospel of Matthew. Seeing some of those dynamics against the background of the associations will also help us better understand what was unique and particular about the Matthean community. In fact, this is what I find missing in the works cited above — in simply stating that the Matthean group is like the voluntary associations they fail to engage what may be as interesting, namely, how they are distinct from the dominant ethos that pervaded the associations.[18]

Using Malina's categories we will examine the stages of group formation which the Matthean group seems to have passed through and which are reflected in the Gospel text. In Matthew's redactional activity we can also see how the writer attempts to address the needs of the group[19] and thus reflects the group's self-definition and structure.[20]

---

16. Malina, 105.

17. Malina (110) calls for a re-doing of the Synoptic story line in light of the forming, storming, norming, performing, and adjourning model. My intent is slightly different — to re-examine the group which gave rise to one of these documents, in light of the first three stages. Throughout his article Malina applies his models to the Jesus movement and to the Pauline communities, but does not explicitly apply them to the communities behind the Gospels themselves.

18. Cf. Jonathan Z. Smith, *Drudgery Divine: On the Comparison of Early Christianities and the Religions of Late Antiquity* (Chicago: University of Chicago Press, 1990), 36-53, esp. 47. This is also true of Weinfeld in his well argued presentation of the similarities between the Qumran community and the voluntary associations. While Saldarini (*Matthew's Christian-Jewish Community*, 120; cf. *Pharisees, Scribes and Sadducees in Palestinian Society: A Sociological Approach* [Wilmington: Michael Glazier, 1988], 68) is correct in his assessment that "no generalizations about Greek associations can be used confidently to describe or define a group," it is still possible to highlight some "typical" features. In holding up the Matthean group against the association inscriptions we are not arguing that they are the same as one particular association but that they have similarities to, and marked differences from, what we can observe in the database of association inscriptions.

19. Stephen C. Barton, "The Communal Dimension of Earliest Christianity: A Critical Survey of the Field," *JTS* 43 (1992): 407.

20. By "structure" I imply their sense of group boundaries and means of internal cohesion; cf. Barton, 407. Cf. Saldarini ("Jewish-Christian Conflict," 39): "the story of Jesus in

The Matthean Community as a Voluntary Association

According to Malina, the first condition for any sort of group formation is "a culture that prepares people for group roles."[21] This indeed we have — during the 1st and 2nd century/ies C.E. there was a proliferation of smaller groups throughout the Roman Empire, so much so that few people would not have some experience of these in one form or another: philosophical schools; professional associations; religious associations; synagogues.[22] We will focus particularly on the voluntary associations, which can be defined as groups of men and/or women organized on the basis of freely chosen membership for a common purpose.[23] The comparison of Christian

---

Matthew reflects the experience of Matthew's community and its social situation." But see Jack Dean Kingsbury on the problem of moving from text to social situation ("Conclusion: Analysis of a Conversation," in Balch, 262).

Matthew addresses his community through his editing of the traditions which have circulated, in oral and literary form (esp. Mark and the Sayings Gospel Q; cf. LaVerdiere and Thompson, 574). In doing so he arrives at an authoritative text for the community, and one which helps provide community definition — the Gospel of Matthew. On the question of the place of Q and Mark in the Matthean community, M. Eugene Boring suggests that they were "authoritative" texts in the Matthean community, and that the community may have been founded by one (or more) of the members of the Q community, with Mark being brought in by a group who joined at a later stage ("The Convergence of Source Analysis, Social History, and Literary Structure in the Gospel of Matthew," *SBL 1994 Seminar Papers.* SBLASP 33 [Atlanta: Scholars, 1994], 587-88). This assumes that the Matthean community is distinct from the Jewish synagogues as a separate group from an early period. Yet Boring wants to view a "Yavnian" experience in 70-90 C.E. as a decisive moment for a breaking away of the Matthean community. This makes little sense if they already have a distinct identity with authoritative texts. My own view is that Q and Mark were used by the Matthean Jewish Christians to recall words and deeds of Jesus. Only when they formed a separate group did they need an authoritative text — the Gospel of Matthew — which incorporated the best of their stories with the community's sense of a distinct identity.

21. Malina, 103.

22. Cf. Malina, 101; see also Richard S. Ascough, *What Are They Saying about the Formation of Pauline Churches?* (New York: Paulist, 1998).

23. See further Ascough, *What Are They Saying?* 74-79; John S. Kloppenborg, "Collegia and *Thiasoi*: Issues in Function, Taxonomy and Membership," in *Voluntary Associations in the Graeco-Roman World,* ed. Kloppenborg and Stephen G. Wilson (London: Routledge, 1996), 16-30; Thomas Schmeller, *Hierarchie und Egalität: Eine sozialgeschichtliche Untersuchung paulinischer Gemeinden und griechisch-römischer Vereine.* SBS 162 [Stuttgart: Katholisches Bibelwerk, 1995], 19-53. A survey of the use of associations in understanding Pauline Christian communities can be found in Ascough, 71-94.

groups with the voluntary associations is warranted since associations were "concerned with the social well being of collective selves," as were the Christian groups in antiquity.[24]

Community Formation — "Forming"

This is the stage in which members of the group first come together and recognize the benefits of mutual interdependence. According to Malina's model, "groups always have a purpose that consists in the perception of some needed and meaningful change."[25] For the Matthean group, the need to organize arose from the perception that the social well-being of those who identified themselves with the Messiah named Jesus was not being enhanced through continued contact with their former small group, i.e., the synagogue. Quite the opposite, in fact.[26]

The exact nature of the break between Matthew's Christian community[27] and the synagogues is a complex problem which others have sum-

---

24. Malina, 107.

25. Malina, 106.

26. Malina (99) attributes the awareness of the need for change within all Christian groups, including Matthew's group, to an experience of the Risen Lord (citing 28:18-20). However, I would suggest that in the case of Matthew the need for a separate group is a secondary development predicated by the conflictual situations the Jewish Christians are experiencing in the synagogue. The perception was not simply the general thought that "something was amiss with Israel" (Malina, 101) but the direct, negative experience of something being amiss for Christians in the synagogues.

27. Graham N. Stanton assumes that Matthew is writing to a number of communities, based on his inability to imagine that the trouble and expense of producing a well-crafted document like the Gospel of Matthew would have been deemed necessary for a single, small group; "Revisiting Matthew's Communities," *SBL 1994 Seminar Papers*. SBLASP 33 (Atlanta: Scholars, 1994), 11-12. However, we have no way of knowing the circumstances of the production of Matthew. Moreover, considerable expense went into the production of inscriptions and memorials by members of small, independent voluntary associations. At the same time, I find myself somewhat persuaded by Stanton's suggestion that the lack of specific details in the community regulations in Matthew suggests a document sent generally to a number of communities rather than one community in a particular situation (Stanton, 12). Thus, I will speak of Matthew's community (singular) but remain open to the possibility that there was a loose confederation of communities. The latter possibility does not undermine my attempt to compare the Matthean situation to the voluntary associations as associations could have loose translocal connections; see

marized more ably than I can.[28] However one understands the relationship of the *Birkat ha-minim* to early Christianity,[29] it seems certain that "Matthew was actively engaged with Jewish rivals."[30] Matthew, and those to whom he writes, were involved in conflict with members of synagogues which are in relatively close proximity to Matthew's group.[31]

Richard S. Ascough, "Translocal Relationships among Voluntary Associations and Early Christianity," *JECS* 5 (1997): 223-41.

28. See Donald Senior, *What Are They Saying about Matthew?* rev. ed. (New York: Paulist, 1996), 7-20; Graham N. Stanton, "The Origin and Purpose of Matthew's Gospel: Matthean Scholarship from 1945-1980," *ANRW* II.25.3 (1985) 1910-21; "The Communities of Matthew," *Int* 46 (1992): 379-91.

29. Of late many are inclined not to see the situation of the rabbis at Yavneh as a large monolithic movement in which the *Birkat ha-minim* was introduced in order to expel Christians *en masse* from the synagogues throughout Palestine and the Diaspora. Rather, "the Yavnean rabbis were a minority, took a long time to formulate their vision and an even longer time to impose it, and, as a result, the *Birkat ha-minim* at first had only a marginal effect on Christians and no discernible effect on the Matthean community at all" (Stephen G. Wilson, *Related Strangers: Jews and Christians 70-170 C.E.* [Minneapolis: Fortress, 1995], 47). See Pieter W. van der Horst, "The Birkat ha-minim in Recent Research," in *Hellenism, Judaism, Christianity: Essays on Their Interaction* (Kampen: Kok Pharos, 1994), 99-111; David E. Aune, "On the Origins of the 'Council of Javneh' Myth," *JBL* 110 (1991): 491-93; Graham N. Stanton, *A Gospel for a New People: Studies in Matthew* (Louisville: Westminster John Knox, 1992), 142-45; Wilson, 46-47.

30. Wilson, 47; LaVerdiere and Thompson, 572-73.

31. The synagogues themselves bear striking similarities to voluntary associations and thus can be classified as such; see E. Earle Ellis, *Pauline Theology: Ministry and Society* (Grand Rapids: Wm. B. Eerdmans, 1989), 122-45; G. P. Richardson, "Early Synagogues as Collegia in the Diaspora and Palestine," in Kloppenborg and Wilson, 90-109. Some of the data is briefly summarized in Duling, "Matthean Brotherhood," 163-64. From the time of Julius Caesar the Romans probably classified synagogues as collegia (Wendy J. Cotter, "The Collegia and Roman Law: State Restrictions on Voluntary Associations 64 B.C.E.–200 C.E.," in Kloppenborg and Wilson, 76-78). In discussing the Pharisees and scribes as members of a voluntary association Saldarini (*Pharisees, Scribes and Sadducees*, 67-70; cf. 216-20) suggests that there are only very general similarities (but see 281). Lloyd Gaston ("Pharisaic Problems," in *Approaches to Ancient Judaism.* N.S. 3, ed. Jacob Neusner [Atlanta: Scholars, 1993], 99-100) moves in a similar direction but even more cautiously. On the rabbis as a collegia, see Irving M. Levey, "Caesarea and the Jews," in *The Joint Expedition to Caesarea Maritima* 1: *Studies in the History of Caesarea Maritima*, ed. Charles T. Fritsch. BASOR 19 (Missoula: Scholars, 1975), 65. A number of studies have also been produced illustrating the similarities between the Qumran documents and the community associated with them and the Greco-Roman voluntary associations; see esp. Weinfeld; Duling, "Matthew 18:15-17"; S. Walker-Ramish ("Graeco-Roman Voluntary Associations and the Damascus Document: A Sociological Analysis," in Kloppenborg and Wilson, 128-45) argues against the connection.

The recounting of the foundational stage of the newly formed Matthean community is retrojected back to the time of Jesus in the narrative. Within the larger (fourth) section of the Gospel (13:53–17:27) Matthew connects the origins of the Church to the failure of Israel to accept Jesus as the Messiah.[32] Thus, this section is concerned with the founding of the *ekklēsia*. Matt. 16:13-20 is central to the section, and it is here that we find the first of three uses of the term *ekklēsia*. Matthew changes the flow of his Markan source so that Peter's confession is no longer rejected or corrected but serves as a blessing in which "Peter is praised as the recipient of a divine revelation (16:17), called the foundation of the Church (16:18), and given special authority (16:19)."[33]

The verses preceding 16:17-19 begin to move the reader to see Jesus in light of the great heroes of the past such as Elijah, Jeremiah, and John the Baptist. However, "it at once becomes apparent that the contrasts are greater than the similarities."[34] As the "Christ, the Son of the living God," Jesus "stands alone." His connection to God thus moves him out of the simply human realm and into the realm of the divine — a divinized hero. This is further supported by texts which refer to his special status: "he will save his people from their sins" (1:21); he is named Emmanuel, "God with us" (1:23); and a heavenly voice declares at his baptism, "this is my beloved Son, with whom I am well pleased" (3:17). Thus, Jesus is not the *human* founder of the *ekklēsia*. The foundational role belongs to Peter.[35]

---

32. W. D. Davies and Dale C. Allison, *The Gospel According to Saint Matthew.* ICC (Edinburgh: T. & T. Clark, 1991) 2:642, 649. Allison and Davies (2:649) note that Matthew's focus on Peter seems to occur in the fourth section of the Gospel due to Matthew's ecclesiology.

33. Daniel J. Harrington, *The Gospel of Matthew.* Sacra Pagina 1 (Collegeville: Liturgical, 1991), 250. Matt. 16:17-19 is a controversial passage fraught with exegetical difficulties (see bibliog. in Davies and Allison, 2:643-47). By discussing it here I do not propose to solve all the problems, nor even to discuss each one in detail. Nevertheless, since this passage is unique to Matthew and has thus been understood to reflect specifically Matthean concerns (Robert H. Gundry, *Matthew: A Commentary on His Handbook for a Mixed Church Under Persecution,* 2nd ed. (Grand Rapids: Wm. B. Eerdmans, 1994), 330-31), it does warrant some attention.

34. Davies and Allison, 2:641.

35. Contra Gundry (334), who argues that Peter represents all the disciples and thus the superstructure of the Church rather than its foundation (cf. Davies and Allison, 2:635, who state that Peter is not placed on the same level as the rest of the disciples). Davies and Allison (2:642-43) understand Peter as a "new Abraham" who stands at the head of a new people. I agree with their assessment that "he is a man with a unique rôle in salvation-

Jesus is rather the *divine patron* of the *ekklēsia*.[36]

After the record of Peter's confession of Jesus' unique identity, Matthew expands the story by first explaining how Simon also came to be named Peter, a fact he has received from Mark (Mark 3:16). J. Andrew Overman points out that "it is Matthew who finds in this name a message for his church and interprets the name accordingly."[37] Thus, Peter *(Petros)* is played off "rock" *(petra)* — "you are Peter, and upon this 'rock' I will build my *ekklēsia*" (16:18).[38] By playing off another reference to *petra* in the Gospel it is clear that Matthew intends Peter to be the *foundation* of the Church (cf. 7:24-25, the story of two types of foundations).[39]

More significantly, Matthew has Jesus point out that Peter's insight did not come through human means. Rather, it was revealed "by my Father in heaven" (16:17b). Thus, it is a divine revelation. As such, "this adds tremendous weight and authority to Peter's position and claims about Jesus."[40] Thus, in 16:17-19 (unique to Matthew) Peter is presented as the

---

history," and that "his faith is the means by which God brings a new people into being." However, for the writer of Matthew, Peter represents the one who was chosen as the founder of the unique, separate community to which Matthew writes. J. Andrew Overman uses the sociological analyses of Max Weber as a lens to understand the passing on of the leadership from the charismatic founder (Jesus) to Peter through "designation"; *Church and Community in Crisis: The Gospel According to Matthew* (Valley Forge: Trinity, 1996), 246-48. Yet surely the context in Matthew, with the climaxing christological confession about Jesus' identity which precedes the "designation," indicates that something more is going on here. Overman (249) rightly notes that "the person and the confession cannot be distinguished here." Peter is thus the human founder of the group. Cf. Crosby (51), who notes that in 16:18 "the foundational function is transferred to Peter." Also Ulrich Luz, *The Theology of the Gospel of Matthew* (Cambridge: Cambridge University Press, 1995), 94.

36. Jesus is also presented elsewhere in Matthew as the mediator of divine revelation: 11:25-27 ("knowledge of the Father"); 13:3-9 ("secrets of the kingdom"). At both the baptism (3:17) and the transfiguration (17:5) a heavenly voice declares "this is my beloved Son." Peter, James, and John experience a vision at the Transfiguration (17:1-8). Cf. in 1:23b Jesus is "Emmanuel . . . God with us." After the Resurrection, wherever two or three are gathered he will be in the midst of them (18:20).

37. Overman, 240.

38. For the plethora of possible interpretations of this phrase and the meaning of "this rock," see Davies and Allison, 2:627; e.g., Peter's faith, Peter's confession, Peter's preaching office, the truth revealed to Peter, the twelve apostles, Jesus, Jesus' teaching, God. On the Old Testament background of the images of "rock" and "keys," see Harrington, 251; Overman, 240-42.

39. Davies and Allison, 2:627, 634; Overman, 240.

40. Overman, 240.

(fictive) founder of the group while Jesus is the deified hero or deity who gives the directives to the founder.[41] In this way, the origins of the group are analogous to the origins of many voluntary associations.

Often the formation and propagation of voluntary associations was given divine sanction. In response to a manifestation of a deity via a dream, vision, or an oracle, an association might be formed to participate in the worship of that deity. An inscription from Philadelphia in Lydia (*SIG*³ 985) records the ordinances given by Zeus to a certain Dionysius while he slept.

> The ordinances given to Dionysius in his sleep were written up giving access into his *oikos* to men and women, free people and slaves. . . . To this man Zeus has given ordinances for the performance of the purifications, the cleansings and the mysteries, in accordance with the ancestral custom and as has now been written. (ll. 4-6, 12-14)

The dream convinces Dionysius either to establish an association in his house *(oikos)* or, more likely, to allow others to have access to an association already existing in his house.

Dreams also play an important part in the expansion of a Delian association of worshipers of Sarapis and Isis (*IG* XI/4 1299).[42] The cult was brought from Egypt by an immigrating devotee. Within two generations this family cult had outgrown the rented premises where the devotees met. The priest Apollonios records:

> the god (Sarapis) revealed to me in a dream that a Sarapeum must be consecrated to him alone, and that he is no longer to be in rented rooms as before, and further that he (Sarapis) will find the place where it (the temple) should be situated and will indicate the location with a sign. And this happened (as he promised). (ll. 13-18)

41. Warren Carter notes how the opening two chapters of Matthew locate the origins of the community in the purposes of God and then in the ministry of Jesus and his call to others to "follow me"; "Community Definition and Matthew's Gospel," *SBL 1997 Seminar Papers.* SBLASP 36 (Atlanta: Scholars, 1997), 647-50.

42. Franciszek Sokolowski briefly discusses this inscription and describes it as recounting the story of a man who, after having Sarapis come to him in his sleep, finds some writing hidden in the frame of the door which instructs him where and how to build the temple (ll. 56-58), which Sokolowski connects to the use of a *Himmelsbriefe;* "Propagation of the Cult of Sarapis and Isis in Greece," *GRBS* 15 (1974): 443. On the use of dreams in the expansion of the cult of Artemis see IEphesos 24.

We have here the move from a private association to a public cult, although it is probable that the private association continued alongside the public cult.[43] Thus, the divinity intervenes in the significant reconfiguration of the group.

In an inscription from Sounion (*IG* II² 1366) it is said of the founder, Xanthos, that "the god chose him" (*airetisantos tou theou;* l. 2). Most probably this is a reference to a divine epiphany. The god may have appeared to Xanthos, either in a dream or "in person," commanding him to build the sanctuary.[44]

These examples show that in presenting the foundation of the *ekklēsia* in terms of a directive from the divinized hero to a specific individual, Matthew's depiction fits one of the characteristic means whereby associations were founded. However, whereas the god might appear in a dream or speak through an oracle, in the case of the foundation of Matthew's community the divine will was revealed at both the supernatural *and* the natural level — supernatural through the revelation of Jesus' true identity to Peter by God (16:17) and natural through the physical presence of the human "Son of the living God" with Peter (16:16).

Community Cohesion — "Storming"

The "storming" stage is the painful process of transition from a collection of individuals to a collective. At this stage there is conflict within the group as individual members assert their own needs through argument and criticism of the leaders.[45] We see this reflected in Matthew. Challenges were being made to the authority of the community and the demands made for membership. False prophets attempted to attract some away while persecutions by both Jews and the civic magistrates were rife. As a result some were leaving the community. In describing the persecutions which the group endures, Matthew has divided and edited a single Markan passage (Mark 13:9-13). In 10:17-25 we read of persecution from outside the community and betrayal within. Matthew continues by drawing on Q 12:8-19, emphasizing that endurance is needed. One must stand firm in one's con-

43. A. D. Nock, *Conversion: The Old and the New in Religion from Alexander the Great to Augustine of Hippo* (1933, repr. Baltimore: Johns Hopkins University Press, 1998), 55.

44. Cf. *CMRDM* 4.137. For other examples of the use of dreams, visions, and oracles see *IG* X/2 255; IPriene 139; IEphesos 24; *SIG*³ 1044.

45. Malina, 104.

victions about Jesus and acknowledge him before others. Failure to do so results in rejection before God (10:32-33).[46] Matthew here inserts another Q passage to which he adds the concluding statement "one's foes will be those of one's own household" (10:36). This clearly echoes 10:21 (par. Mark 13:12) where brothers and fathers and children are in conflict. Yet in 10:25 Matthew added "If they have called the master of the house Beelzebul, how much more will they malign those of his household *(tous oikiakous autou)*." Clearly this is a reference to the Matthean community as a (fictive) kin-based relationship. Thus, when Matthew indicates that foes will come from one's own household (10:21, 35-36), it is suggestive not only of divisions among families but divisions within the Christian group itself. Hence, "brother will deliver up brother to death" *(paradōsei de adelphos adelphon eis thanaton,* 10:21).

We see this further in 24:9-14, the other pericope in which Matthew has adapted Mark 13:9-13, where we read

> Then they will hand you over to be tortured and will put you to death; and you will be hated by all nations because of my name. Then many will fall away, and they will betray one another and hate one another. And many false prophets will arise and lead many astray. And because of the increase of lawlessness, the love of many will grow cold. But the one who endures to the end will be saved. And this good news of the kingdom will be proclaimed throughout the world, as a testimony to all the nations; and then the end will come.

Clearly internal tensions have affected the group, indicating that it has experienced what Malina calls the "storming" stage of community formation. This passage was meant to "explain the attrition within the group, and to support those who remained but were nevertheless troubled by the doubts departing members had spawned."[47] This is further confirmed in

46. The narrative works on two levels, that of the narrative world and that of the world of the readers. Thus, while the earlier part of the mission instructions (10:5-6) would seem to be confined to Jesus' disciples (remain within the house of Israel), the latter part refers to experiences of the community after the death and resurrection of Jesus (10:16-23). See Donald Senior, *The Gospel of Matthew* (Nashville: Abingdon, 1997), 117-18; also Davies and Allison, 2:179-80.

47. Overman, 331. Overman (332) points out that the phrase "hate one another" stands in direct contrast to the love command that was the summation of the Law within the Matthean community.

the regulations concerning forgiveness and reconciliation, which suggest a time when conflict was rife but hope was still held that members would return (18:21-35).

Not only are internal tensions among group members evident in the text, something more sinister is afoot. These texts clearly reflect the Matthean community's experience of physical persecution.[48] The most obvious source of this persecution in the Matthean picture is the Jewish synagogues. The disciples will be delivered *(paradidōmi)* up to "their synagogues" (10:17), clearly indicating a Jewish assembly.[49]

The first few verses of Matthew 24:9-12 read: "Then they will deliver you up to tribulation, and put you to death; and you will be hated by all nations for my name's sake" (24:9-10). This can be connected with 10:18, "you will be dragged before governors *(hēgemonas)* and kings *(basileis)* because of me." This is clearly a reference to the persecution of the Matthean Christians by Roman authorities. Nevertheless, most commentators struggle to determine what exactly the nature of charges against the Matthean Christians would be — "We are not given sufficient information to know how and why the members ended up in court."[50] Various suggestions have been made such as the Christian movement being perceived as "suspect," or "deviant," or "dangerous," or "seditious," or "lawless," but little detail is given to suggest why or how they were so perceived.[51]

I would suggest that it is similar to the official Roman sanctions

48. Overman, 155; Leon Morris, *The Gospel According to Matthew* (Grand Rapids: Wm. B. Eerdmans, 1992), 600; Alfred Plummer, *An Exegetical Commentary on the Gospel of According to St. Matthew* (1915; repr. Grand Rapids: Baker, 1982), 331.

49. *Paradidōmi* is the term used of Jesus being handed over to Pilate by the Jews (27:2, 18), and by Pilate to soldiers for crucifixion (27:26; Overman, 154).

50. Overman, 156. Often no reason for the persecution is given except a general response to evangelization; see Davies and Allison, 2:183-84; Craig C. Blomberg, *Matthew.* New American Commentary 22 (Nashville: Broadman, 1992), 174; Morris, 254; Harrington, 333-34; Donald A. Hagner, *Matthew 1–13.* WBC 33A (Dallas: Word, 1993), 277; Gundry, 478-79. Daniel Patte (*The Gospel According to Matthew: A Structural Commentary on Matthew's Faith* [1987; repr. Valley Forge: Trinity, 1996], 149) assumes that in 10:18 it is the Jews who drag the Matthean Christians before the Roman authorities, but this is not necessarily the case for 24:9-10. Within the eschatological discourse of ch. 24 the persecutions are one of the signs of the coming parousia of Jesus.

51. Overman (156) suggests that they were seen as seditious in the tradition of John the Baptist and Jesus because they emulated similar behavior, but this is pure speculation. Overman (157) also suggests that the picture of them "on the run" from town to town is perhaps hyperbolic. However, it may reflect their recent recruitment efforts.

against voluntary associations. Matthew is often read in light of Christians being singled out by the authorities, but they may be no more singled out than other association members were. Members of voluntary associations often suffered at the hands of others, particularly those in authority. At various points during the Roman period attempts were made to suppress voluntary associations.[52] As early as 186 B.C.E. the Roman senate acted against an association of worshipers of Dionysos. The Senate dissolved the collegia in 64 B.C.E. and enacted two futher decrees against association in 56-55 B.C.E. In 49 B.C.E. a *Lex Julia* banned all associations, except those which had been established for a long time.[53]

At the beginning of the 1st century the number of associations had grown once again. In an attempt to control the associations, Augustus passed a law that every association must be sanctioned by the senate or emperor.[54] This was continued under successive emperors during the 1st century but was enforced only sporadically.[55] An exchange between Pliny, governor of Bithynia, and the Emperor Trajan over the formation of a firemen's guild *(heraeria)* illustrates that official wariness over such groups continued into the 2nd century (*Epistulae* 10.33-34; cf. 10.92).

All of this suggests that during the 1st and early 2nd centuries care had to be taken by those who regularly gathered as a group for social or cultic purposes. Despite the prohibition against such associations,

> these measures do not seem to have been uniformly enforced. If Clau-
> dius, Nero, and Trajan are seen to suppress the collegia, it is because
> these clubs continued to spring up and grow whenever the political cli-
> mate allowed them to do so.[56]

It is into this general context of official suspicion of associations, alongside their continued existence, that we might view the formation of the Matthean Christian community. Encounters with the authorities are to be avoided at all cost. At 5:25-26 Matthew includes a Q text which advocates

---

52. For details of the following summary, see Cotter, "The Collegia and Roman Law," 74-89.

53. Jewish groups gained expemption through this provision (Cotter, "The Collegia and Roman Law," 76-78; Richardson, 93), although later they were occasionally disbanded (e.g., temporarily under Claudius; Cotter, 78).

54. See *CIL* VI 2193 (= *ILS* 4966); cf. Suetonius *Vitae,* "Augustus" 32.1; *CIL* VI 2193.

55. Cotter, "The Collegia and Roman Law," 88.

56. Cotter, "The Collegia and Roman Law," 88.

reconciliation with an accuser before one gets to court. Not to do so will involve imprisonment and fines. Matthew connects this saying to Jesus' advice to reconcile with one's brother even if it means interrupting participation in worship (5:21-24). Divisions within the community itself will not only result in some members leaving but will also be brought to the attention of the civic (Roman) authorities who are only too eager to suppress such newly forming groups.

The connection of the persecution sayings with apocalyptic visions indicates that for Matthew "betrayal and falling away from the group as a result of this political and civil pressure were seen as an indication that the end was near."[57] However, the storming stage is also the stage at which hope for success and for betterment is instilled within the group for those who are members. We find this hope for the community reflected in the Beatitudes (5:3-12), which reinforce the blessing of God upon them despite their "underdog" status.

Community Relations — "Norming"

"The norming stage is marked by interpersonal conflict resolution in favour of mutually agreed upon patterns of behaviour. . . . norming involves group members in the attempt to resolve earlier conflicts, often by negotiating clearer guidelines for group behaviour."[58] It "involves group members in the attempt to resolve earlier conflicts, often by negotiating clear guidelines for group behaviour."[59] There are a number of ways in which Matthew evidences a concern with community definition: "by naming, by separation and social organization, by association with a group, by practices and ritual, by invective against opponents, by claims to the exclusive center for revelation, or by claims to be the true heirs and interpreters of a tradition."[60] I want to highlight some of these features of community definition and examine them in light of the voluntary associations to see what light can be shed on the Matthean group's practices.

57. Overman, 158; cf. 332-33.
58. Malina, 104.
59. Malina, 104; cf. Saldarini, *Matthew's Christian-Jewish Community,* 89-90.
60. Carter, 637.

111

Community Designations

Most commentators have noted Matthew's distinctive use of the term *ekklēsia* in his Gospel.[61] The term is used three times in two verses:

16:18: "And I tell you, you are Peter, and on this rock I will build my *ekklēsia*, and the gates of Hades will not prevail against it."

18:17: "If the member refuses to listen to them, tell it to the *ekklēsia*; and if the offender refuses to listen even to the *ekklēsia*, let such a one be to you as a Gentile and a tax collector."

The Matthean use of the term *ekklēsia* is often highlighted in discussions of the Christian community's relationship to Judaism. Most often the LXX background is cited in order to show how the title was derived from the community's roots in Judaism.[62] The word *ekklēsia* is used more than 100

---

61. Davies and Allison (2:629, 635) suggest that Matthew uses two slightly different meanings for *ekklēsia* — the universal Church in 16:18 and the local assembly in 18:17. However, they do not show why this is the case, nor do I think it is self-evidently obvious why this would be the case for Matthew's audience. Certainly it is the predominant way of understanding these verses in later Christian history, but this need not be read back into Matthew (cf. Saldarini, *Matthew's Christian-Jewish Community*, 116, 118).

62. So Floyd V. Filson, *A Commentary on the Gospel According to St. Matthew*, 2nd ed. Black's New Testament Commentaries (London: A. & C. Black, 1971), 187; David Hill, *The Gospel of Matthew*. NCBC (Grand Rapids: Eerdmans, 1972), 261; Hubert Frankemölle, *Jahwebund und Kirche Christi*. NTAbh n.s. 10 (Münster: Aschendorff, 1974), summarized in Senior, *What Are They Saying about Matthew?* 90-91; Morris, 424-25; Blomberg, 252-53; John J. Kilgallen, *A Brief Commentary on the Gospel of Matthew* (Lewiston: Mellen, 1992), 132; Gundry, 332-33 (on 335 he states that Matthew's composition of 16:17-19 in Greek eliminates the quest for the right Semitic word behind his use of *ekklēsia* but does not investigate the background of the word in the Greek world). Davies and Allison (2:629) state that "it is doubted whether the background to early Christian usage is to be found in the LXX and it must be conceded that the NT uses of *ekklēsia* sometimes lack LXX parallels." Despite this, they only look to Jewish literature for antecedents of early Christian self-identity and never do investigate the background of the term outside of the Jewish world. Plummer (253) goes so far as to suggest that *ekklēsia* at 18:17 indicates the local Jewish assembly rather than the Christian community.

In a modified assessment of the position, Saldarini argues that Matthew is not using *ekklēsia* as a title for his group (*Matthew's Christian-Jewish Community*, 116, 119-20), but Saldarini still understands the primary referent of *ekklēsia* to lie in the LXX (117). The term is used to indicate that Matthew's community is "the assembly *(ekklēsia)* of Israel according to the teachings of Jesus" as distinct from "the assembly of Israel" (119). Saldarini is quite

times in the LXX, in most instances as a translation for the Hebrew *qhl.* However, *synagōgē* is the more frequently chosen word as a translation of *qhl.*[63] Few scholars address cogently the issue of why the Christian groups would choose to use *ekklēsia* over *synagōgē*. Duling breezes too quickly over the issue when he notes that "given the Septuagint rendering of Hebrew 'assembly' *(qahal)* as both *synagoge* and *ekklesia* and the relation of these two terms to the 'house-synagogue' and the 'house-church,' it is naturally the central option for the Matthean group."[64] Yet *ekklēsia* is not *the* central option; *synagōgē* is *also* an option — an option which the Matthean group (and other Christian groups) did *not* adopt. Clearly, the Matthean Christians wanted to "differentiate" themselves from Jewish groups.[65] Thus, the LXX use of the term *ekklēsia* is not necessarily the primary reference for their group designation. If they saw themselves as the "true" Israel, why not retain the designator *synagōgē*? If they saw themselves as distinct and outside of Judaism, why the need to find antecedents in the LXX?

Again the voluntary associations can be helpful. Despite McCready's claim that "there is little evidence that voluntary associations or clubs used the word *ekklesia* as a community designation,"[66] there are a few examples: one from Samos;[67] *OGIS* 488 (Kastollos near Philadelphia, 2nd century C.E.); *IGLAM* 1381 (Aspendus [Pamphylia]); *IGLAM* 1382 (Aspendus); IDelos 1519 (196 B.C.E.). The most obvious source from which these associations have taken over the term is the civic government (not the LXX!),

---

right in observing that Matthew's use of *ekklēsia* "must be determined from immediate literary and social context and not by usage in other Christian literature" (116, 118; contra Stanton, "Revisiting Matthew's Communities," 16). Yet the use of this term as a title in the civic environment of antiquity makes Saldarini's argument that it has no titular function in Matthew unlikely. The term shows up in Matthew at precisely those places where the later community is in view and one would expect a title to be used.

63. W. O. McCready, "*Ecclesia* and Voluntary Associations," in Kloppenborg and Wilson, 60; K. L. Schmidt, "ἐκκλησία," *TDNT* 3 (1965): 513-14, esp. n. 25.

64. Duling, "Matthean Brotherhood," 164.

65. Cf. Luz (97): Matthew's group "has a new name — 'my "congregation"', as distinct from the old 'congregation', Israel." Harrington (248, 269) notes that the difference in terminology is for differentiation, and suggests that Jewish Christians have adopted the "Greek title" for their communities (251). However, he does not explain what he means by this.

66. McCready, 62.

67. E. G. L. Ziebarth, *Das griechische Vereinswesen* (1896, repr. Wiesbaden: Martin Sändig, 1969), 116 no. 3.

where the word was commonly used of "an assembly of the citizens of a 'free' city."[68] The use of *ekklēsia* was similar to the use of other civic terms used by the associations, such as *taxis, phylē, hairesis, kollēgion, syllogos, synteleia, synedrion, systēma, synodos, koinon.*[69] "In the environment of Greek cities, the term *ekklēsia* would almost certainly be understood (by all involved) as one of the names for a voluntary association."[70]

The Matthean Christians would hear *ekklēsia* as marking them off as distinct from the Jewish *synagōgai* and as designating them as similar in structure to a voluntary association.[71] By adopting the title *ekklēsia* for the community, the Matthean Christians are standing in clear *contrast* to the Jewish groups who have used the term *synagōgē.* This contrast is made even stronger through the language of "their/your synagogues" (4:23; 9:35; 10:17; 12:9; 13:54; 23:34)[72] and the synagogues of the "hypocrites" (6:2; cf. 6:5; 23:13-26). In choosing *ekklēsia* Matthew wants the newly founded group to be readily understood as a different *type* of association than the Jewish associations from which he and his companions have been expelled.[73]

---

68. Wendy J. Cotter, "Woman's Authority Roles in Paul's Churches: Countercultural or Conventional?" *NovT* 36 (1994): 370.

69. See Franz Poland, *Geschichte des griechischen Vereinswesens* (1909, repr. Leipzig: Zentral-Antiquariat der DDR, 1967), 152-68.

70. John S. Kloppenborg, "Edwin Hatch, Churches and *Collegia*," in *Origins and Method: Towards a New Understanding of Judaism and Christianity,* ed. Bradley H. McLean. JSNTSup 86 (Sheffield: JSOT, 1993), 231. Saldarini (*Matthew's Christian-Jewish Community,* 116-17) points out the use of *ekklēsia* by voluntary associations but does not use it as background for Matthew's group. His note (117; cf. 265 n. 135) that it is not a technical term for a cultic group does not subtract from the fact that it was used for associations. There is such a wide variety of terms used of associations in antiquity that it would be difficult to argue that a "technical term" would need to be used in order to identify an association as such.

71. Saldarini (*Matthew's Christian-Jewish Community,* 117) is probably correct in his assessment that both the general Greek usage and the LXX were sources for Matthew's choice of the term.

72. In all but the first case the use of "their/your" is unique to Matthew. Matt. 4:23 comes from Mark 1:39, which L. Michael White suggests was the literary prototype for the remainder; "Crisis Management and Boundary Maintenance: The Social Location of the Matthean Community," in Balch, 215 n. 17.

73. This is emphasized by Matthew's placement on Jesus' lips the phrase "my *ekklēsia*" (*mou tēn ekklēsian,* 16:18) in contrast to "their" synagogues (Crosby, 51).

Conflict Resolution

It is clear that Matthew's community had experienced a time of internal conflict and division and had created regulations by which such conflict could be resolved. This is seen particularly in the community discourse of ch. 18 but also in the regulations concerning respect for the brethren (5:1–7:29) and elsewhere in the Gospel.[74] In the sayings on forgiveness (18:15-22) instructions are given concerning a community member found to be in sin.[75] A process is to be followed when dealing with an erring member. If after a confrontation s/he does not change ways, then the next step is undertaken. The steps are:

1. an individual approaches the erring member
2. a group of two or three approach the erring member so that they may act as witnesses
3. the erring member's ways are brought before the entire community (*ekklēsia*)
4. the erring member is expelled by the group

If at any point in the process the erring member verbalizes a desire to change and be reintegrated into the group, then those overseeing the process must accept that member back into fellowship. There is no limit on how often such a person may be confronted and ask for forgiveness (this is the import of Jesus advocating forgiveness "seventy times seven" [18:22]).[76]

With this communal context for conflict resolution in mind, we turn again to the voluntary associations. A number of regulations from volun-

74. Cf. LaVerdiere and Thompson, 579; William G. Thompson, "An Historical Perspective in the Gospel of Matthew," *JBL* 93 (1974): 261.

75. Thompson (*Matthew's Advice to a Divided Community*, 258) is clearly correct when he notes that "the narrative introductions situate Mt 17,22–18,35 within Matthew, and its situation implies that this passage was particularly relevant to the Matthean community." He goes on to state that 18:1-20 "reveal a divided community. . . . sin was disrupting the Matthean community, and the need for fraternal correction was urgent" (259). Where I would disagree is in his suggestion that 17:22–18:35 is to be seen as "proverbial" advice because it is not legal or prescriptive (264). I do think it is meant to function prescriptively within the community — Barton (407) calls Matthew 18 "a kind of 'community rule' to deal with matters of internal discipline."

76. Luz, 106.

tary associations indicate that agonistic situations were common within such groups.[77] For example, the 2nd-century c.e. rule of the Iobacchi (*IG* II² 1368; Athens) states that:

> If anyone begins a fight or if someone is found disorderly *(heurethē tis akosmōn)*, or if someone comes and sits in someone else's seat or is insulting or abuses someone else . . . the one who committed the insult or the abuse shall pay to the association 25 drachmae and the one who was the cause of the fight shall pay the same 25 drachmae or not come to any more meetings of the Iobacchi until he pays. (ll. 72-83)

Anyone singled out by an official for having caused a disturbance is ejected from the meeting, if not voluntarily then by a group of "bouncers" *(hippoi)*. If one member strikes another member, the one struck is to file a report with the priest, who in turn convenes a meeting of the entire group who vote on a verdict. The resulting penalty is expulsion "for as long as it seems appropriate" as well as a fine. The same penalty applies to the one who is struck if he takes the matter outside of the group to the public courts.[78]

A 4th-century b.c.e. inscription from an Athenian association stipulates that anyone who attempts to introduce legislation which goes against that already agreed upon by the membership is to be fined (*IG* II² 1361; see also *IG* II² 1275). In *P.Lond.* 2710 members are forbidden "to make factions . . . to enter into one another's pedigrees at the banquet, or to abuse one another at the banquet or chatter or to indict or charge one another or to resign during the course of the year or to bring the drinking to naught." A section concerning the "disorderly" *(akosmountōn)* in the regulations of the mysteries of Andania (*IG* V/1 1390; 96 b.c.e.) begins

---

77. Such regulations seem also to have had legal force. There are instances where members or relatives of members bring a civil suit against the association for not carrying out the contracted duties; see *P.Enteuxeis* 1.20.

78. John S. Kloppenborg has shown how Paul's injunction against taking one another to court in 1 Cor. 6:1-11 betrays a problem within the Corinthian congregation which is common within the voluntary associations; "Egalitarianism in the Myth and Rhetoric of Pauline Churches," in *Reimagining Christian Origins*, ed. Elizabeth A. Castelli and Hal Taussig (Valley Forge: Trinity, 1996), 247-63. Schmeller (86-87) arrives at a similar conclusion. We might also note the similarity with Matt. 5:25. The similarity between the statutes concerning an erring member in 18:15-17 and the Iobacchi inscription (and the Qumran community documents) is noted by Weinfeld, 49; and expanded by Duling, "Matthew 18:15-17," esp. 263-66; cf. Duling, "Matthean Brotherhood," 167, 168.

> And whenever the sacrifices and mysteries are celebrated, let everyone keep silent and listen to the things announced. And let the officers flog the disobedient and those who live indecently and prevent them from (participating) in the mysteries. (ll. 39-41).

A similar injunction against those are disorderly in a procession is found in *LSAM* 9, although the punishment here is a beating with a rod.

In *CIL* XIV 2112 (2nd century c.e.) any member who disrupts the banquet or speaks abusively of another or causes an uproar shall be fined. If a complaint is to be made, it is to be brought up at a business meeting rather than at a banquet. *P.Cairo dem.* 30605 (157/156 b.c.e.) imposes fines for a member who does not provide what is required for the festival. More interestingly, in another set of regulations from the same Egyptian religious association (*P.Cairo dem.* 30606; 158-157 b.c.e.), a fine is levied upon a member who brings a complaint before the civic authorities before bringing it before the membership of the group. Fines are also imposed for insults (e.g., "you are a leper"), striking another member, and refusal to attend a meeting. In the case of insults, the erring member is expelled from the group. If two members meet on the road and one asks the other for money, presumably out of need, the one asked must give or else be fined by the group. The exception is a clause which states that the one who is reluctant to give must swear an oath before the god that he cannot afford to give anything.

A similar concern for fellow members is expressed in *P.Mich.Teb.* 243 (early imperial period; cf. *P.Mich.Teb.* 244). The usual financial penalties are levied against members who fail to meet their responsibilities, who misconduct themselves in public, at banquets, or during the funerary ceremonies (including failure to shave), or who fail to attend a meeting. It also stipulates that "If a member ignores someone who is in distress and does not assist in helping him out of his trouble, he shall pay 8 drachmae."

These regulations from voluntary associations give some indication of the type of disturbances that could occur at meetings (fighting, disruptions of order and ceremony, abuse of others) or between members (failure to care), along with guidance on how to deal with such (fines, floggings, and expulsion). In most cases the erring member is brought before the entire group and the punishment proclaimed and exacted publicly. These regulations of a number of voluntary associations also show that regularly occurring agonistic community interaction required that restrictions be placed on members who were in conflict with one another both during the meetings of the association and outside of the meetings. Recalling Matthew's injunctions against an erring member and the number of times one must forgive another, we can assume, I think, that such conflictual situations were regular occurrences within the Matthean Christian community. Thus we see a similarity between this Christian community and the voluntary associations in terms of both internal conflict among members and regulated conflict resolution.[79]

Other passages might also be indicated in this. In 5:21-24[80] a member *(adelphos)* is warned that bearing anger internally against another member will result in "judgment" *(krisis)* and articulating insults ("says to his brother 'raka'") will result in being brought before the "council." This "council" or *synedrion* is usually thought to be the Jewish Sanhedrin,[81] but it could also indicate the collective membership of the Matthean Christian group.[82] Within the Matthean community, persistence and intensification

79. One might also ask whether being handed over to councils (*synedria*, plural) and the "flogging" in the synagogues referred to in 10:17 (a passage unique to Matthew) is meted out upon individual Christians who have remained within the synagogue groups and are punished for seemingly disrupting group cohesion, as is the case with punishments in other voluntary associations. In the current context in Matthew it applies to the mission commission of the group members as a warning against what to expect as they spread the message.

80. This is unique to Matthew, but is joined with a Q text about making amends with one's accuser on the way to court (Q 12:58-59).

81. See W. C. Allen, *A Critical and Exegetical Commentary on the Gospel According to St. Matthew,* 3rd ed. ICC (Edinburgh: T. & T. Clark, 1912), 48; E. Lohse, "συνέδριον," *TDNT* 7 (1971): 867; Filson, 85; Davies and Allison, 1 (1988): 514; Morris, 115; Hagner, 116; cf. Gundry, 85. Craig S. Keener understands it with reference to a heavenly Sanhedrin; "Matthew 5:22 and the Heavenly Court," *ExpTim* 99 (1987): 46.

82. Others have suggested a smaller group within the Matthean Christian community, responsible for church discipline; so Hill, 121; Manfred Weise, "Mt 5 21f — ein Zeugnis sakraler Rechtsprechung in der Urgemeinde," *ZNW* 49 (1958): 117-19. The word *synedrion* is used for non-Jewish voluntary associations (see Poland, 156-58) and is thus applicable to the Matthean community. Davies and Allison (1:514) state that the lack of attestation in New Testament times for *synedrion* as "a church body responsible for discipline of church members" indicates that the reference must be to the Jerusalem high council or a local court; cf. Robert Guelich, *The Sermon on the Mount: A Foundation for Understanding* (Dallas: Word, 1982), 187. However, they overlook the adoption of the term by local voluntary associations. The word *synedrion* is used of the college of presbyters envisioned as part of a three-tiered church organization put forth by Ignatius of Antioch (*Magn.* 6.1; *Phld.* 8.1). The word, like so many used by the voluntary associations, Christian groups, and the synagogues, was taken from the civic government.

of the insults will result in the council's judgment, the "hell of fire," perhaps a locution for expulsion.[83]

The primary difference between the Matthean Christians and the voluntary associations in terms of conflict resolution is the emphasis within this Christian group on forgiveness — not defending one's honor according to the typical patterns.[84] In fact, the regulations concerning community discipline are prefaced with Jesus' sayings about humility (18:1-5), proper treatment of the defenseless (18:6-9), and the importance of "little ones" in the kingdom (18:10-14).[85] The onus is placed on the one

83. Stanton uses "the very stringent moral requirements (5:20, 48; 18:8-9; 19:11-12) and the strong internal discipline of Christian communities (18:5-19)" as evidence that the Matthean communities were minority, sectarian groups; *Int* 46 (1992): 386. In light of the evidence from voluntary associations this statement may need some nuancing. While the sectarian nature of such groups can be shown, their "minority" status might have been over-emphasized — there were lots of other groups expressing similar forms of community and experiencing community in similar ways.

84. Kloppenborg ("Egalitarianism," 259) suggests that the primary difference between Christian groups and associations is that the Christians "did not use the blunt instruments of fining or expelling those who threatened the stability of the group" but rather "a rhetoric of belonging based on the language of 'brother- and sisterhood,' was nurtured." In general, this is the case. However, one should note that the language of "brotherhood" can be found in some association inscriptions (*contra* Kloppenborg, "Egalitarianism," 259; Saldarini, *Matthew's Christian-Jewish Community*, 93). Nevertheless, it is not a particularly common designation (cf. Adolf von Harnack, *The Mission and Expansion of Christianity in the First Three Centuries* [1908, repr. New York: Harper, 1962] 1:405-6 n. 1). Duling makes clear the emphasis on "brotherhood" in Matthew ("Matthean Brotherhood," 164-72) but makes little reference to the usage in the associations. For evidence for the use of "brothers" in associations, see *TAMSup* III 201; *OGIS* 51 (cf. *OGIS* 50); *P.Paris* 42; see also Poland, 56; Franz Bömer, *Untersuchungen über die Religion der Sklaven in Griechenland und Rom* 1 (Wiesbaden: Steiner, 1958), 72-78; G. Adolf Deissmann, *Bible Studies: Contributions, Chiefly from Papyri and Inscriptions, to the History of the Language, the Literature, and the Religion of Hellenistic Judaism and Primitive Christianity* (Edinburgh: T. & T. Clark, 1901), 88; MM (1914), 9. In Latin inscriptions one also finds reference to members of associations as *fratres* (*CIL* VI 377, 406, 7487, 10681, 21812; see Kloppenborg, "Edwin Hatch, Churches and *Collegia*," 216 n. 17).

85. Matt. 24:9-13 (Matthean additions to Mark) suggests that many will leave the community and join with others. The exclusivity demanded within Christian groups would strike the ancient as odd as many joined more than one association. Once the erring Christian was convinced of the need to adhere only to the Matthean group, regulations were in place to bring them back into the community (18:15-17; on these regulations see Thompson, *Matthew's Advice to a Divided Community*, 262-63). Thompson (263) rightly points out that it is not a specific group(s) that is defecting but individuals.

who is wronged *not* to act as one would expect — rather s/he should forgive "seventy times seven" (18:22).[86]

As we noted above, when one does confront an erring member, the steps by which one does so insure confidentiality at first and allow the person to change course before being brought before the entire group. By structuring conflict resolution around personal confrontation before recourse to public exposure, honor codes are set off to one side. The dialogue is to be private rather than public.[87] It is only after such steps have been taken that the public pronouncement and expulsion are carried out. The erring member must not persist in his or her ways once s/he becomes aware of the conflictual situation. If one knows one has wronged another member, then one is to stop what one is doing, even if in the midst of ritual, and go and be reconciled (5:24; cf. vv. 25-26). The agonistic claims for honor expressed through the conflictual situations are to be put aside. We see this also in Matthew's adaptation of Q 6:29-30 in which one does not retaliate (5:38-42), Q 6:37-38, 41-42 where one is warned about trying to correct another without first examining oneself (7:1-5), and Q 6:29b-30 where one is to give beyond what one is asked (5:40, 42).

Egalitarianism

This emphasis on forgiveness and the nondefense of one's honor raises another important issue, that of the hierarchical versus egalitarian nature of the group. As Stephen C. Barton notes, "Potential sources of tension and conflict within the group are addressed by the attempt to encourage an ideal of the community as a non-hierarchical brotherhood (Matt. 23:8-10), whose dominant ethos is one of forgiveness and pastoral care for the one who 'goes astray.'"[88] Such egalitarianism may "represent the author's ideology about formal organization,"[89] but the struggle over its implementation is evidenced in the text, particularly in contexts of leadership within the community.[90]

---

86. Luz (106-8) points out the tension within these texts, which indicate a community which exercises discipline and expulsion, yet holds to an ideal of forgiveness.

87. Saldarini (*Matthew's Christian-Jewish Community*, 103) calls the binding relationships of the group "more personal than structured."

88. Barton, 408.

89. Duling, *BTB* 25 (1995): 188.

90. For a detailed study of this issue, see Dennis C. Duling, "'Egalitarian' Ideology, Leadership, and Factional Conflict within the Matthean Group," *BTB* 27 (1997): 124-37.

Evidence for leadership within the community includes the power to "bind and loose" being conveyed to Peter (16:19), the contrast of "their" scribes (7:29) with scribes "trained for the kingdom of heaven" (13:52),[91] and a possible reference to a "council" (*synedrion*) to which erring members are responsible (5:22). There are also a number of references to people in positions of leadership, such as apostles (10:2), prophets (5:10-12; 11:9; 10:40-42; 13:57; 21:11, 23-27; 23:29-36), teachers (5:19; 28:20), and wise men (23:34).[92] Nevertheless, those in leadership positions are warned against declaring themselves with titles of honor such as rabbi, father, teacher (23:8-10). There is a clear contrast to the synagogues here.[93] At the same time, "Matthew presents [the community's] governance as a theocracy focussing not on offices and officials but on the community of disciples which does God's will revealed by Jesus (1:21; 11:25-27; 12:46-50)."[94] The process of discipline through which a member must go involves the entire community rather than a single leader or a group of leaders.[95]

91. Duling ("Matthean Brotherhood," 172-75) discusses the implications of 8:19; 13:52; and 23:34 for the existence of a scribal leadership in Matthew, although he sees it as "marginal" scribal leadership with respect to the dominant leadership of scribes within the larger society. Stanton ("Revisiting Matthew's Communities," 20) notes his agreement with the traditional view that the "scribe trained for the kingdom" is "the evangelist's own self-portrait"; see O. L. Cope, *Matthew: A Scribe Trained for the Kingdom of Heaven.* CBQMS 5 (Washington: Catholic Biblical Association, 1976).

92. See Duling, "Matthean Brotherhood," 178-79; Luz, 105. Duling (*BTB* 25 [1995]: 189) also includes "righteous men" (10:41-42) as a leadership title. Stanton ("Revisiting Matthew's Communities," 19) understands this as a designation for a group within the Matthean communities (likewise "the prophets"). Stanton (20) also suggests that the "wise men" are the same as "the prophets."

93. Edgar Krentz, "Community and Character: Matthew's Vision of the Church," *SBL 1987 Seminar Papers.* SBLASP 26 (Atlanta: Scholars, 1987), 569; Wilson, 52. Krentz (569) points out that all of these "are titles of honor for teachers of the Law inside Judaism." But, at least in the case of *patēr* and "teacher," they are not exclusive to Judaism.

94. Carter, 650; cf. Krentz, 572. We noted earlier that Peter was given authority to "bind and to loose" (16:19). However, this authority is also granted to the entire community (18:18). Overman (243) suggests that "this very fact highlights the Matthean ideal that leadership and community coalesce. There were leaders and authoritative roles operative in Matthew's church, but he tried to view the community as the primary focus of attention and the locus of authority and wisdom." Cf. Benedict T. Viviano, "Social World and Community Leadership: The Case of Matthew 23:1-12, 34," *JSNT* 39 (1990): 16; C. E. Carlston, "Christology and Church in Matthew," in *The Four Gospels 1992,* ed. Frans van Segbroeck et al. BETL 100 (Leuven: Leuven University Press, 1992), 1302-3.

95. Carter, 652.

Carter points to a number of other egalitarian structures evidenced in Matthew:

> Women are not to be objects of male lust and power. The warnings against adultery are severe. . . . Children are valued and model important characteristics of the community's existence (19:13-15; cf. 2:1-23; 18:1-14). Excessive wealth is to be redistributed and used for the poor (19:16-30; 6:19-34). Community members are to live not as masters but slaves (20:17-28).[96]

In sum, the typical Greco-Roman household structures are overturned within the community itself in an attempt at egalitarianism.[97] Yet at the same time there remain in the community a structure and leadership which in themselves point to a *de facto* hierarchy.[98]

In this data one can see similarity *and* difference with the voluntary associations. Within many associations there was also both hierarchy and equality.[99] The hierarchy existed among the founder and the officials of the association, many of whom received larger portions of the meat from the sacrifices than the general membership. However, among the members themselves it is not uncommon to find citizens and noncitizens, masters and slaves, and men and women, rich and poor, all fellowshiping together in one association.[100] Thus, in its inclusivity and egalitarianism the

---

96. Carter, 652.

97. Kathleen E. Corley, *Private Women, Public Meals: Social Conflict in the Synoptic Tradition* (Peabody: Hendrickson, 1993), 178; cf. Carter, 652. See also Antoinette C. Wire, "Gender Roles in a Scribal Community," in Balch, 87-121; Elaine M. Wainwright, *Towards a Feminist Critical Reading of the Gospel According to Matthew*. BZNW 60 (Berlin: de Gruyter, 1991).

98. Stanton, "Revisiting Matthew's Communities," 20-21. Saldarini's assessment is that since Matthew "eschews many, but not all, official roles and titles (23:1-12 versus 23:34), his group must have some formal organization but is not highly institutional"; *Matthew's Christian-Jewish Community*, 86. Krentz (572-73) understands there to be a group of Christian leaders in the Matthean community, which Matthew opposes with his vision of an egalitarian community.

99. Cf. Schmeller, 42.

100. Professional/trade associations would be the most socially homogeneous (Schmeller, 49), other types of associations less so. In comparing Pauline groups to the associations Wayne A. Meeks suggests that the Christian groups were more inclusive in terms of social stratification than were the voluntary associations; *The First Urban Christians: The Social World of the Apostle Paul* (New Haven: Yale University Press, 1983), 79; so also

Matthean community is similar to the general egalitarianism of the associations.[101]

The difference between the Matthean group and the associations lies in the emphasis put on titles of honor within the associations. Officials were common in the associations and there was a "positive exuberance" with granting titles to functionaries.[102] Officials were responsible for the sacrifices, banquets, and festivals (priests; priestesses), the collection and disbursement of monies (treasurers), and for the convening and chairing of meetings (presidents). A person might be elected to one of these positions by the members of the association, or in some cases the office would be purchased by the highest bidder. Either way, serving in such a capacity often could bring with it a heavy financial burden as the official was required to expend his or her own money in carrying out the requisite duties. In exchange, of course, he or she received multiple honors (statues, crowns, proclamations, inscriptions) from the association members.[103]

The quest for honors was promoted as a means to encourage members to contribute more and more lavishly to the social practices of the association. It was encouraged within the associations by appeals to *philotimia*. For example, in *IG* II² 1263 (Piraeus, 300 B.C.E.) the secretary of an association is honored with the erection of a statue, "so that also the others shall be zealous for honor (*philotimōntai*) among the members, knowing that they will receive thanks from the members deserving of benefaction."[104] In contrast, within the Matthean group not only are titles and leadership positions subdued, one's piety (almsgiving, prayer, fasting)

G. Schöllgen, "Hausgemeinden, *oikos*-Ekklesiologie, und monarchischer Episcopat," *JAC* 31 (1988): 74-75. However, see Kloppenborg ("Edwin Hatch, Churches and *Collegia*," 234-36), who argues that although membership within both types of "groups" was inclusive to some degree, the "inclusivity" of Paul's churches has been exaggerated, as has been the exclusivity of associations.

101. Wainwright (355) concludes that "the Matthean vision of *ekklēsia* has been shown to be inclusive, legitimating, therefore, structures and practices within the community that allowed for women's participation together with men in a way that was not always possible in the prevailing patriarchal culture." Yet it is precisely within the confines of voluntary (religious) associations that such inclusivity was possible and was often practiced.

102. Meeks, 134. Often these officials imitated both the titles and functions of civic officials; Meeks, 31, 134.

103. For example, see IDelos 1521; *IG* II² 1263, 1291, 1292, 1317; IKios 22.

104. See also *IG* II² 1271; 1273.A; 1277; 1292; 1314; 1315; 1369; *IG* XII/5 606; IDelos 1519.

is not to be displayed externally but in secret (6:1-18). Unlike the members of associations, the Matthean Christians are to evidence humility and service (23:11-12).[105]

Co-operative Work — "Performing"

At the fourth stage of group cohesion there is an ability to look outward, beyond the formative stages of the group towards establishing the vision which first inspired the formation of the group — in Malina's words the "performing" stage.

> Members take social roles that make the group more rewarding to all. They work together co-operatively to achieve mutual goals.[106]

This is encapsulated in the Great Commission of 28:19-20. This is the present experience of the Matthean community.[107] It is only when the gospel has been preached to the entire world that the end will come about and the strife and persecutions that the Matthean Christians are suffering will come to an end (24:14).

Thompson noted that Matthew stresses four themes which, I would suggest, are indicative of the "performing" stage of the Matthean community: emphasis on the Gentile mission rather than simply a mission to Jews; acceptance of an independent identity apart from the developing Yavnian Judaism; community coherence and mutuality as a basis for the Gentile mission; and final judgment at the return of the Son of Man as a motivation for the Gentile mission.[108] The Gospel of Matthew itself repre-

---

105. Saldarini suggests that Matthew's particular type of egalitarianism is typical of sects and reform movements and sees Matthew's group as such within Judaism; "Delegitimation of Leaders in Matthew 23," *CBQ* 54 (1992): 671. However, since it is different than other types of associations, this "sectarian" nature of the group can be broadened to the wider Greco-Roman context. The same can be said of Luz' analysis (105). Luz understands the Matthean community as having "many structural elements in common with a sect visibly in the process of self-definition." Yet his definition of a "sect" (105 n. 5) also describes many voluntary associations (see esp. *SIG*³ 985).

106. Malina, 105.

107. Pheme Perkins, "Matthew 28:16-20, Resurrection, Ecclesiology and Mission," *SBL 1993 Seminar Papers.* SBLASP 32 (Atlanta: Scholars, 1993), 587.

108. LaVerdiere and Thompson, 574-82.

sents the end result of their "forming, storming, and norming" and a movement towards "performing." Nevertheless, Matthew's community is not just outward looking. They are also inwardly focused. Much of Matthew's instructional material is meant not just to record what decisions have been made in the group but is meant to continue to guide relationships within the group for some time to come.[109]

Conclusion

Duling suggests that the Matthean group is "beginning to move to a level of assimilation, formal organization, development of norms and style of leadership which suggest that it might be called an 'incipient corporation.'"[110] I have attempted to show, by using Malina's categories, that in fact, the Matthean group has already moved beyond "incipient corporation." By the time the Gospel is written down the group has gone through the first three stages of community definition — community formation, community cohesion, and community regulations. Throughout this process they reflect characteristic features of many voluntary associations of antiquity: a divine patron who speaks to a human founder ("forming"); internal divisions and external pressures ("storming"); and community designations and regulations ("norming"). The Gospel concludes by turning the group to the "performing" stage, when group members work cooperatively towards a particular goal.[111]

The Gospel of Matthew reflects the group's manifesto — it sets the

109. Cf. Overman, 337-38.

110. Duling, "Matthean Brotherhood," 159; cf. 161.

111. Malina, 105. "Our New Testament documents come from storming and norming situations for the most part" (Malina, 106; cf. 110 and 113 n. 8). Others have noted the "community building" function of the Gospels; see Carter, 637. Carter examines how Matthew uses encomia in his attempt at community definition and building. He notes three types of concerns evidenced in writers of *bioi* (which he suggests is the genre of Matthew), which are loosely similar to the three stages identified by Malina: the "community's origin, accomplishments or institutions, and deeds and virtues" (647). Matthew's Gospel can be generically a *bios* and at the same time a "foundation document"; see Stanton, "Revisiting Matthew's Communities," 10. It is also an apologetic work, providing "legitimating answers" for the membership; Stanton, *Int* 46 (1992): 388. At the time of the writing of the Gospel of Matthew the community had not undergone the fifth and final stage — "adjourning."

agenda and defines the parameters of belonging to the group.[112] This is why both the Sayings Gospel Q and the Gospel of Mark are inadequate — they are not tailored for the specific needs of the newly forming group. In setting this agenda within a narrative framework, the Gospel of Matthew conveys the past history of the group and offers hope for success for the members. It tells the story of the one to whom the group is devoted, one who faced difficult odds and overcame even death, and it promises that those who belong to the group will do likewise.

112. As Barton (407) points out, there are two aspects to the editing of the Jesus traditions which meet the needs of the community: "community self-definition, and the maintenance of group boundaries and internal cohesion." As "second-generation" literature the Gospels are "community forming literature" (see Overman, 246-48).

Greco-Roman Apotheosis Traditions
and the Resurrection Appearances in Matthew

WENDY COTTER, C.S.J.

Introduction

Unlike Mark or Q, the Matthean Gospel concludes with a report of post-Resurrection appearances, one to the women followers just after they receive the angel's message at the tomb (28:8-10) and the other to the disciples on a mountain in Galilee (28:16-20). In that last scene, Jesus claims his authorization over heaven and earth and commissions his disciples to make disciples of the whole world.

These stories are intriguing and invite a wide variety of scholarly questions. One of them is the reason for their late appearance. Why do they appear for the first time in a Gospel at the end of the 1st century? May we discover the particular reason for their articulations in the Sitz im Leben of the Matthean community?

The "Commissioning of Jesus' Disciples" (28:16-20) has claimed special attention since, as Otto Michel observed, it seems to hold the key to the entire Gospel.[1] Whether we conduct an exegetical examination from the vantage of form criticism or from Matthean redaction, it is plain that a range of Old Testament and intertestamental allusions are deliberately interwoven in this account. The sheer volume of the scholarship on this pericope makes any itemized review an impossibility here. Let us turn to a

---

1. Otto Michel, "Der Abschluss des Mattaüsevangeliums," *EvT* 10 (1950): 21.

strong representative case which seems to summarize the work done to date, the 1992 article by W. D. Davies and Dale C. Allison, Jr., "Matt. 28:16-20: Texts Behind the Text."[2] While the point of the article is to argue for a three-part stratification of textual influences on the narrative, it is not their proposal that I am endorsing, but rather their succinct and rich review of scholarly research relative to the major Old Testament influences on the story.

As most Matthean scholars,[3] Davies and Allison are persuaded that Benjamin J. Hubbard's 1974 monograph, *The Matthean Redaction of a Primitive Apostolic Commissioning,*[4] has correctly identified the form of 28:16-20 as a prophetic commissioning. Just as God commissions Moses and Moses commissions Joshua, so too Jesus commissions his disciples.

Davies and Allison hold that at a secondary stage, i.e., the pre-Matthean stage, there was an insertion of a midrash on the vision of the Son of Humanity in Dan. 7:13-14 (LXX).

13 I saw in the night visions, and behold, with the clouds of heaven
      there came one like a son of Man,
  and he came to the Ancient of Days
  and was presented before him.
14 And to him was given dominion and glory and kingdom
  that all peoples, nations, and languages
  should serve him;
  his dominion is an everlasting dominion,
  which shall not pass away,
  and his kingdom one that shall not be destroyed.

For evidence of this intended reference, they rely on Jane Schaberg's 1982 monograph, *The Father, Son, and the Holy Spirit,*[5] which illustrates the seven elements of internal coherence between the accounts:

---

2. *RHPR* 72 (1992): 89-98.
3. E.g., Pheme Perkins, *Resurrection: New Testament Witness and Contemporary Reflection* (Garden City: Doubleday, 1984), 131; Jerome H. Neyrey, S.J., *The Resurrection Stories* (Wilmington: Michael Glazier, 1988), 25-30; Gerd Lüdemann, *The Resurrection of Jesus: History, Experience, Theology* (Minneapolis: Fortress, 1994), 134-35; Donald Senior, *The Gospel of Matthew* (Nashville: Abingdon, 1997), 173.
4. SBLDS 19 (Missoula: Scholars, 1974).
5. SBLDS 61 (Chico: Scholars, 1982), 114.

1. common vocabulary: *edothe, exousia, panta ta ethne*
2. the word order of *edothe* + dative pronoun + *exousia*
3. a "heavenly triad" likeness: Ancient of Days, Son of Man, the angels (in Matthew the angel element is taken by Holy Spirit)
4. repetition of *pas* (Daniel twice and Matthew three times)
5. same concern: "the transfer of power from a divine figure to a human or quasi-human figure, after a struggle and victory"[6]
6. mention of implications for "all the nations"
7. presentation of a scene of worship of the main figure: the Son of Humanity in Daniel, Jesus in Matthew

The third and final stage of the account, according to Davies and Allison, is the redaction of Matthew, who inserted certain obvious references to Moses such as his commissioning of Joshua, and the combined effect of Moses allusions: the mountain, the order to go, the command to observe, and the promise of presence.

In whatever order these allusions were interwoven in the account, the evidence of their deliberate intended presence in the narrative is, in my view, indisputable. In this story, Jesus does indeed commission his followers, he does fulfill the glorious expectation of a coming Son of Man, and the smaller elements of mountain and of comisssioning certainly evoke the image of the greatest of all Jewish leaders, Moses.

But the question that is even more basic remains to be asked. How were these Old Testament allusions meant to function in a story of a hero returned from the dead? For the basic genre of the account cannot really be satisfied with the commissioning stories of the Old Testament since this event is clearly outshone by the fact of the hero's appearance after death! Surely this feature takes greater precedence over parallels with Old Testament commissioning accounts! This major claim of the Christian community, i.e., the appearance of Jesus to his disciples after his death, does not have obvious precedents in Old Testament traditions. Something as major as this claim for Jesus' apearance must be properly contextualized before the significance of the Old Testament allusions we have identified (commissioning accounts, Son of Man promises, and Mosaic references) can be properly interpreted.

The story of a human hero who returns from the dead in order to

---

6. Schaberg, 114.

commission followers is simply not a tradition to be identified in Jewish religious texts. But such claims did indeed exist for heroes and kings, where the exalted ruler received his divine *apotheosis,* an elevation to immortality. These types of story first arising in the Hellenistic and Greco-Roman period would even influence some intertestamental Jewish narratives about ancient heroes, as we shall show.

In this article, I will first explain the main features of *apotheosis* as promulgated to the populace of the Mediterranean world, via Roman political power, and then show how the Old Testament allusions seen in 28:16-20 take on their meaning against such a backdrop.

Ideas of Apotheosis

John E. Alsup's 1975 dissertation, *The Post-Resurrection Appearance Stories of the Gospel Tradition,*[7] includes a history-of-religions examination of certain examples of *apotheosis* narratives known to the ancient world. He observes no chronological order for the narratives he cites, discussing Apollonius of Tyana (1st century C.E.); Romulus (reported by Ennius, 239 B.C.E.–169 B.C.E.); and three legendary figures: Aristeas of Proconnesus, reported by Herodotus in his *Persian Wars* (440 B.C.E.); Cleomedes of Astypaleia, from Pausanias' *Descriptions of Greece* (150-200 C.E.); and Alcmene, who had a cult in Thebes (cf. Plutarch's *Lives*). Alsup also includes two figures from Lucian's satirical works: Peregrinus Proteus, from *The End of Peregrinus;* and Demainete, from *The Lover of Lies;* both of whom are supposed to have received an *apotheosis.* Amazingly, at the conclusion of his comparisons between these accounts and the Resurrection appearance stories, Alsup dismisses any influences from the *apotheosis* ideas, in favor of "Jewish anthropomorphic theophanies." For him, God's appearance to Abraham, to Moses, and to other Jewish heroes seems the pattern that has generated the account of Jesus' Resurrection appearances to his disciples. Alsup gives little importance to the difference between the God of all Creation appearing to a prophet and Jesus as a hero risen from the dead appearing to his apostles. But even if one could support Alsup's conclusion, his "either-or" method is inappropriate for the syncretistic sentiment and practice of the Greco-Roman world. Any number of religious influences might well be interwoven

7. (London: S.P.C.K., 1975).

in an account, and the presence of some Jewish allusion to a God's appearance does not dismiss the possibility that a heroic *apotheosis* tradition has also been employed, especially when Jesus, like the heroes of *apotheosis* legends, is human and then experiences death/transformation.

The scope of this article does not allow a full discussion of *apotheosis* as it was understood in the Greco-Roman world, but rather only the most pertinent features and texts will be presented. As noted, *apotheosis* refers to a human hero's elevation to immortal life among the gods after his/her death. In the private world, families might — and often did — claim that a certain deceased member had been taken to heaven to be among the gods. The criteria for these private family members are never articulated and were surely based on the goodness of the deceased. However, the public announcement of a hero's *apotheosis* was another matter, and this subject moves us immediately to the class of Greek and Roman kings, Roman emperors, and certain high-ranking military heroes.

While scholars remind us that *apotheosis* ideas in the West were foreign to native Roman sensibilities, and were borrowed from the Greeks, by the 1st century C.E. evidence shows that concepts of *apotheosis* had already been appropriated by the Roman state and were used for political propaganda throughout the Empire.

The Mediterranean world had become familiar with the idea of the divinized hero from the time of Alexander the Great's death. Alexander's successors made sure that his *apotheosis* was promulgated in every way possible, in particular through coins where the image of his ecstatic face was featured. Until that time, only deities were accorded the privilege of representation on coins.[8] In this bold move, Alexander's successors introduced the ecstatic image of Alexander, his large upward gaze and parted lips expressive of his heavenly exaltation, his new and rightful place among the gods forever.[9]

The first signs of Roman political efforts to appropriate the *apotheosis* and use it to their political advantage are discussed in Hans Peter L'Orange's interesting and erudite essay, "The Hellenistic Saviour-type invades Rome."[10] There, he cites the evidence of the image of Scipio

---

8. Hans Peter L'Orange, *Apotheosis in Ancient Portraiture*, 2nd ed. (1947; repr. New Rochelle: Caratzas Brothers, 1982).

9. L'Orange, 1-49.

10. L'Orange, 39-53.

Africanus' face wearing the same ecstatic expression of Alexander, imprinted on coins struck in his memory as early as 91 B.C.E. This image copies a Hellenistic monument raised to Scipio's honor dated ca. the 2nd century B.C.E.[11] The next notable Roman figure to be immortalized on the coins is Pompey, whose family struck the coins in his memory in 46-45 B.C.E., again with the *apotheosis*-type expression of Alexander.[12] L'Orange observes:

> These portraits of Scipio and Pompey furnish, in their historical context, a particularly clear expression of the religious ruler-idea of Hellenism which was so prominently to the fore in Rome during the last centuries of the republic.[13]

Although illustrations of the divinized-ruler are interesting evidence of a readiness in the populace to accept heavenly exaltation, it is even more to the point to explore narratives which claim *apotheosis* and narrate its occurrence. Research shows that such narratives are reserved for a few very prominent political figures. The most important and famous example for the Roman state was that of Romulus, the founder of Rome. The elements in the narrative of his *apotheosis* seem to have set the criteria for authentic *apotheosis* of any other rulers, at least up until the end of the 1st century C.E. All Roman authors who mention Romulus' *apotheosis* seem to rely on Ennius (259-169 B.C.E.), although his account itself is not extant. I will treat two genres that address the *apotheosis* of Romulus, a narrative by Plutarch and an epic poem by Ovid, his *Metamorphoses*. Although Plutarch postdates Ovid, we will present his account first because the narrative version of the *apotheosis* will help supply the elements to which the epic poem of Ovid will refer.

11. L'Orange, 49.
12. L'Orange, 52.
13. L'Orange, 53.

Plutarch (late 1st century C.E.)

The Death and Translation of Romulus[14]
(The nobles and the king, Romulus,
are gathered just outside the city)

Strange and unaccountable disorders with incredible changes filled the air; the light of the sun failed, and night came down upon them, not with peace and quiet, but with the awful peals of thunder and furious blasts driving rain from every quarter, during which the multitude dispersed and fled, but the nobles gathered closely together, and when the storm had ceased, and the sun shone out, and the multitude, now gathered together again in the same place as before anxiously sought their king, the nobles would not suffer them to inquire into his disappearance nor busy themselves about it, but exhorted them all to honour and revere Romulus, since he had been caught up into heaven, and was to be a benevolent god for them [*hos anerpasmenon eis theous kai theon eumene genesomenon*] instead of a good king.[15]

[*Some people explain the disappearance of Romulus as a deception by the patricians whom they accuse of murdering their king, Romulus. We will see that this is mentioned in the subsequent appearance story of Romulus to the patrician, Proculus*]

The Appearance Story

At this pass, then, it is said that one of the patricians, a man of noblest birth, and of most reputable character, a trusted and intimate friend also of Romulus himself, and one of the colonists from Alba, Julius Proculus by name, went into the forum and solemnly swore by the most sacred emblems before all the people that, as he was travelling on the road, he had seen Romulus coming to meet him, fair and stately to the eye as never before, and arrayed in bright and shining armour. He himself, then, affrighted at the sight had said, "O King [Romulus], what possessed thee, or what purpose had thou, that thou has left us patricians a

---

14. I am indebted to John E. Alsup for the following treatment of Romulus' *apotheosis* (Alsup, *The Post-Resurrection Appearance Stories*, 225).

15. Plutarch "Romulus," *Lives* 27.7.

prey to unjust and wicked accusations, and the whole city sorrowing without end at the loss of its father?"

Whereupon Romulus had replied: "It was the pleasure of the gods, O Proculus, from whom I came, that I should be with mankind only a short time, and that after founding a city destined to be the greatest on earth for empire and glory, I should dwell again in heaven. So farewell, and tell the Romans that if they practice self-restraint, and add to it valour, they will reach the utmost heights of human power. And I will be your propitious deity, Quirinus."

These things seemed to the Romans worthy of belief, from the character of the man who related them, and from the oath which he had taken; moreover, some influence from heaven also, akin to inspiration, laid hold upon their emotions, for no man contradicted Proculus, but all put aside suspicion and calumny and prayed to Quirinus, and honoured him as a god. (28.1-3)

There are three points to observe here. First, the credible witness to the hero's *apotheosis* would prove to be a criterion for the Roman state before any formal pronouncement of *apotheosis* of a hero, at least up until the end of the 1st century c.e. Second, Romulus returns from the dead in order to give a counsel to Proculus for the whole of the Roman people, to direct them to continued supremacy. Their valor will allow them to reach the "utmost heights of human power." The political significance of a hero's *apotheosis* is obvious. His counsels are the will of the gods. If the Romans are masters of the civilized world it is due to their greater virtue and valor, i.e., their superiority over others. So the *apotheosis* serves the successors of the hero as legitimation of their rule. Finally, it is notable here that Romulus promises a constant presence with the people, to watch over them as their new deity. This shows us that along with the *apotheosis* was a sense of the divinized hero now a constant companion of his people.

This legend of Romulus' *apotheosis* was deliberately promulgated throughout the Mediterranean, especially in the writers of the Augustine period. References occur in Livy's *History* 1.16; in Cicero's *De Republica* 2.17; Dionysus of Halicarnassus 2.56 (his mention of the legend is to dismiss the *apotheosis* as the patrician cover-up story for their murder of Romulus); and Ovid in two works, the *Fasti* 2.491ff.; and *Metamorphosis* 14.806ff.

Ovid *(43-17 B.C.E.)*

The *Metamorphosis* was composed during Augustus' administration at a time when the emperor was trying to consolidate his power and inculcate in the Roman people as sense of confidence and pride in their own religion and myth. Not only does Ovid's poem serve Augustus' project, but it especially serves Augustus himself, hailing him as a heavenly designated ruler for the world, as we shall see.

Metamorphosis 14.804-51
(The god Mars, said to be the father of Romulus speaks to Jupiter about bringing his son Romulus to heaven)

The time is come, O father, since the Roman state stands firm on strong foundations and no longer hangs on one man's strength alone, to grant the reward which was promised to me and to thy worthy grandson, to take him from earth and set him in the heavens.

Once to me, in full council of the gods . . . thou didst declare: "One shall there be whom thou shalt bear up to the azure blue of heaven.'

Now let the full meaning of thy words be ratified."

The Omnipotent Father nodded his assent; then, hiding all the sky with his dark clouds, *he filled the earth with thunder and lightning.* Gradivus [an epithet of Mars] *knew this for the assured sign of the translation* [italics mine] which he had promised him; and leaning on his spear, dauntless he mounted his chariot drawn by steeds straining beneath the bloody yoke, and swung the loud-resounding lash. Gliding downward through the air, he halted on the summit of the wooded Palatine. There, as Ilia's son was giving kindly judgment to his citizens, he caught him up from earth. His mortal part dissolved into thin air, as a leaden bullet hurled by a broad sling is wont to melt away in the mid-heavens. And now a fair form clothes him, worthier of the high couches of the gods, such form as has Quirinus, clad in the sacred robe.

Note that Ovid explains the translation of the mortal with a metaphor of the speeding bullet. The "mortal part" dissolves away as the hero rises with such rapidity to the heavens.

From these two accounts it is fair to say that the most basic elements of Romulus' *apotheosis* are (a) a body that vanishes into the air; (b) his visitation to a credible witness; (c) the purpose of appearance is to give an exhortation to his subjects; and (d) he wants to promise to be with the Romans as their new deity. Romulus' *apotheosis* seems to have been the ideal for all other political figures to be publicly acclaimed as *apotheosized.*

Excursus: Romulus' Legend Known to the Fathers

The legend of Romulus' *apotheosis* would hardly be of import if there was no evidence that it had moved beyond the gates of Rome, or if it had fallen away from the public gaze by the end of the 1st century B.C.E., but in fact, it was widespread throughout the empire, and the devotions continued as did the temples right through to the days of Augustine, as he himself mentions. The legend of Romulus was brought into the apologies and the treatises of the Fathers of the Church, and although this article cannot provide an exhaustive study of their treatment of it, a few examples will provide helpful evidence about its widespread character and constant promulgation by the Romans. We will draw from the work of Tertullian, Minucius Felix, Arnobius, and Augustine.

Tertullian (ca. 150-155 C.E.) makes several references to Romulus, among them this passage from *Ad Nationes* in which he holds up Aeneas and Romulus for scorn. Aeneas was a coward, and Romulus, although pronounced a god, was in his lifetime a murderer of his brother and a rapist:

> What other glorious achievement can be related of Aeneas, but that he was nowhere to be seen in the fight on the field of Laurentum? Following his bent, perhaps he fled a second time as a fugitive from the battle. In like manner, Romulus posthumously becomes a god. Was it because he founded the city? . . . To be sure Romulus slew his brother in the bargain, and trickishly he ravished some foreign virgins. Therefore of course he becomes a god, and therefore a Quirinus ("god of the spear"), because then their fathers had to use the spear on his account.[16]

Minucius Felix (200-250 C.E.) simply dismisses the legend of Romulus with his reference to the perjury of Proculus. Notice that he knows the power of the witness in any credible *apotheosis* claim.

---

16. Tertullian *Ad Nationes* 3.2.9; *The Ante-Nicene Fathers*, ed. Alexander Roberts and James Donaldson (Grand Rapids: Wm. B. Eerdmans, 1979) 3:138.

It is needless to go through each individual case, and to develop the entire series of that race, since in its first parents their mortality is proved, and must have flowed down into the rest by the very law of their succession, unless perhaps you fancy that they were gods after death; as by the perjury of Proculus, Romulus became a god.[17]

Arnobius stands out for his use of the Romulus legend, not to denounce its claims, but rather to draw on the popularity and acceptability of "Father Romulus" in order to claim the legitimacy of similar Christian claims for their own hero Jesus. In the text that follows, notice that Arnobius has chosen to accept that the senators did indeed tear apart Romulus' body. But Arnobius does not thereby discount the possibility of *apotheosis*. He shows that he likewise accepts that Father Romulus ascended into the heavens. By accepting the "rumored" end of Romulus, i.e., his murder by the senators, as well as the claim of Romulus' *apotheosis*, Arnobius creates a more obvious parallel between the exalted divinized hero worshipped by the Romans and the Christian hero Jesus.

> Father Romulus himself, who was torn in pieces by the hands of a hundred senators, do you not call Quirinus Martius, and do you not honour him with priests and with gorgeous couches, and do you not worship him in most spacious temples; and in addition to all this, do you not affirm that he has ascended into heaven? Either, therefore, you too are to be laughed at, who regard as gods men slain by the most cruel tortures; or if there is sure ground for your thinking that you should do so, allow us too to feel assured for what causes and on what grounds we do this.[18]

We should comment on Arnobius' mention of the worship of Quirinus "in most spacious temples" as proof of the way the Romans institutionalized his legend for the public.

The most extensive treatment of Romulus' legend in comparison to Christ is made in Augustine's *The City of God*. Augustine's charge that Rome has forced Romulus' devotion on the people of the Empire supplies evidence of its widespread character. The legend of Romulus was exported everywhere in the Mediterranean world.

---

17. Minucius Felix *The Octavius* 4.23; *The Ante-Nicene Fathers* 4:187.

18. Arnobius *The Seven Books of Arnobius Against the Heathen* 6.1.41; *The Ante-Nicene Fathers* 6:424.

It was necessary that succeeding generations should preserve the tradition of their [Rome's] ancestors; that, drinking in this superstition with their mother's milk, the [Roman] state might grow and come to such power that it might dictate this belief, as from a point of vantage, to all the nations over whom its sway extended. And these nations, though they might not believe that Romulus was a god, at least said so, that they might not give offence to their sovereign state by refusing to give its founder that title which was given him by Rome, which had adopted this belief, not by a love of error, but an error of love. . . .

And did a single nation worship Romulus among its gods, unless it were forced through fear of the Roman name? . . .

And thus the dread of some slight indignation, which it was supposed, perhaps groundlessly, might exist in the minds of the Romans, constrained some states who were subject to Rome to worship Romulus as a god.[19]

Many of the Fathers ridicule Romulus' *apotheosis* as concocted by the state and contrast it negatively with the heavenly authorization of Jesus by God. It is fair to note here that for these Fathers living in the 2nd century C.E. and beyond, this contrast seemed all the more obvious in their day because at the end of the 1st century, the public witness to the *apotheosized* emperor was no longer required. Rather, a ritual was inserted into the funeral proceedings whereby, as soon as the funeral pyre was ignited, an eagle was released as a public sign of the emperor's ascent into heaven. The artificiality, the institutionalization of an emperor's *apotheosis,* only served to emphasize the contrast. But our point is this: whether Romulus' *apotheosis* was judged artificial or believable, its mention by so many sources, including the Christian Fathers, shows that it continued to be known, and that Romulus' legend held parallels close enough to Jesus' *apotheosis* to draw fire from Christian apologists.

The Apotheosis of Julius Caesar

The two Roman leaders whose supporters pressed for state recognition of their *apotheosis* are Julius Caesar and Octavian (Augustus Caesar). The cir-

---

19. Augustine *City of God* 6; *Nicene and Post-Nicene Fathers,* ed. Philip Schaff (Grand Rapids: Wm B. Eerdmans, 1977), 1st ser. 2:483.

cumstances of Julius Caesar's death already threatened the possibilities for claims of *apotheosis*. In the days following his assassination, charges were still made that Caesar had had ambitions to establish a monarchy. Meantime, Octavian, his adoptive son and heir, pressed the senate to declare Julius *divus*. In preparation, Octavian was trying to raise the money necessary to hold commemorative games in Julius Caesar's honor. Meanwhile, no credible witness had come forward to testify before the senate that he had witnessed Caesar's *apotheosis*. The fact that this mattered illustrates to us that Romulus was being used as the model.

Octavian went ahead with the games, and as luck would have it, a comet appeared in the sky for the seven days during which the memorial games were underway. Octavian used the comet to say that it was the sign of Caesar's having found a new place in the heavens among the gods. Thus, *everyone* who had seen the comet was Caesar's witness that he had attained divine life in heaven forever. Pliny the Elder reports Octavian's interpretation:

> This comet, *the people thought* [italics mine], indicated that Caesar's soul had been received among the immortal gods. For that reason this symbol is placed above the head of the statue of Caesar which I consecrated in the Forum soon after.[20]

Although Octavian's interpretation of the comet solved the problem of the lack of a witness, there was also the problem that Caesar's body had not vanished in his death. It is in Ovid's *Metamorphoses* that we find an explanation as to why it lay on the Forum floor. According to Ovid, Venus, Julius Caesar's divine mother, could not bear to see her own son's body vanish and this is why Jupiter had not caused it to dissolve.

In the speech that follows it is not only this feature of the *apotheosis* that receives an explanation. Jupiter consoles Venus with a prophecy about the future and Caesar's "son," i.e., Octavian, Caesar Augustus. Ovid uses this opportunity to prophesy that Julius Caesar's successor will carry on for him for a long time until he too would "attain the heavenly seats and his related stars." Thus Ovid not only includes a "prophecy" that affirms the sanctity of Augustus' own administration, but also a prophecy of his own *apotheosis*.

---

20. Pliny the Elder *Natural History*. 22.94. See also Vergil *Ecl.* 9.47. I owe this reference to Lily Ross Taylor, *The Divinity of the Roman Emperor* (Middletown, Conn.: American Philological Society, 1931), 91 n. 21.

Ovid *Metamorphosis* 15
(Julius Caesar has entered the Forum, and Jupiter now tries to console Venus, who wants to protect Julius from the assassins)

Jupiter: This son of thine has fulfilled his allotted time and his years are finished which he owed to earth. That as a god he may enter heaven and have his place in temples on earth, you and his son shall accomplish . . .

(Here Ovid includes a prophecy about Augustus, the divine Julius' son)

Whatsoever heritable land the earth contains shall be his [Octavian/Augustus'] and the sea also shall come beneath his sway.[21]
  When peace has been bestowed upon all lands he shall turn his mind to the rights of the citizens, and as a most righteous jurist promote the laws.

  By his own good example shall he direct the ways of men and,
  looking forward to the future time and coming generations,
  he shall bid his son [i.e., Tiberius] born of his chaste wife
      [i.e., Livia],
  to bear his name and the burden of his cares;
  and not till he as an old man shall have equalled Nestor's years
  shall he attain the heavenly seats and his related stars.

(Then Jupiter orders Venus to catch up the soul of Julius Caesar)

Meanwhile do thou catch up this soul [Julius Caesar's] from the slain body and make him a star in order that ever it may be the divine Julius who looks forth upon our Capitol and Forum from his lofty temple.

(Here we see Ovid making the homage to Caesar the fulfillment of God's own will and command . . .)

(Now the apotheosis)

Scarce had he [Jupiter] spoken when fostering Venus took her place within the senate-house, unseen by all, caught up the passing soul of her Caesar from his body, *and not suffering it to vanish into the air,* she bore it

---

21. This is a reference to Octavian's triumph at Actium in 31 B.C.E.

toward the stars of heaven. And as she bore it she felt it glow and burn, and released it from her bosom. Higher than the moon, it mounted up and, leaving behind it a fiery train, gleamed as a star. [italics mine][22]

The Prophecy from Caesar's Star about His Son's Rule

Julius Caesar's "soul," the star, views the earth and can see the future. From this celestial advantage the divine Julius is able to prophesy about his son, Augustus.

It is important here to note the way that divine authority in the cosmos is seen to be divided between Jupiter and Augustus so that we can later contrast it with how Matthew understands Jesus' command and authorization:

Ovid *Metamorphosis* 15.849-70

And now beholding the good deeds of his son,
he [Julius Caesar] confesses that they are greater than his own,
and rejoices to be surpassed by him.
And though the son forbids that his own deeds be set
    above his father's
Fame, unfettered and obedient to no one's will,
exalts him [Augustus] in spite of his desire, and in this
    one thing opposes his commands.
. . . .
Jupiter controls the heights of heaven and the kingdom
    of the triformed universe;
but the earth is under Augustus' sway.
Each is both sire and ruler [italics mine].
O gods, I pray you, comrades of Aeneas, . . . you native gods of Italy,
and you Quirinus, Father of our city, and all other deities,
far distant be that day and later than our own time
    when Augustus, abandoning the world he rules,
shall mount to heaven and there, removed from our presence,
    listen to our prayers!

---

22. Ovid *Metamorphosis* 15.843-48.

There are a number of concepts articulated here that have import for our reconstruction of authority for earthly decisions and the effects of a ruler's *apotheosis*. Ovid grants to Jupiter the "tri-formed universe," i.e., the cosmos as a whole, and, as a special region of power, "the heights of heaven." The realm of the earth is under Caesar, "but the earth is under Augustus' sway." When Ovid underlies this division with "Each is both sire and ruler," he expresses a sort of independence of power enjoyed by the empowered ruler. But Caesar is not turning to Jupiter for his decisions. The idea is that, once empowered or authorized, Caesar exercises that authority as he sees fit. But at death, and with his *apotheosis,* the ruler moves to his glorious rest, and the power over earth is transferred to his successor, the newly authorized ruler of earth. This means that the rulings of the Caesars should be viewed as rightfully authorized by heaven and willed by the gods for the good of the earth.

The Apotheosis of Caesar Augustus

The empire was still young when Augustus died in 14 C.E. As noted above, formal state appropriation of *apotheosis* was only beginning. Although Augustus had made a show of refusing public acclaim during his life, he cultivated the mystique of the divinely authorized leader, as his efforts with respect to Julius Caesar's *apotheosis* also make clear. When Augustus died, he was granted recognition as divine immediately. Unlike Julius Caesar's case, there was no conflict or problematic physical situation to require special pleading in the face of the expected criteria. The necessary witness to swear he had seen Augustus was credible enough, an ex-praetor. Suetonius reports:

> Though it was decided not to pay him [Augustus] excessive honours, he was given two funeral eulogies — by Tiberius from the forecourt of Julius Caesar's Temple, and by Tiberias' son, Drusus, from the Old Rostra — after which a party of senators shouldered the body and took it to the Campus Martius, where it was burned; and an ex-praetor actually swore that he had seen Augustus' spirit soaring up to Heaven through the flames.[23]

23. Suetonius "Divus Augustus," *The Twelve Caesars* 2.100; trans. Robert Graves (Middlesex: Penguin, 1957).

From his distance, Dio casts a wintery eye on such claim as we see in his report about Livia's "gift" to Numerius Atticus, the witness to Augustus' *apotheosis:*

> she [Livia, Augustus' wife] bestowed a million sesterces upon a certain Numerius Atticus, a senator and ex-praetor, because he swore that he had seen Augustus ascending to heaven after the manner of which tradition tells concerning Proculus [the witness] and Romulus.[24]

Note the reference to Romulus, as the model for such divinizations, the expectation that a credible witness be able to swear to the event. Thanks to Numerius Atticus, that criterion had been fulfilled and the senate now had the official evidence it required to make a public acclamation of Augustus as a *divus* taking his place among the gods. Once this approval was given, the political machinery of Rome sent notices around the conquered world. It would have been naive in the extreme for cities not to see in the proclamation an invitation for formal celebrations and honor offered to Caesar Augustus and his family. Augustus' divinity was announced on the coins. Cities would beg to acknowledge Caesar's divinity through temples and priesthoods and sacred brotherhoods, and in smaller ways, by honorific plaques and monuments.

The raising of temples to the *apotheosized* emperor does not of course suggest that he was now on an equal footing with the great gods of the Roman pantheon. A. D. Nock brings attention to the necessary distinction in the *Cambridge Ancient History,* in which he notes: "Dedications to deified rulers are all of the nature of homage and not of worship in the full sense."[25] And with relation to the real world of adminstration, the emperor's divinization through *apotheosis* meant that he had moved on, a point underlined by the sardonic comment of Tacitus about the life in the court:

> After an appropriate funeral, Augustus was declared a god
>   and decreed a temple,
> But the target of every prayer was Tiberius.[26]

---

24. Dio Cassius *Roman History* 56.46.1-3.

25. *Cambridge Ancient History*[1] 10 (Cambridge: Cambridge University Press, 1934): 481.

26. Tacitus *Annals of Imperial Rome* 1.10; trans. Michael Grant (Middlesex: Penguin, 1981).

All Authority Is Given to Me on Earth

The dour Tiberius might lack Augustus' polish and charism, but he knew how to use Augustus' *apotheosis* to political advantage. Impatient with these supernatural honors awarded a mere political administrator, Tiberius knew enough to foster them, because to have a divinized adoptive father places a holy cast around one's own accession to office. So, for example, to the people of Gythium in the Peloponnese who had sent Tiberius a list of special honors they were awarding the deified Augustus, the emperor wrote:

> I approve the idea that all men generally and particularly your city should reserve the honors which belong to the gods for the benefactions which my father conferred on the human race.[27]

Tiberius granted a broad array of cities permission to institute a host of honors of various kinds to Augustus. Some cities like Herod's Caesarea in Palestine already boasted a magnificent temple to "Rome and Augustus," a beautiful and imposing edifice which dominated the harbor there.

The Hero's Accession to Divinity Flows Backward to Consecrate the Actions of His Earthly Life

The granting of *apotheosis* to a hero opens to the door to a sanctification of his commands in his earthly life. This attribution was relatively easy in Augustus' case, since even during his lifetime he was extravagantly praised as divine by delegations from the East. Certainly the Roman "Pax" he established for 45 years was his major contribution to the Mediterranean world.

Very interestingly, even a Jewish intellectual like Philo praises Augustus using miraculous feats ordinarily granted to a god:

> The whole human race exhausted by mutual slaughter was on the verge of utter destruction, had it not been for one man and leader, Austustus whom men fitly call the averter of evil. This is the Caesar who calmed the torrential storms on every side, who healed pestilences common to Greeks and barbarians.[28]

---

27. Taylor, 231ff.
28. Philo "Embassy to Gaius," *Philo* 10.144-45 (London: Heinemann, 1962).

Here, the exercise of legitimate and heavenly approved authority amounts to a holy act for the world's salvation. It is no surprise to find the epithet *soter* on countless plaques raised in honor to an emperor, and certainly to Augustus.

But these attributions of divinity would move even back as far as to Augustus' birth! If the emperor could be said to have been born from the union of a god with a mortal, then his divinity was not due to authorization of a virtuous man, but a recognition of the man's very nature, god/man. In these two accounts from Suetonius, Augustus is shown to be in the same glorious category as Alexander the Great.

In the first story, Suetonius presents an account he found in a book called *Theologumena* by Asclepiades of Mendes. Everyone will recognize here the influence of the legend of Alexander the Great's divine paternity:

> that Augustus' mother Atia had been in the temple of Apollo with her married women friends when a serpent entered her and glided away again. And even though she purified herself on awakening, a mark of a serpent appeared on her body and made her ashamed to visit the public baths and more . . . and the birth of Augustus nine months later suggested a divine paternity. Atia dreamed that her intestines were carried up to Heaven and overhung all lands and seas; and Octavius [her husband] dreamed that the sun rose from between her thighs.[29]

(And Atia did give birth just as the senate was meeting for an important decision.)

> At this Publius Nigidius Figulus the astrologer, hearing at what hour the child had been delivered, cried out: *"The ruler of the world is now born."*

And Suetonius adds "Everyone believes this story."[30]

In a second account, Suetonius recalls a prophecy given to Augustus' father with a singular linkage between Augustus and Alexander the Great. The second dream clearly moves Augustus ahead of Alexander, and places him as expressing in his person the power of Jupiter on earth:

> When Augustus' father Octavius was passing through the wilder parts of Thrace, he came to a grove dedicated to Father Liber (Dionysus) and

29. Suetonius "Divus Augustus," *The Twelve Caesars* 94.
30. Suetonius "Divus Augustus," *The Twelve Caesars* 94.

consulted the priests about his son's destiny. After performing certain barbaric rights, they gave him the same response as Figulus; for the wine they had poured over the altar caused a pillar of flame to shoot up far above the roof of the shrine into the sky — a sign never before granted except to Alexander the Great when he sacrificed at that very altar.

That same night Octavius had another dream: his son appeared in superhuman majesty, armed with the thunderbolt, sceptre and regal ornaments of Jupiter Best and Greatest, crowned with a solar diadem, and riding in a belaurelled chariot drawn by twelve dazzling horses.[31]

As we have said, this promulgation of Augustus' divinity by the Roman senate can be dated to 14 C.E., the year of his death. This means that even if certain peoples east of Rome had not been familiar with the ideas of *apotheosis* (and this would be difficult to imagine since the concepts came from the East), the state-empowering propaganda of the Romans would have made sure that the claims and their signficance would be very plain indeed. Any hero granted *apotheosis* has been approved by heaven and is granted an eternal place among the gods.

The Jewish Community Claims Apotheosis for Moses

One sign of the sigificance of the claim of *apotheosis* for a hero that has wide significance throughout the Mediterranean world is Philo's appeal to it in his desception of the death of Moses. Even though Deut. 34:1-8 states that Moses' body was buried, Philo's composition illustrates his conviction that the exalted status of Moses surely allows an articulation of his heavenly ascent.

First, with regard to the status of Moses as presented by Philo, it is pertinent to compare his description with what this same author awarded to Augustus. We have already noted that he describes the emperor's administration using metaphors of the miraculous, i.e., worldwide healing of pestilences and the calming of storms. For Moses, however, Philo sets aside the far more special claims that Moses is both a king and god. Moses' authority over the earth allows him to be seen as a "partner" of God.

---

31. Suetonius "Divus Augustus," *The Twelve Caesars* 94.

Since God judged him worthy to appear as a *partner of his own posses-sions,* He gave into his hands the whole world as a portion well fitted for his heir.

Therefore, each element obeyed him as its master, changed its natural properties and submitted to his command, and this perhaps is no won-der. For if as the proverb says, what belongs to friends is common, and the prophet is called the friend of God it would follow that he shares also God's possessions so far as it is serviceable. . . .

Again was not the joy of his partnership with the Father and Maker of all magnified also by the honour of being deemed worthy to bear the same title? For he was named god and king of the whole nation.[32]

Philo concludes Moses life with this *apotheosis* narrative:

Afterwards the time came when he had to make his pilgrimage from earth to heaven, and leave this mortal life for immortality, summoned thither by the Father *Who resolved his twofold nature of soul and body into a single unity, transforming his whole being into mind, pure as the sunlight.* Indeed, we find him possessed by the spirit, no longer uttering general truths to the whole nation but prophesying to each tribe in par-ticular. . . .

When he was already being exalted and stood at the very barrier, ready at the signal to direct his upward flight to heaven, the divine spirit fell upon him and he prophesied with discernment while still alive the story of his own death; told how the end came; told how he was buried with none present, surely by no mortal hands but by immortal powers; how also he was not laid to rest in the tomb of his forefathers but was given a monument of special dignity which no man has ever seen; how all the nation wept and mourned for him a whole month and made open dis-play, private and public of their sorrow in memory of his vast benevo-lence and watchful care for each one of them and for all.

Such as recorded in the Holy Scriptures, was the life and such the end of Moses, king, lawgiver, high priest, prophet.[33]

We can see here something of the element found in Ovid's *Metamor-phoses,* that, like Julius Caesar in his *apotheosis,* Moses too can see into the future and prophesy. Unlike the Roman exaltations, Moses' story admits to

32. Philo *Moses* 1.155-56, 158 (London: Heinemann, 1959).
33. Philo *Moses* 2.288, 291-92.

no witnesses for his ascent into heaven. But while Philo follows Deut. 34:6 that Moses was buried, he uses the traditions about his unknown grave to insert the element of Moses' burial being accomplished in secret by "immortal powers." Moreover, Philo also moves from the idea of a grave or tomb to the notion of a monument, "how he was not laid to rest in the tomb [taphos] of his forefathers but was given a monument [mnema] of special dignity which no man has ever seen."[34] By moving from the idea of tomb to that of monument, Philo shifts away from the testimony to the burial of the actual corpse, to the memorial raised to a hero's status. This repeats the same movement that we see in the Roman state, where the state elevated huge monuments to the *apotheosized* emperors, while the relatives discreetly visited the buried ashes in the family tomb. That is, for the Roman state, there was always tension between the *apotheosized* emperor's monument and his tomb.

Philo's description uses the mystery around Moses to support the idea that Moses enjoyed *apotheosis*.

John J. Collins has shown that certain other groups within Judaism provide modifications of the *apotheosis* claims in order to claim the exalted status of their ancient heroes.[35] Collins observes, "the idea that righteous human beings will have thrones in heaven as an eschatological reward becomes current from the first century C.E."[36] Collins' observation shows not only how widespread the effect of Roman propaganda was about signs of divine exaltation of heroes, but also the ways that certain communities modified those *apotheosis* ideas. Instead of a heavenly enthronement of the hero, a divine vision takes him up to heaven for a journey there. As the earliest example, Collins cites the Book of Watchers in 1 Enoch, where that patriarch is said to ascend to the heavens; a second example is provided in the book of Daniel in the person of the coming Son of Humanity. No formal ceremony of his enthronement occurs, but rather he can claim as his own "dominion, glory and kingship," which Collins rightly notes is tantamount to the same thing.

The element of the hero's heavenly vision allows him to return to the living with a report of his experience there. Collins isolates a hymn which

---

34. Philo *Moses* 2.291.

35. John J. Collins, "A Throne in the Heavens: Apotheosis in pre-Christian Judaism," in *Death, Ecstasy and Other Worldly Journeys*, ed. Collins and Michael Fishbane (Saratoga Springs, N.Y.: State University of New York Press, 1995), 43-58.

36. Collins, 50.

occurs at the end of "The Community Rule" in which the hymnist claims that he has sat among the gods, and received his own apotheosis:

> My eyes have gazed on that which is eternal,
> on wisdom concealed from men,
> on knowledge and wise design (hidden) from the sons of men,
> on a fountain of righteousness and on a storehouse of power,
> on a spring of glory (hidden) from the assembly of flesh.
> God has given them to His chosen ones as an everlasting possession,
> and has caused them to inherit the lot of the Holy Ones.
> He has joined their assembly to the Sons of Heaven
> to be a Council of the Community,
> a foundation of the Building of Holiness,
> an eternal Plantation throughout all ages to come.[37]

In relation to the other texts of this set, we can see with Collins that the ideas found in this hymn are normative and not in any way odd or unknown.

This evidence suggests to us that *apotheosis* was understood around the Mediterranean as a powerful expression of a hero's great status before God and before the world.

The Apotheosis of Jesus in 28:19-20

It is fair to say that the scene found in 28:16-20 would be understood by a Greco-Roman audience, Jew or Gentile, as an *apotheosis* of Jesus. Matthew concludes his Gospel with the appearance of the hero whose body has been transformed so that it is fitting for paradise. Credibly witnessed by his own disciples, the divinized Jesus first announces his cosmic authorization to his followers (v. 18), and then exercises that authority in a mandate to them that they spend the remaining time making disciples of the world, "all the nations" (vv. 19-20a). His final message is a reminder of his constant presence until the end time (v. 20b-d.)

However, Matthew sets Jesus apart and above all other *apotheosized* hero/gods in his new authorization, his exercise of cosmic power. Jesus' first

---

37. 1QS 11:5-9; trans. Geza Vermes, *The Dead Sea Scrolls in English* (Harmondsworth: Penguin, 1975), 92-93.

pronouncement to his disciples states: "All authority has been given to me in heaven and on earth" (28:18). Even in the case of Ovid's most lavish poetic praise of Augustus' authority, it was confined to the earth, for Ovid recognizes that to Jupiter belongs "the realm of heaven and the three-tiered universe." Moreover, Augustus' authority belongs to his mortal life. With his *apotheosis,* as with all other heroes', the authority is passed on to the successor. But Jesus' authorization over both heaven and earth has *begun* with his *apotheosis.* His appearance to his followers is not to pass on his authority but to use his authority to commission his disciples in their new project. Whereas previously in Jesus' lifetime the gospel had been directed to "the lost sheep of Israel," the gospel is now to stretch out to "all the nations," a universal scope to match the cosmic empowering of the *apotheosized* Jesus. The disciples now will be empowered by Jesus to "teach," a prerogative of Jesus alone throughout his earthly life. Now the disciples too are newly authorized in their turn to teach what Jesus has commanded them to everyone, to fulfill this initiative of their newly *apotheosized* Lord.

We also notice that the character of Jesus' authorization differs dramatically from that of the Roman commanders/emperors. While Romulus and his successors have an ultimate goal of superiority over the world, Jesus mandates a goal of world discipleship, world community with him. And here it is especially pertinent to observe that discipleship in this evangelist's Gospel is noted for its features of not only loyal and devoted obedience to Jesus, but, as we see especially in 18:1-35, a personal and community righteousness, responsibility for the common good, mature and compassionate leadership, protectiveness towards the weak and sinful, wise guardianship of the community.

Here we should note that Jesus in 28:19-20 shows that his community is indeed expecting an end time, but not soon! Features of apocalyptic sensibilities are not evident here at all. The world is worthy of Jesus' compassion and the mandate of the disciples to bring its inhabitants to discipleship. And Matthew's community is clearly depending on this mandating scene of Jesus to explain the delay of the end time, i.e., to bring the world to discipleship. Furthermore, Jesus' reassurance that he will be with the community until the end time seems more appropriate and significant for a community who has accepted a delay in the parousia. Thus, Matthew's scene does not belong in a category of apocalyptic materials, but rather easily takes its place in the world of the *apotheosis* accounts usually granted to kings/rulers and heroes.

Whether or not the listener to this Gospel would have been ready to believe the claims that Matthew makes for Jesus in the *apotheosis*, the claim itself is clear. Jesus has been divinized and given a total cosmic imperium, a directing authorization for the remaining history of the cosmos.

The exaltation of Jesus in this *apotheosis*, as in the case of other *apotheosized* heroes, causes the sanctification to flow backwards over the acts of the hero's life, right back to the moment of his conception. The Gospel shows that indeed Jesus has fulfilled the divine portents attending his birth, the dreams that protect his life, the astral sign that guides the magi to fall before him (2:1-12). The meaning of that prostration before the child takes on its full clarity as the *apotheosized* Jesus proclaims his cosmic authorization and commands his disciples to go make disciples of *panta ta ethne*. These magi show the direction of the gospel until the end of time.

We notice that the cosmic claims for divine authorization of Jesus in this *apotheosis* scene are understandable to anyone in the ancient world because *apotheosis* was already known through the propaganda of Alexander's followers and then through that of the Romans. There is no necessity for reference to any Jewish hero or Jewish text to see that Jesus is being adored as divine hero empowered as Lord of heaven and earth. Yet Matthew has deliberately appealed to Old Testament texts in his description of Jesus' *apotheosis*, and our task now is to observe how these references affect this important scene.

The Function of the Old Testament References in 28:16-20

The actual description of Jesus' appearance after his death has already been recognized by scholars to suggest the fulfillment of the promised Son of Humanity in the book of Daniel. As converts Jew or Gentile probed the significance of Jesus' appearance, the backdrop of Daniel thus points to the Jewish Deity as the One who authorizes Jesus, and who thus authorizes the community. Jesus' empowerment itself recalls the traditional calls to God's prophets, and thus Jesus is shown to be in continuity with those great heroes of Jewish tradition, and in particular the greatest of them, Moses. By these allusions Matthew points the convert to the sources that inform and direct the Christian community, i.e., Jewish tradition. There will be no allusions to Homer anywhere in this material, no direct allusions to Alexander or Romulus. Rather, Jesus' cosmic role is meant to find its truest significance within the revelations of the Jewish Deity, and in the allusions to the heroes of Jewish tradition Jesus' fulfillment of God's promises reveals his most profound identity. For in fact, Jesus is shown to surpass all these Jewish heroes. If Moses does stand in the background of this account as the figure with whom Jesus' role is in dialogue, as Davies and Allison hold, Moses has already been outshone by the glorious Lord Jesus of Matthew's Resurrection narrative. For Moses had to hand over his authorization to another at his death or *apotheosis,* and he was not empowered with cosmic authority for all time and never granted the singular title of Son as it is stipulated for Jesus in this Gospel.

Thus Matthew's Old Testament references properly contextualize the *apotheosis* of Jesus, so that its meaning is only fully appreciated, as this community sees it, if it is interpreted against the backdrop of Jewish religious tradition, the tradition which is foundational for this Jesus community.

Our current studies of this pericope have easily seen these Old Testament references, but we have not seen the basic *apotheosis* story that they modify and contextualize. But if we fail to recognize the *apotheosis* influences, and the way that they had been applied to the politically mighty world leaders of the ancient world, the claim being made by Matthew for the audiences who heard this story cannot be properly reconstructed. That is, if our scholarship is confined only to explore the stories from Jewish traditions to which Matthew alludes, without seeing the *apotheosis* story that forms the basic narrative, we are left with the particularizations, the modifications, but not the major proclamation it makes to the Greco-Roman world. Once it is seen how easily Matthew has placed Jesus in the same category as the most exalted emperors and rulers, we see how the listeners understand the worldwide and eternal significance of the kind of power that Jesus holds. The power that an emperor wielded throughout the empire was immensely practical. For Jesus to be given such authority now for all time, and such imminence to the community, suggests to the audience that even now the great Lord Jesus has a close and practical care for the entire world. It is in this way that Jesus fulfills the role of the coming Son of Humanity. It has often been observed by Matthean scholars that in Matthew's Gospel, the kingdom of heaven seems very closely connected to the kingdom of earth. This scene of Jesus' *apotheosis* explains why that is true. Jesus has not ascended to the couches of the gods, as in the case of the emperors, but has even more fully taken authority of earth and heaven too, to guide the cosmos through to the end time.

While Matthew's text makes allusion to Jewish traditions in order to contextualize the religious tradition which informs the significance both of Jesus and of the community, the story presented is one of Jesus' *apotheosis* which would be clear in its basic claims for anyone in the Greco-Roman world, Jew or Gentile. This account plainly proclaims Jesus' divinity as Lord in a universal manner. And thus, the very vehicle that Matthew used to announce the mission to the whole world is an account perfectly understandable in its claims to anyone from that world. Thus form and function unite to serve the mandate of Jesus in a story that is as universal as Jesus' command commissions his disciples to be.

The Birth Narrative of Matthew

JACK DEAN KINGSBURY

(18) Now the birth (origin) of Jesus Messiah was thus. After his mother, Mary, had been betrothed to Joseph, before they had come together, she was found pregnant from the Holy Spirit. (19) Then Joseph, her husband, because he was righteous and did not want to make a public example of her, resolved to divorce her secretly. (20) And after he had pondered these things, behold, an angel from the Lord appeared to him in a dream, saying, "Joseph, son of David, do not be afraid to take Mary to be your wife. For that which is conceived in her is from the Holy Spirit. (21) She shall bear a son, and you shall call his name Jesus. For he shall save his people from their sins." (22) Now all this happened in order that what was said by the Lord through the prophet might be fulfilled: (23) "Behold, the virgin shall conceive and shall bear a son, and they shall call his name Emmanuel (which means, 'God with us')." (24) Now Joseph arose from sleep and did as the angel from the Lord commanded, and he took his wife. (25) And he did not attempt to have relations with her until she had borne a son. And he called his name Jesus. (Matt. 1:18-25)

As is apparent, this text is usually associated with Christmas, which the Church celebrates as the Feast of the Nativity of Our Lord. It tells of Joseph

---

This address is in memory of William Thompson, who was not only a scholar and pastor but also a friend. In writing it, I did not so much have the expert in mind as preachers, priests, and students, to whom Bill ministered so very well.

and Mary, of Mary's giving birth to Jesus, and of the guidance God gives Joseph through the visitation of an angel. All these persons and themes relate to the Christian worship of the newborn Christ-child amidst the singing of carols, the readings from scripture, the nativity creche up front, and the Christmas tree adorned with a star on top.

Today, however, we turn to this text not because we celebrate Christmas, but because we want to explore it in terms of how it is related to the Gospel-story Matthew narrates. This story, we know, is about Jesus of Nazareth, from conception and birth to death and resurrection. As with any story, this one too has a beginning, middle, and end. In the beginning (1:1–4:16), Matthew introduces the reader to Jesus, who is the story's protagonist. In the middle (4:17–16:20), Matthew tells of Jesus' public ministry to Israel (4:17–11:1) and of Israel's repudiation of Jesus (11:2–16:20). And in the end (16:21–28:20), Matthew tells of Jesus' journey to Jerusalem and of his suffering, death, and resurrection.

Noteworthy is the place this text occupies within Matthew's Gospel-story. It is situated not only in the beginning phase of the story but even at its very head, namely, within ch. 1 and immediately following the genealogy of Jesus (1:1-17). The result is that this text becomes only the second pericope, or paragraph, in the story. Such positioning of the text becomes especially important for interpreting it in terms of its relationship to its context.

In the opening words of the text (1:18-25), the interpreter encounters the central hermeneutical question it poses. In v. 18a the Greek term *genesis* occurs. If one consults a Greek-English lexicon, one discovers that *genesis* can have a wide range of English meanings, depending upon the context in which it is found. Here in v. 18a the history of interpretation shows that commentators have preferred to translate *genesis* in one of two ways. The first is to render it as "birth." This way is deeply rooted in tradition, as apparent from the fact that "birth" is the meaning the translators of virtually every English Bible intended to be read aloud in public worship have given it.

The second way in which commentators have rendered *genesis* is "origin," a more recent translation. Indeed, not until the latter half of the 20th century did commentators choose "origin" with any frequency as the translation of *genesis*.

155

To determine whether *genesis* is to be rendered as "birth" or "origin," the key question the interpreter must ask is this: What literary and theological difference does the one or the other translation make? The answer is that the difference is much in every way. It is so because the manner in which *genesis* is translated controls the interpreter's entire understanding of the text.

Should the interpreter take the meaning of *genesis* to be that of "birth," the assumption he or she necessarily makes is that Matthew would have the reader construe the focus of 1:18-25 as resting on the one event in Jesus' life of his birth. To assume this, however, is also to assume that Matthew invites the reader to understand 1:18-25 as being the counterpart to Luke's narrative of Jesus' birth, which is found in his Gospel at 2:1-20. To capture the flavor of Luke 2:1-20, recall the following words:

> And so it was, that, while they [Joseph and Mary] were there, the days were accomplished that she should be delivered. And she brought forth her firstborn son, and wrapped him in swaddling clothes, and laid him in a manger; because there was no room for them in the inn. (Luke 2:6-7 KJV)

In view of these words, one cannot doubt but that Luke's intention in 2:1-20 is to hold up to theological reflection the event of Jesus' birth. Because Jesus' birth is so clearly the focus of Luke 2, the Church, in having selected it as the Gospel appointed to be read at the Feast of the Nativity of Our Lord (i.e., each Christmas Day), has unquestionably chosen aright.

Still, should Jesus' birth be the focus of Luke 2, can it legitimately be argued that Jesus' birth must also be the focus of Matt. 1:18-25? Or, to put the question differently, if the Greek term *genesis* in 1:18a is translated not as "birth" but as "origin," what effect does this have on the interpreter's understanding of 1:18-25?

If *genesis* in 1:18a is translated as "origin," the immediate effect is to abolish any notion that the point of 1:18-25 is to hold up to theological reflection the one event in Jesus' life of his birth. The term "origin" is much broader in scope than "birth." "Origin" has to do with relationships: one's relationship to mother, to father, to lineage and forebears, and even to one's own people, or nation. Does 1:18-25, however, address relationships such as these? If one considers the account in conjunction with the genealogy preceding it (1:1-17), the answer is "Yes." In the genealogy and 1:18-25,

Matthew summons the reader to reflect on Jesus' relationship to Mary, to Joseph, to the lineage of David and Abraham, and even, as we shall see, to his relationship to God. Provisionally, therefore, one may confidently conclude that the proper translation of *genesis* is not that of "birth" but of "origin" and that the opening words of v. 18a are to be read: "Now the 'origin' of Jesus Christ was thus."

Interpreters outline texts because outlines provide them with a valuable tool in their search for understanding. If a text is outlined properly, interpreters can trace the movement of the writer's thought. Sometimes interpreters can even uncover an element, or factor, common to every major part of the text. Should they be successful at this, they can reasonably be certain that they have placed their finger on the main topic or theme of the text.

Throughout the history of interpretation, 1:18-25 has been outlined in three chief ways. Each way leads to a fundamentally different construal of the text. Prior to the Enlightenment and rise of historical consciousness, the principal way in which commentators outlined the text was dogmatic in nature. Specifically, many commentators looked upon vv. 18-21 as leading up to the text's culmination in vv. 22-23, in which Old Testament prophecy is quoted, and vv. 24-25 as declining from this culmination. By locating the culmination of the text in vv. 22-23, commentators laid interpretive stress on the theological pattern of "promise and fulfillment." In support of this, they supposed that one had only to appeal to the wording of vv. 22-23:

> (22) Now all this happened in order that what was said by the Lord through *the prophet* might be *fulfilled:* (23) "Behold, the virgin shall conceive and shall bear a son, and they shall call his name Emmanuel (which means, 'God with us')."

Convinced that this dogmatic pattern of promise and fulfillment was anchored in the text itself, commentators advanced an understanding of the text that went something like this: In the human affairs surrounding Joseph's betrothal to Mary, his struggle to resolve the problem of Mary's unlawful pregnancy, his taking of Mary to be his wife, and his naming of Jesus, God was at work to bring to fulfillment the prophecy of Isa. 7:14, which foretold of the divine conception and birth of Jesus. The focal theme of the text, therefore, is that of God's fulfillment of ancient prophecy, and all parts of the text undergird this theme.

With the coming of the Enlightenment and the rise of rationalism and then liberalism in the 18th, 19th, and 20th centuries, commentators in droves forsook the dogmatic approach to 1:18-25 and replaced it with a radically historical approach. Gone was any stress on God's acting directly in the affairs of humankind, which meant that the theological pattern of promise and fulfillment or belief that God caused the miraculous conception of Jesus in Mary was all but abandoned. Instead, interpretation became governed by the axioms and rules of historical method. When such axioms and rules are applied to 1:18-25, the result is predictable: the account is said to focus not on God's activity but on the actions of Joseph, and the text is then read and outlined as a story in which Joseph becomes the protagonist.

To illustrate, it is Joseph to whom Mary is betrothed. It is Joseph who must wrestle with the problem of Mary's unanticipated pregnancy. It is Joseph who, because of his righteousness and compassion, decides he must divorce Mary but determines to do so as leniently as possible. It is Joseph who hears the voice of an angel in a dream and has·a change of mind. It is Joseph who arises from sleep and takes Mary to be his wife. And it is Joseph who gives Mary's son the name of Jesus. From the standpoint of historical method, commentators regarded 1:18-25 as a story featuring Joseph that could be analyzed to set aside the Church's dogma of the virginal conception and to figure out what "really happened" relative to the events surrounding the birth of Jesus.

The third chief way in which 1:18-25 has been outlined and interpreted did not arise until the latter half of the 20th century. This way is neither dogmatic nor radically historical in nature. Instead it is literary and focuses on the narrative flow of the text. In principle, this narrative approach eschews neither the dogma of the Church nor the circumstances of history. Its purpose is to guide the interpreter to read and outline 1:18-25 in the manner in which the writer, through rhetorical and linguistic clues embedded in the text, invites readers to do so. At bottom, the issue at stake becomes this: How does "Matthew," as author and narrator, lead the interpreter-reader to outline and comprehend 1:18-25?

One way to answer this question is to take note of the alternation that occurs in the text: on the one hand, the narrator directly addresses the reader; on the other hand, the narrator tells the story about Jesus' origin. In v. 18a Matthew, in his own voice as narrator, speaks directly to the reader. He gives no indication that any character within the story, neither Joseph nor Mary, overhears his words. In direct address, Matthew informs the reader that the story he is about to narrate has to do with Jesus' origin. The idea is that the reader know the theme of this story and be prepared to be informed about it.

In vv. 18b-21 Matthew begins the narration of the story. Notice that once he begins, the narration flows seamlessly. At the end of v. 21, however, Matthew suddenly halts the narration. Having thus broken it off, he once again, in vv. 22-23, turns to the reader. In direct address and again speaking past the characters within the story, Matthew calls the reader's attention to the divine fulfillment of Old Testament prophecy. Then, returning to his narration in vv. 24-25, Matthew picks up on the story as though he had never disrupted it and concludes it.

In sum, when one outlines the text of 1:18-25 in accordance with narrative theory, one discovers that the text falls into four, easily discernible parts that are demarcated by Matthew's alternation between direct address to the reader and narration of the story of Jesus' origin. With this narrative outline of the text before us, we can next ask whether all four parts of the text have any single element in common.

In Part I (v. 18a), the apparent awkwardness of the language ("Of Jesus Christ his origin was thus") suggests that the element "Jesus Christ" stands out. "Jesus Christ" is a name. But if one investigates Matthew's use of the Greek term *christos,* one learns that he overwhelmingly employs it, not as the name "Christ," but as the title "Messiah" ("Anointed One"). For Matthew, the purpose of the name "Jesus Christ" is to raise the claim that "Jesus is the Christ," i.e., "the Messiah." Once this is apparent, one can recognize that the element that stands out most prominently in v. 18a is the name "Christ," which connotes "Messiah."

In Part II (vv. 18b-21), Matthew begins the narration of the story of Jesus' origin and guides it to its high point in the angel's declaration to Joseph in a dream, "She [Mary] shall bear a son, and you shall call his name Jesus. For he shall save his people from their sins" (v. 21). In the latter half of v. 21, Matthew takes pains to translate the name "Jesus" in such fashion as to highlight the theme "to save." By thus taking the trouble to translate

159

"Jesus," Matthew calls attention to its importance and indicates that the interpretive stress in Part II is, for a second time in 1:18-25, on a name of Jesus. As Matthew reveals, "Jesus" connotes Savior in the sense that, in him, God saves, or God is salvation.

In Part III (vv. 22-23), Matthew again directly addresses the reader but not characters within the story. Once more he privileges the reader, this time with inside information about the fulfillment of divine prophecy. In quoting from the prophet Isaiah, Matthew ascribes yet a third name to Jesus, "Emmanuel," and underscores its peculiar significance by translating it for the reader: "They shall call his name Emmanuel (which means, 'God with us')" (v. 23). Hence, also in Part III Matthew highlights a name of Jesus.

In Part IV (vv. 24-25), Matthew concludes his narration of the story. Guiding the story to its overall culmination, Matthew tells the reader, "And he [Joseph] called his name Jesus." For a fourth consecutive time, therefore, Matthew lays stress on a name of Jesus and, for a second time, this name is the personal one of "Jesus." Hence, the pattern in Matthew's narration of 1:18-25 is clear: Each part of the text finds its climax in the citation of a name of Jesus.

This four-part, narrative outline of 1:18-25 shows that the topic or theme all parts have in common is that of a name of Jesus. The upshot is that two interrelated questions posed so forcefully above suddenly become answerable: the proper translation of *genesis* and the focus of the text. Conclusively, we can now say that the focus of 1:18-25 does not lie on the event of Jesus' birth and that the purpose of the text cannot therefore be that of holding up this event to theological reflection. Matt. 1:18-25 is not the counterpart to Luke 2:1-20. The proper translation of *genesis* is not "birth" but "origin," and the outline that best captures the text's focus is neither the dogmatic one, which locates the center of the text in Matthew's quotation of the Old Testament, nor the historical one, which places the stress on Joseph. On the contrary, the outline that points most convincingly to the focus of the text is the narrative one, which makes fourfold reference to three different names of Jesus. It follows, therefore, that the purpose of 1:18-25 is to hold up names of Jesus to theological reflection. Though Jesus is indeed the son born to Mary, it is his identity as "Messiah" (v. 18a), "Jesus" (vv. 18b-21, 24-25), and "Emmanuel" (vv. 22-23) that is emphasized. Neither the theological theme of promise and fulfillment nor a purely historical description of the human circumstances surrounding

Jesus' birth is paramount. Instead, the theology and meaning of the text reside above all in the interpretation of Jesus' three names.

Since the focus of 1:18-25 is on names of Jesus, the interpreter must discern their significance. How would Matthew invite the reader to understand them?

The first name is that of "Christ," or "Messiah" (v. 18a). In v. 17, which summarizes the genealogy, Matthew explains the name of "Messiah" in these words: "Now all the generations from Abraham to David are fourteen generations, and from David to the Babylonian captivity fourteen generations, and from the Babylonian captivity to the Messiah fourteen generations." What is striking about these words is the division of Jesus' genealogy into sections of fourteen generations each. By so dividing the genealogy, Matthew discloses the awesome claim he makes on his own behalf as author and narrator, namely, that he is privy to the "thinking of God" (16:23b). Here in v. 17, Matthew reveals his knowledge of God's thinking both by showing how God has guided the whole of Israel's history and by noting which persons and events function as the principal markers in this history: Abraham, the father in whom Israel's history began; King David, in whom Israel's history reached its apex; the Babylonian captivity, in which Israel's history sank to its depths; and the Messiah, in whom Israel's history has reached its eschatological culmination. In thus setting forth the divine pattern in terms of which Israel's history has unfolded, Matthew asserts that he knows both the place of the Messiah in history and his identity. Who is the Messiah and what is his place? The Messiah, Matthew declares, is the Son of David and the Son of Abraham, the one in whom Israel's history has climbed from its depths in the Babylonian captivity to attain to its eschatological culmination. With this declaration as background, Matthew, in 1:18-25, enlarges on the identity of the Messiah. Who, then, is the Messiah? The Messiah is not only the Son of David and the Son of Abraham but also the son born of the virgin Mary who was conceived not by Joseph but by the Holy Spirit.

In vv. 18b-21 Matthew calls attention to "Jesus," a personal name. Beginning his narration of the story about Jesus' origin, Matthew tells the reader that Joseph is commanded by the angel to designate as "Jesus" the son whom Mary will bear. So that the reader might know the meaning of "Jesus," Matthew interprets it: "for he will save his people from their sins"

161

(v. 21). In vv. 18b-21, therefore, Matthew uses the name of "Jesus" to inform the reader about what the son born to Mary will do. What will Mary's son do? He will save his people from their sins.

In vv. 22-23 Matthew focuses on the name of "Emmanuel." Interrupting his narration, Matthew addresses the reader for a second time in a private aside. His word to the reader is that, in the human circumstances surrounding Joseph and Mary, one is to see God's hand at work. Indeed, in such circumstances God has brought to eschatological fulfillment the Old Testament prophecy uttered by Isaiah according to which a virgin shall conceive and bear a son called "Emmanuel" (Isa. 7:14). The name "Emmanuel," Matthew says, means "God with us."

By interpreting the name "Emmanuel," Matthew points to its importance. First, however, the reader must decide who the "they" is who will call Jesus Emmanuel. Is this "they" Joseph and Mary? No, because it is Joseph alone whom the angel commands to give Jesus his name (v. 21), and Joseph complies with this command (v. 25). In fact, the pronoun "they" in v. 23 can have only one antecedent in 1:18-25: "the people" whom Jesus will save from their sins (v. 21). Once this becomes clear, the importance of Emmanuel leaps to light.

"Emmanuel" is different in character from either "Messiah" or "Jesus." Whereas "Messiah" informs the reader of the identity of the son born to Mary and "Jesus" explains what Mary's son will accomplish, "Emmanuel" is a confessional name. It is confessional in the sense that the only persons who will utter it are those who look upon the figure of Jesus and profess that in him "God is with us," that God has, through Jesus' conception and birth, inaugurated the eschatological age of salvation. Effectively, these persons, or "his people," will be disciples of Jesus. Such disciples will belong to the Church (16:18), acknowledge Jesus to be their Savior from sins (1:21), and perceive that in him God has drawn near in his gracious rule to proffer humans salvation (v. 23; 4:17).

At bottom, therefore, 1:18-25 shows itself to be a text of names. In all four parts, interpretational stress lies on one of three names by which Mary's son is to be called: "Messiah," "Jesus," and "Emmanuel." Whereas the force of the name "Messiah" is to identify Mary's son, the force of the names "Jesus" and "Emmanuel" is to inform the reader of what Mary's son will do and how the reader is to assess his eschatological significance. Who is the son born to Mary? As the genealogy has said, he is Israel's kingly Messiah who stands in the line of David and Abraham and in whom Israel's entire history attains to its eschatological culmination. What will Mary's son do? He will save his people from their sins. What is his eschatological significance? In his conception and birth, God has drawn near to be "with us" and hence to inaugurate the age of salvation. In short, Matthew places 1:18-25 virtually at the head of his Gospel-story so as to introduce the reader to Jesus by highlighting his identity as Messiah, his mission as Savior from sins, and his significance as the one in whom God proffers eschatological salvation.

As has been noted, the story of Jesus' origin is embedded in a context, and this context is, most immediately, the genealogy of Jesus (1:1-17). One indication of this is the words with which the story begins: "the origin of Jesus Messiah" (1:18a). These words point directly to the opening words of the genealogy, "Book of the origin of Jesus Messiah" (1:1a).

We observed above that, in the genealogy, Matthew tells of Jesus' lineage by tracing it from Abraham through King David and the Babylonian captivity to Jesus himself, who is Israel's Messiah. The thing to notice is that Matthew does not merely list the names of Jesus' forebears but presents them in narrative form according to a fixed pattern: "Abraham fathered Isaac, and Isaac fathered Jacob, and Jacob fathered Judah . . . and Eliud fathered Eleazar, and Eleazar fathered Matthan, and Matthan fathered Joseph" (1:2, 15-16). Through use of the verb "to father" and the formula of "A fathered B, and B fathered C," Matthew shows the reader that he begins the narration of his Gospel-story already with the genealogy (1:2). The fact that Matthew narrates the genealogy is further indication of how closely he has tied the story of Jesus' origin (1:18-25) to Jesus' genealogy (1:1-17); together, the two units form a larger section.

At the end of the genealogy, Matthew suddenly breaks the narrative pattern to which the reader has become accustomed. At v. 16 Matthew does not write, as the reader would anticipate, that "Jacob fathered Joseph, and Joseph fathered Jesus," but that "Jacob fathered Joseph, the husband of Mary, from whom was born Jesus who is called Messiah." The point to be made is that at the place in the genealogy where Matthew narrates the last link, he startles the reader by breaking the pattern, or formula, he has otherwise followed throughout the genealogy. Moreover, by breaking this pattern, Matthew confronts the reader with an astonishing problem, to wit: How can Jesus, who is called Messiah, legitimately be said to be the Son of

David (1:1, 6, 17) if Joseph son of David (1:16, 20) is not his father and Mary, his mother, does not come from the line of David?

It is immediately following the genealogy, in the story of Jesus' origin (1:18-25), that Matthew addresses this problem of the broken link (1:16). This, too, shows that both story and genealogy belong together in one section. Specifically, Matthew solves the genealogical problem in the last verse of the story: Jesus, who is called Messiah, can legitimately be said to be the Son of David (1:1) because, although Joseph son of David is not his father and his mother, Mary, does not descend from the line of David, Joseph — on divine command from the angel of the Lord (1:21) — gives Jesus his name and thus adopts him into the line of David (1:25).

Accordingly, with Joseph's adoption of Jesus into the line of David, Matthew gives answer to the problem with which he confronted the reader in the last link of the genealogy. Still, even at this Matthew does not leave the reader to suppose that David, together with Abraham, constitutes the ultimate source of Jesus' origin (1:1). On the contrary, Matthew has, at four places in 1:18-25, pointed the reader beyond Jesus' Davidic sonship: (a) in v. 18 he narrates that "she [Mary] was found pregnant from the Holy Spirit"; (b) in v. 20 he depicts the angel as announcing the same to Joseph, "For that which is conceived in her is from the Holy Spirit"; (c) in v. 23 he draws on the Old Testament to declare, "Behold, the virgin shall conceive and bear a son"; and (d) in v. 25 he recounts that "he [Joseph] did not even attempt to have relations with her until she had borne a son." Taken together, these various assertions have adumbrated to the reader that, although Jesus is Son of David by adoption, his ultimate origin lies in God: God, by the creative power of his Holy Spirit and totally apart from any male such as Joseph, caused Jesus to be conceived in his mother, Mary, who was a virgin, and to be born.

This grand claim Matthew makes through the text of 1:18-25 reveals why this text, when all is said and done, resists being construed as a story about the "birth" of Jesus and must be read as a story about Jesus' "origin." If one takes account of the twin facts that the chief emphasis of the text is on names of Jesus (vv. 18a, 21, 23, 25) and that the text demands to be read in close conjunction with the genealogy (1:1-17), one recognizes that the text's intention is best explicated along such lines as the following. Jesus, the son born to Mary, is the kingly Messiah of Israel in whom Israel's entire history, begun in Abraham, reaches its eschatological culmination. Adopted by Joseph into the line of David, Jesus can legitimately be called the Son of David and the Son of Abraham. Ultimately, however, Jesus has his origin in God, which means he is the Son of God, for he was conceived in Mary, a virgin, by a creative act of God's Holy Spirit. As Messiah, Son of David, Son of Abraham, and Son of God, Jesus' mission will be to save his people, the disciples who will constitute his Church, from their sins. By so doing, Jesus will inaugurate the eschatological age of salvation.

By introducing Jesus at the outset of his Gospel-story through a genealogy and story about his origin, Matthew succeeds, in merely two paragraphs, in informing the reader of the identity and ancestry of his story's protagonist and of the protagonist's ultimate origin, ministry, and eschatological significance. Following his narration of genealogy and story, Matthew — author and narrator — has only one essential task remaining: to fill the reader in on all the details.

Reading Matthew without Anti-Semitism

ANTHONY J. SALDARINI

As the 20th century ends, both thematic words in the title of this study, "reading" and "anti-Semitism" have become loaded, multivalent terms in biblical studies. When I began to read Matthew in Greek more than 35 years ago, I read it in the language of the New Testament, understanding the words and sentences as best I could. As I learned about 1st-century Judaism and Christianity, I read Matthew as the 1st-century audience would have done so. When I learned the Christian theological tradition, I read Matthew as it was received in the Christian community through its worship, teaching, prayer, and theology. Now in a period of critical theory, postmodernism, and deconstruction, I read the Gospel of Matthew against the grain in order to correct its defects and uncover the hidden potentialities of the text. Most cogently and starkly for me, in the ecumenical and post-Holocaust era, I read Matthew in my Christian, Catholic Church, but always with Jews by my side — occasionally physically present, but always in my mind and heart. So I necessarily read Matthew against the dominant supersessionist theological tradition and against the inner Jewish polemics of the text. As a Christian, I also read to affirm Matthew's teaching about God and Jesus Christ apart from the author's bitter disputes with his opponents in the Jewish community.

Reading Matthew without anti-Semitism seems easy at first because Matthew is not anti-Semitic in relation to the 19th-century term "anti-Semitism," which was based on now discredited racial theories. New Testament scholars usually refer to polemics as anti-Jewish rather than anti-Semitic. Fair enough, but in my interpretation Matthew is not even anti-Jewish, since I see him as a Jewish teacher in conflict with other Jewish teachers in the broadly diverse Jewish community of the eastern Mediterranean at the end of the 1st century.[1] That historical reconstruction hardly takes care of the problem, however. In our world Matthew is still used in an anti-Jewish way in Christian theology. The traditional interpretation of Matthew has contributed substantially to the anti-Semitism which led to the Holocaust. So let the terms "anti-Semitism" and "anti-Judaism" stand.[2]

How shall we read Matthew today? How shall we educate Christian clergy and teachers not to use the Pharisees as paradigms of hypocrisy or legalism since their listeners will hear slanders against Jews in our community today? How shall we affirm the salvific teaching, death, and resurrection of Jesus without denigrating the Jewish community's faithful commitment to God's covenant and varied observance of God's law enshrined in the Hebrew Bible and the Talmud?

The Gospel of Matthew in the Late First Century

Let us begin with a quick review of what Matthew's narrative says about Jews. Though many treatments of the Gospel of Matthew refer facilely to Matthew's attacks on and rejection of Judaism or Jews, in fact the *leaders* of Israel are the only groups unequivocally attacked and rejected by Matthew.[3] The Pharisees, scribes, chief priests, elders of the people, who appear frequently, and the Sadducees (16:1; 22:23) and Herodians (22:16) function in special ways within Matthew's narrative.[4] The Pharisees and

1. See Anthony J. Saldarini, *Matthew's Christian-Jewish Community* (Chicago: University of Chicago Press, 1994).

2. The recent Vatican document, "We Remember: A Reflection on the Shoah," written by the Commission for Religious Relations with the Jews, speciously tries to separate theological anti-Judaism from neo-pagan Nazi anti-Semitism (sections II and IV). Historians had uncovered the links between these traditions well before the commission tried to minimize them.

3. Saldarini, *Matthew's Christian-Jewish Community*, ch. 3. Hostility to the leadership within the Jewish community is common in Jewish literature. See J. Andrew Overman, *Matthew's Gospel and Formative Judaism: The Social World of the Matthean Community* (Minneapolis: Fortress, 1990), 19-23, 141-47.

4. For the leaders as a corporate character in the plot, see Jack Dean Kingsbury, *Mat-

167

scribes appear in both Galilee and Jerusalem and dog Jesus' footsteps everywhere. They argue with Jesus over sabbath observance, food laws, ritual purity, blasphemy, the signs of his ministry, and his authority.[5] In Jerusalem the national leadership, the chief priests, elders, and (high-ranking) scribes seek to blunt Jesus' influence on the crowds. All are members of the ruling classes who oppose Jesus' popular authority with the people. Matthew views them as evil and hypocritical blind guides (23:13-36) who have misled the crowds, who are "sheep without a shepherd" (10:6). Matthew and his group in the late 1st century, like Jesus and his disciples, competed with Jewish community leaders for the hearts of the Jewish community. Matthew sought to tear down the effective authority of the community leaders and to exercise his own leadership in order to bring about the reforms which Jesus taught and to turn the Jewish community toward a recognition of Jesus as Messiah, Son of God and Son of Man sent by God to Israel and the Gentiles. Matthew failed to convince most of his fellow Jews, but his Gospel succeeded with Gentiles in the next generation beyond his wildest dream.

Despite Matthew's highly negative view of the Jewish leaders, their behavior, analyzed according to conventional social norms, was neither unusual nor evil. Though the scribes and Pharisees ask Jesus hostile questions and bring negative charges against him, they never engage in extended vilification of Jesus (in contrast to Jesus' polemics against them in Matthew).[6] Matthew raises questions and controversies between Jesus and the Pharisees and scribes which are normal and legitimate matters for discussion in 1st-century Judaism. They raise questions about proper sabbath observance (12:2, 10), divorce (19:3), association with sinners (9:11), blasphemy (9:3), handwashing (15:2), the signs of Jesus' authority (12:38;

---

thew as Story, 2nd ed. (Philadelphia: Fortress, 1988), 17-23. See also his study, "The Developing Conflict Between Jesus and the Jewish Leaders in Matthew's Gospel: A Literary-Critical Study," CBQ 49 (1987): 57-73. I have not seen Mark Allan Powell, The Religious Leaders in Matthew: A Literary Critical Approach (Ph.D. diss., Union Theological Seminary in Virginia, 1988).

5. For a complete account of their characterization in Matthew, their agendas, and the historicity of Matthew's account, see Anthony J. Saldarini, Pharisees, Scribes and Sadducees in Palestinian Society (Wilmington: Glazier, 1988), 157-73; and Matthew's Christian-Jewish Community, ch. 6.

6. The restricting of the Pharisaic polemics against Jesus may be part of Matthew's narrative technique which emphasizes the charges against the Jewish leaders and minimizes any objections to Jesus.

16:1), and taxes (22:15-22). The one explicitly hostile charge against Jesus is a "witchcraft accusation," i.e., a claim that he is demon possessed (9:34; 12:24), to which Jesus provides a lengthy defense in ch. 12.[7] All of these disputes over Jewish law and the disputants' status and authority in the community are normal conflicts found in any society. The laws and customs discussed by Jesus and the leaders are part of the standard fare found in other Jewish literature in late antiquity. The disagreements and conflicts are legitimate and normal. Similarly, the disputes over Jesus' authority in Jerusalem (chs. 21-22), involving the chief priests and elders, are to be expected when a popular teacher with no official standing gains a following in the capital city. Thus the common Christian interpretation of the Jewish leaders as corrupt monsters or willful rebels against God does not accord with history.

What is Matthew doing with his polemics? The author of Matthew seeks specifically to delegitimate the traditional, established leadership of the Jewish community and thus legitimate his own group and its authority.[8] The origin, structure, and tone of the attack on the Pharisees and scribes strongly support the thesis that the author of Matthew is engaged in lively and serious controversy with his fellow late 1st-century Jews and that he is specifically attacking the leaders of the Jewish community through Jesus' polemic against the scribes and Pharisees.[9] Clearly the author of Matthew is dissatisfied with the Jewish community in his city or

7. Bruce J. Malina and Jerome H. Neyrey, *Calling Jesus Names: The Social Value of Labels in Matthew* (Sonoma: Polebridge, 1988), chs. 1-2, esp. ch. 1, analyze the traditional nature of this type of attack in detail and its desired effects. For the legal disputes, see Saldarini, *Matthew's Christian-Jewish Community,* ch. 6.

8. A similar approach to these materials has been taken by Benedict T. Viviano, "Social World and Community Leadership: The Case of Matthew 23:1-12, 34," *JSNT* 39 (1990): 3-21.

9. In reality scribes were found at every level of society and did not form a cohesive group. Some of them were surely officials and teachers and thus had contact and conflict with Jesus. The Pharisees had a program for reform of Jewish society and had won influence and sometimes power in society since the Hasmonean period. Neither group was in control of society; the Roman government, the chief priests and families in Jerusalem, and Herod Antipas in Galilee had that role. The author of Matthew describes the scribes and Pharisees as lower level officials, i.e., as just the type of Jewish leader who would have interacted with Jesus and the small, new Christian-Jewish group. Scribes, Pharisees, and the leaders of the Jewish community in Matthew's day had recognized power and status in the community and sought to preserve it by receiving public honor and titles and by controlling the interpretation of community custom and justice. See Saldarini, *Pharisees, Scribes and Sadducees*.

area. As is true in other parts of the Gospel, he does not deny the fundamental legitimacy of Israel, its law, and its community structures. To do so would be to destroy the basis for his own group which was so closely tied to Israel. Rather, he attacks the legitimacy of the leaders' rule over the Jewish community by attacking their personal integrity and the accuracy of their interpretation of Jewish law and the divine will.

Replacement Theology and Salvation History

Throughout Christian history interpreters have imposed upon the Gospel of Matthew a variety of theological schemes of salvation history unwarranted by the text. These supposed expressions of God's plan for humanity and God's Church have reduced the Jewish community and its covenant with God to irrelevance by claiming that the new covenant superseded the old or that the Church replaced Israel as a true or new Israel. These theories, from the mid-2nd century on, have done incalculable harm to the Jewish community and caused the deaths of many Jews. They have also biased the interpretation of the Gospel of Matthew. The parable of the wicked tenants in the vineyard (21:33-46) is perhaps the most egregious and enduring case of eisegesis. The tenants refuse to pay their rent to the owner, abusing agents sent to collect, and eventually killing the owner's son. According to the standard interpretation, the tenants represent Israel refusing to obey God and killing God's son Jesus. As a result "the kingdom of God will be taken away from you and given to a nation *(ethnos)* producing the fruits of it" (21:43). Most commentators understand this *ethnos* as the gentile Church replacing Israel.

Numerous problems beset this interpretation and the supersessionist replacement theology which motivates it. First, the addressees of the parable are unclear. Those who respond to Jesus in 21:41 are identified only as "they"; in the Gospel context the closest antecedent is the chief priests and elders of the people in v. 23. In the narrative following the parable, the chief priests and Pharisees realize that Jesus is speaking about them (21:45). So the parable addresses and speaks about the leaders of the Jewish community. Consequently, the group from whom the kingdom is taken away is not Israel, but the leaders of Israel who, in Matthew's view, have failed in their responsibilities to God by opposing Jesus. Second, the symbolic use of the vineyard in the Gospel parable clearly derives from the Hebrew Bible. However, the parallel is less with the famous vineyard parable in Isa. 5:1-5 than with Isa. 3:13-15. In Isa. 5 the vineyard, which symbolizes Israel, fails to produce good fruit and is uprooted. However, in Matthew the vineyard is faultlessly fruitful and only its tenants are unsatisfactory. In contrast, both Matthew and Isa. 3 blame the community *leaders* for misappropriation of the vineyard. Isaiah says:

> The Lord rises to argue his case;
> he stands to judge the peoples.
> The Lord enters into judgment
> with the elders and princes of his people:
> It is you who have devoured the vineyard;
> the spoil of the poor is in your houses.
> What do you mean by crushing my people,
> by grinding the face of the poor?
> says the Lord God of hosts.
>
> (Isa. 3:13-15)

The leaders do not respond to and obey God, but rather oppress and mislead the people. Thus the judgment in Isa. 3 as in Matthew's parable rests upon the leaders of Israel who oppose the teachings of Isaiah and Matthew.

What of the *ethnos,* the so-called "nation"? First, contrary to many careless formulations, the text does not refer to a *new* nation or *new, true* Israel (a 2nd-century Christian category). Nor does the singular form refer to "the nations," i.e., the Gentiles or non-Jews, as it does in the Greek translation of the Bible. The word *ethnos* has a variety of meanings in Greek. In Homer *ethnos* may mean a number of people living together, a (often military) company or body of men, and a band of comrades. It is also used of a large number of people (an *ethnos* of people) and of an ethnic group or tribe with its own proper name. After Homer *ethnos* acquired the common meanings "people" and "nation," referring to a group of people with cultural, linguistic, geographical, or political unity.[10] In the Roman period the Latin word *provincia* ("province") was translated into Greek as *ethnos;* it referred to a somewhat coherent body of people, at least

---

10. The subdivision of an *ethnos* was often designated a *genos,* i.e., a clan (Lat. *gens*). In the Aphrodisias reliefs of the various *ethne* conquered by the Romans, each relief is identified by an inscription using the word *ethnos,* e.g., *ethnous Ioudaion.* See R. R. R. Smith, "*Simulacra Gentium:* The *Ethne* from the Sebasteion at Aphrodisias," *JRS* 78 (1988): 50-77.

bureaucratically speaking. The Greeks had ethnocentric usages for the plural *ethne* as a designation for non-Greek nations or peoples and for rural folk in contrast to city people.

More germane to its use in Matthew, *ethnos* is also used in the Hellenistic-Roman period to refer to a variety of specialized groups such as guilds and trade associations.[11] A social class of people can be referred to as an *ethnos,* as can a caste or other political subdivision. For example, Plato used *ethne* for the various groups who have different functions and stations in his ideal city (*Republic* 421c). Finally, orders of priests can be referred to as holy *ethne.*

This variety of Greek usage makes it far from inevitable that the statement, "The kingdom of God will be taken away from you and given to an *ethnei* [dative case] producing the fruits of it" (21:43), refers to a new nation of Gentiles to replace the old, rejected nation, Israel.[12] *Ethnos* should not be translated in 21:43 as "nation" because the followers of Jesus were not a nation or ethnic group. The *ethnos* which produces fruit certainly refers to a group which believes in Jesus, but what group and what kind of group? The author of Matthew does not say that these believers-in-Jesus are a new or true Israel, nor a replacement for Israel. Commentators who claim that Matthew implies this are reading in 2nd-century Christian theology. Rather, the author of Matthew almost certainly refers to his own group of Jews who follow Jesus as the *ethnos* which produces the fruit of

11. H. G. Liddell-Robert Scott-H. S. Jones-Roderick MacKenzie, *A Greek-English Lexicon,* rev. ed. (Oxford: Clarendon, 1940), 682a, citing the Petrie papyri of the 3rd century B.C.E. For the classic study of these associations, see Franz Poland, *Geschichte der griechischen Vereinswesens* (Leipzig: Teubner, 1909), who traces a wide variety of terms and types of association. The best recent collection of essays on this topic is John S. Kloppenborg and Stephen G. Wilson, eds., *Voluntary Associations in the Graeco-Roman World* (London: Routledge, 1996).

12. Douglas R. A. Hare, "The Rejection of the Jews in the Synoptic Gospels and Acts," in *Antisemitism and the Foundations of Christianity,* ed. Alan Davies (New York: Paulist, 1979), 27-47, takes this verse as a rejection of "Israel according to the flesh" (38-39). Note his use of Pauline language (1 Cor. 10:18), which is not appropriate to Matthew's categories. Hare also holds (153) that the kingdom of God is being transferred to another people *(ethnos),* not to a new or true Israel. Wolfgang Trilling earlier had argued that Matthew's community saw itself as a true Israel, but still associated with unfaithful Israel (*Die Wahre Israel: Studien zur Theologie des Matthäusevangelium,* 3rd ed. SANT 10 [Munich: Kosel, 1964], 95, 224, passim). See Amy-Jill Levine, *The Social and Ethnic Dimensions of Matthean Salvation History* (Lewiston: Edwin Mellen, 1988), 206-11, for a discussion of the passage and references to other authors.

the kingdom.[13] He uses the term *ethnos* of his own group with the less usual, but still ordinary, meaning of a voluntary organization or small social group. The Matthean *ethnos* is a sub-group within the larger Jewish community which seeks to lead the members of the Jewish community to Jesus. Thus the narrative criticizes the Jewish leadership for rejecting God's message, brought by his accredited messenger, Jesus. The parable assumes that the vineyard (Israel), though it has been badly managed, can be given to other tenants (leaders) who will make it bear fruit (21:41). Thus the *ethnos* bearing (lit., "making") fruit (21:43) is a new group of tenants who will lead Israel and give the owner, God, his share of the fruits at the appropriate time (v. 41). Those who are rejected, the previous leaders, are a group who do not act appropriately by producing fruit for the owner.[14] The vineyard, Israel, remains the same; sub-groups of leaders within Israel are blamed or praised.[15] The *ethnos* of leaders which can lead Israel well is, of course, Matthew and his community of followers of Jesus.

Matthean Polemics

The preceding analysis of just one parable shows that careful attention to both the text and the world behind the text can dispel traditional but inaccu-

13. See Graham N. Stanton, "The Gospel of Matthew and Judaism," *BJRL* 66 (1984): 269, for the suggestion that the stone which is rejected (21:42) refers to the rejection of the Matthean group by the leaders of the Jewish community.

14. In 1 Macc. 1:29-40 the Mysarch sent by Antiochus IV plundered Jerusalem and built the Akra (a citadel). In it he stationed a "sinful *ethnos,* lawless *(paranomous)* men" (1:34) who kept Jerusalem subjugated. This ethnos is a group of people left in charge of Seleucid interests. They are judged by the author of 1 Maccabees to be an evil leadership group, much like the group condemned in Matt. 21. Commentators identify this "sinful *ethnos* (variously translated as "breed, race, people")" as Jews loyal to the Seleucids. This interpretation also fits biblical usage. See Jonathan A. Goldstein, *1 Maccabees.* AB 41 (Garden City: Doubleday, 1976), 123-24, 219-20.

15. Ernst Lohmeyer, *Das Evangelium des Matthäus,* ed. W. Schmauch, 2nd ed. KEK (Göttingen: Vandenhoeck & Ruprecht, 1958), 315, argues that *ethnos* refers to a portion of the historical people Israel. He suggests that it refers to a community living among the Jewish people and knowing itself as the true eschatological Israel. For a similar usage of *ethnos,* see Acts 21. Paul brings alms to the Jewish community of believers-in-Jesus and offers sacrifices at the temple. Defending his actions after his arrest, he says that he was bringing alms and sacrificial gifts to his *ethnos* in Jerusalem (Acts 24:17). His *ethnos* is both the whole Judean Jewish community and a subgroup of those Jews, the followers of Jesus.

rate anti-Jewish interpretations of Matthew and, more importantly, expose the theological paradigms we modern commentators bring to the text. However, such laborious analyses still do not explain the presence of such virulent attacks against Matthew's opponents in the Gospel nor what to do with them. Even granting that the author of Matthew attacks only the Jewish leaders, his polemics against his opponents hardly accord with his instruction to love your enemies (5:44). He conforms, rather, to the norms of Second Temple polemics among Jewish sects and the Greco-Roman practices of rhetorical vituperation and blame against philosophical and political opponents.[16] Further, polemical language fills the Hebrew Bible and serves as a model for later Jewish and Christian writing. From the prophetic attacks on idolaters, to the postexilic struggles between competing Jewish groups, on to the civil strife of the Maccabean period, and the claims and counterclaims of Jewish sects during the Roman period, both inner Jewish arguments and attacks on outsiders abound. Divisions among competing groups of priests seeking to guide the Jewish community in Judea appear from the 5th century on. They disagreed about how the sacrifices were to be done, what calendar was to be followed, how priestly purity was to be maintained, how sabbath was to be observed, what relationships were to be maintained with the nations, and a host of other practical and theoretical matters. In such a political, social, religious context groups which passionately believed in their outlooks, positions, and ways of life created modes of speech to articulate their experience, argued for their own views, and attacked their opponents as wrong-headed and evil. The priests and people who were out of power protested against political and economic oppression of the powerless and the poor. With a sectarian outlook which proclaimed their own justice and their opponents' wickedness, such groups urged faithfulness until God would intervene apocalyptically to reward the good and destroy the evil. This faithful minority, as always, was looked upon as deviant by the majority who controlled society. Apocalyptic literature is especially polemical against the powerful on behalf of groups who are weak. Divine intervention, final judgment, and punishment of the evil derives from these concerns. The threat of Hellenization, the Maccabean uprising, Hasmonean civil conflict, unrest during Herod's reign, and finally the two wars against Rome encouraged polemics against those inside and outside Israel.

16. See Luke T. Johnson, "The New Testament's Anti-Jewish Slander and the Conventions of Ancient Polemic," *JBL* 108 (1989): 419-41.

The Qumran *pesharim*, commentaries on scripture, from the 1st century B.C.E. and C.E. exemplify this genre. They reflect a later generation's perception of the Qumran group's history and its evaluation of its early struggles and enemies. A passage from the Habakkuk *pesher* is typical:

> "For the violence to Lebanon will cover you and the assault of beasts will destroy you on account of human bloodshed and violence (done to) the land, the town and all who inhabit it." (Hab. 2:17)
>
> *The interpretation of the passage* concerns the *Wicked Priest* to pay him his due inasmuch as he dealt wickedly with the poor ones;
> - for "Lebanon" is the council of the community, and
> - the "beasts" are the simple ones of Judah, those who observe the Law
> - [It is the Wicked Priest] whom God will sentence to complete destruction because he plotted to destroy completely the poor ones.
>
> And when *it says* "on account of the bloodshed of the town and violence (done to) the land" (Hab. 2:17b)
>
> *the interpretation of it:*
> - the "town" is Jerusalem, where the *Wicked Priest* committed abominable deeds and defiled God's sanctuary.
> - And "violence (done to) the land" (refers to) the cities of Judah, where he stole the wealth of the poor ones.
>
> (1QpHab 11:17–12:10)

All the conflicting players in this interpretation are from governing and priestly classes in Jerusalem and the people in Judean villages. All accept the same Bible from the same God and profess to follow the same commandments and way of life. But they differ to the death, as do many groups today.

In Greco-Roman literature too, epideictic rhetoric or the encomium honors people with praises for their powers, status, virtue, and accomplishments. The same genre turned on its head shames and blames others with crass and ruthless vituperation for their misdeeds and failures as well as their low status and weakness. Though Matthew reverses Greco-Roman and Jewish values by praising Jesus' "dishonorable" death and valuing his lowly disciples, he does so using the polemical genres of Greek and Jewish literature.[17] Matthew lays on the slander and vilification as well as any

---

17. Sean Freyne, "Vilifying the Other and Defining the Self: Matthew's and John's

other author in antiquity. His unjust characterization of the Pharisees as hypocrites (ch. 23) has become, with the help of Christian tradition, a normative usage in the English dictionary.

So maybe polemics are all right. Matthew's all-out attacks did meet the cultural expectations of his Greek-speaking Jewish audience for a vigorous attack on the practices and outlooks of their opponents in the Jewish community. Regrettably, as admirable as much of Matthew's teaching has been and is for the Christian Church, we must part company with him here. Even if his polemics were within in the 1st-century Jewish community and thus not anti-Semitic or anti-Jewish, inner-cultural polemics can kill. Even though polemics against enemies are as old as writing, even though everyone does it, even though polemical tirades have a long and "respectable" history and seem to be a permanent aspect of human society and religion, we cannot accept these conflicts as normal any more than we can accept the Holocaust as inevitable. In antiquity Jew killed Jew in the Maccabean and Herodian periods and Christian killed Christian in the East and in the West. In the past few years in Ireland, the former Yugoslavia, and Rwanda, Christian has killed Christian. Words easily turn into deeds. Especially in a world of mass media, rhetorical demonization of others easily turns speakers and audiences into beasts capable of ruthless violence and cruelty.

But why does Matthew engage so extensively in attacks on his opponents, the leaders of the Jewish community? In terms of the sociology of knowledge, as synthesized and developed by Peter Berger and Thomas Luckmann,[18] society is created and experienced as an objective reality through processes of institutionalization. The objective and necessary nature of these institutions is justified, explained, and passed on to new generations by the processes of legitimation.[19] The meanings attached to disparate social institutions are integrated into a symbolic universe which is a coherent and comprehensive explanation for all of life in a given society. "Legitimation 'explains' the institutional order by ascribing cognitive va-

Anti-Jewish Polemic in Focus," in *"To See Ourselves as Others See Us": Christians, Jews, "Others" in Late Antiquity,* ed. Jacob Neusner and Ernest Frerichs (Chico: Scholars, 1985), 117-43.

18. Peter Berger and Thomas Luckmann, *The Social Construction of Reality: A Treatise in the Sociology of Knowledge* (Garden City: Doubleday, 1966), 92-128.

19. Berger and Luckmann, 61-62, 93. Berger and Luckmann effectively describe the social processes of legitimation at a very abstract level. The neo-Kantian presuppositions of their epistemology are not being utilized or espoused here.

lidity to its objectivated meanings. Legitimation justifies the institutional order by giving a normative dignity to its practical imperatives."[20] Note that knowledge and values are inextricably linked. First we become convinced of the way things are, and then we affirm certain values appropriate to reality as we perceive it.

When two groups conflict with one another, usually their irreconcilable symbolic universes and institutional structures come into conflict. When a large group is faced with a dissident small group (a sect or heresy in the religious sphere), it responds by rearranging its legitimations in order to reaffirm its symbolic universe and institutions.[21] It also attacks the other group by a process called nihilation and rejects it by assigning it a lower ontological status. The established group may also try to explain away the dissident group through apologetics which account for its deviance through the cognitive terms of the larger group's symbolic universe and by ascribing the disagreement to the misunderstandings and bad faith of the smaller group.

Matthew and his small deviant group of Jews who follow Jesus seek to break up the symbolic universe of their opponents and the theories which legitimate their various institutions. In short, Matthew seeks to "delegitimate" his opponents.[22] He is not denying the whole Jewish symbolic universe and system and replacing it with Christianity, as many hold. Rather, the author of Matthew proposes from within the Jewish symbolic world an alternative understanding and actualization of life as a faithful response to God. He seeks to delegitimate his opponents' interpretation of Judaism.[23] Consequently he reduces the plausibility of his opponents' symbolic universe by creating contradictions in it as well as conflicts in values, a different symbolic center (Jesus), and a modified understanding of God's will (the kingdom of heaven). In addition, he de-emphasizes certain sectarian practices and values (purity and tithes) and stresses alternative practices and values. Finally, just as the larger body accounts for the deviance of the smaller body by attributing to it error and bad faith, Matthew delegitimates the Jewish leaders and their interpretation of the Jewish symbolic universe and institutions by accusing them (the leaders, not the

20. Berger and Luckmann, 86.
21. Berger and Luckmann, 106-9.
22. Berger and Luckmann, 94-95.
23. For a more extended treatment of Matt. 23, see Anthony J. Saldarini, "Delegitimation of Leaders in Matthew 23," *CBQ* 54 (1992): 659-80.

people whom he hopes to attract) of bad faith, misunderstanding of scripture, and malfeasance in their duties.

The rearrangement of the Jewish symbolic world according to the teachings of Jesus which was proposed by Matthew did not attract the majority of Jews in the late 1st century. Rather, it led in the next generation to further changes and separation of the Jewish and gentile followers of Jesus from the Jewish community. Yet both then and today the Jewish and Christian symbolic universes overlap substantially, sharing language, metaphors, texts, affirmations about God and the world, and commitments to God and community. Paradoxically, this shared life world has intensified polemics and persecution. How would I say nasty things about Advaita-Vedanta Hindus? I don't know enough to attack them effectively. But in the case of Jews, our shared world places both love and hate close at hand.

The intensity of conflict between related groups and the delegitimation of the Jewish leaders reach a climax in Matthew's seven "woes" or curses in ch. 23. The author of Matthew begins by acknowledging the authority of the scribes and Pharisees and then undercutting it with attacks on their titles, laws, and intentions and by proposing an alternative model of community leadership.[24] His introductory acknowledgment of the authority of the scribes and Pharisees is strikingly contradictory to the argument of the chapter and has long troubled New Testament commentators: "The scribes and Pharisees sit on Moses' seat; so practice and observe whatever they tell you, but not what they do; for they preach but do not practice" (23:2-3).[25] Even if this saying is a pre-Matthean, Jewish-Christian tradition,[26] its use by Matthew must be explained. In citing this affirmation of the authority of the scribes and Pharisees, Matthew admits either the official positions of his opponents in the Jewish community or their

24. The attack on the scribes and Pharisees is made by Jesus in Jerusalem as a climax to his attack on the Jerusalem authorities in chs. 21-22. The narrative place, Jerusalem, and the time of the attack, just before Jesus' arrest, indicate that Matthew is opposing the highest Jewish authorities in their entirety.

25. Note that at the beginning of the Sermon on the Mount, in which Jesus teaches authoritatively, he sits.

26. Commentators typically assign these verses to the Jewish-Christian stratum of tradition and then depict Matthew as preserving but disagreeing with them. In these types of interpretations commentators have difficulty showing why Matthew would preserve them and what use he makes of them. See Joachim Gnilka, *Das Matthäusevangelium.* HTKNT (Freiburg: Herder, 1988), 2:271-72, for sharply differing views on the tradition history of 23:1-12.

influence on those in power. The emerging coalitions seeking power after the destruction of the temple in 70 C.E. contained elements of the Second Temple Pharisaic and scribal groups. It seems that these groups had attained some power or important influence in Matthew's area. Matthew, facing with this kind of competition, and especially with a wholesale rejection of Jesus and his interpretation of scripture and law, attacks the rival leaders and those who have followed them. In the same sentence in which he acknowledges their de facto power, he attacks their conduct of office. He levels against them the usual charge of hypocrisy (23:4-7) and introduces the discussion of a new model of leadership (vv. 8-12), which he supports with an attack on the traditional, institutional forms of Jewish leadership and its interpretation of community norms. He attacks the scribes and Pharisees for failing to practice Judaism sincerely, to guide others to live Judaism correctly, to interpret the Bible adequately, and to attend to the major principles of the law and Jewish way of life. The scribes and Pharisees are used as negative examples for how a community leader should act (23:4-7) and contrasted with proper community leaders who should not use titles such as "rabbi" and "master" but should rather be notable for their lowliness (vv. 8-12).[27]

Matthew uses the scribes and Pharisees as negative examples to define true leadership. He also denounces them in order to legitimate the authority of his new group against the more established authorities in the Jewish community. The powers and status of the established authorities are graphically portrayed (23:4-7): they impose burdens, wear special insignia, claim privileged positions, and seek public honor. Against this common Near Eastern social hierarchy, Matthew forbids the use of titles and the exercise of highly authoritative roles (23:8-12). The followers of Jesus must avoid honorific titles because Jesus is the one leader and all his followers are brethren who are to be "servants" to one another. This resistance to hierarchically structured roles plus the emphasis on equality is typical of sects and reform movements.[28] All the members have begun a new life together and are to participate fully and equally in the emerging

27. David E. Garland, *The Intention of Matthew 23*. NovTSup 52 (Leiden: Brill, 1979), 53-54.

28. Classically, sects have been contrasted with Church, e.g., by Ernst Troeltsch. For a modern, broad typology of sects and their characteristics, see Bryan R. Wilson, *Magic and the Millennium: A Sociological Study of Religious Movements of Protest Among Tribal and Third-World Peoples* (New York: Harper & Row, 1973), Introduction and chs. 1-2.

community. The Matthean group, which is being rejected by a broad constituency in the Jewish community, is being forced into the role of a sect which defines itself by differing from the traditional mode of community organization. Usually, the elders of established families and officials appointed by the government oversaw the application of community laws and customs, adjudicated disputes, and maintained public order. The members of Matthew's community have been cut off from their network of family and friends and begun a new, nontraditional association. Matthew's attack on the established authorities intends to weaken their legitimacy and to establish the authority of his group and its claim to be the genuine leaders of Judaism.

Matthew's attack on his opponents in ch. 23 is part of an ongoing confrontation throughout the Gospel. Here and in many other polemical passages Matthew exhibits the characteristics of a sectarian group protecting itself from the dominant social institution and from rival sects. Matthew attacks the community norms proposed by rival leaders, including several cited in ch. 23, and modifies many points of law and practice to conform to the teachings of Jesus and the way of life which derives from his teaching. Like any good sectarian leader, the author of Matthew claims to have the only legitimate interpretation of the practice of many Jewish customs, all of which he interprets in relationship to Jesus.

Matthew's attack on the Jewish community leadership is contained in seven woe oracles,[29] in which Jesus condemns the scribes and Pharisees (23:13, 15, 16, 23, 25, 27, 29).[30] His opening formula, "Woe to you, scribes and Pharisees, hypocrites" (used six times), drives home the contrast between inner attitudes and outward behavior, a contrast found also in the

---

29. Woe oracles are found frequently in prophetic literature, either individually (Amos 5:18; 6:1; Isa. 1:4; 3:11; 10:5) or in series (5:8-24). The woe is usually followed by a participle describing the criticized action or by a noun giving a negative characterization of the person. Appended to the woe may be a variety of forms, such as rhetorical questions, threats, etc. A woe oracle is a mild form of curse which functions as a public denunciation. Woes may have been adapted from wisdom literature. Lief E. Vaage relates the woes to Greek rhetorical contrasts between appearances and reality and shows how this type of critique of human blindness and untempered zeal has been transformed into a polemic which serves to justify Matthew's group; "The Woes in Q (and Matthew and Luke): Deciphering the Rhetoric of Criticism," *SBL 1988 Seminar Papers*. SBLASP 27 (Atlanta: Scholars, 1988), 603, 605.

30. The "woe" in 23:14 is rejected by most textual critics. It is missing from many manuscripts, interrupts the topical arrangement of the woes, and increases the number of woes from seven to eight.

Sermon on the Mount.[31] The central charge that the Jewish leaders are insincere and of ill will and the image of blindness, repeated five times, undercuts their leadership authority (see also 15:14).[32] The woe oracles are not a random selection of complaints, but a structured series of charges aimed at key aspects of the leadership roles exercised in the Jewish community. The first two woes concern rival interpretations of community identity. According to Matthew, the Jewish leaders prevent their members from following Jesus' teachings and attract Gentiles to their way of life in the Jewish community, thus frustrating the major goal of Matthew's community, teaching all nations to observe Jesus' commands (28:20). Matthew charges that his rivals' teachings frustrate God's purpose embodied in Jesus' message of the kingdom of heaven. The next three woes, concerned with oaths, tithes, and purity, attack prevailing interpretations of the law, economy, and customs which hold the Jewish community together and

31. The Sermon on the Mount (chs. 5–7) and the woes against the scribes and Pharisees are respectively the first and last lengthy public teachings of Jesus. For the correlation of eschatological blessings and curses, see W. D. Davies and Dale C. Allison, *The Gospel According to Saint Matthew.* ICC (Edinburgh: T. & T. Clark, 1988), 1:432-33. In both Jesus is said to teach both the crowds and disciples (5:1; 23:1). The Beatitudes, like the woes, stress the inner attitudes of the group and the patterns of its behavior. Its members should be merciful, meek, pure of heart, and peacemakers; they mourn and seek justice; they know suffering for they are poor in spirit and persecuted (the beginning and end of the series). The sense one has of this group is that it is neither powerful nor established. It seeks to make the best of its minority, deviant status. The reward offered both at the beginning and end of the Beatitudes (5:3, 10) to those who adhere to this code is the kingdom of heaven, i.e., life under the rule of God rather than the unreliable Jewish authorities excoriated in chs. 6, 23, and elsewhere in the Gospel. They will see God, possess the land, and enjoy justice, mercy, peace, and comfort. This is in direct contradiction to the society promoted by the scribes and Pharisees which, according to Matthew's tendentious view, neglects justice and mercy (23:23), places burdens on people (v. 4), keeps cups and dishes pure, but not hearts (v. 25), appears just, but is hypocritical (v. 28), and kills God's messengers (vv. 30-31) rather than creating peace and harmony. Thus Matthew brackets his account of Jesus' deeds and teaching with a vision of a new society (chs. 5–7) and an attack on an alternate program (ch. 23). It should be noted that both have succeeded quite well for almost 2000 years.

32. The term "hypocrite" originally referred to a mask used in the theater. It then became used for insincerity and pretense. It also is used of the misplaced and mistaken zeal of the scribes and Pharisees; see Garland, 96-116. This kind of an attack on the hypocrisy of Jewish leaders is found in Pss. Sol. 4. Hypocrisy makes it difficult to know the actual commitment of a person to a culture, religion, or system and so it inhibits strong relationships among people. Hence it is despised. See Hans Mol, *Identity and the Sacred: A Sketch for a New Social-Scientific Theory of Religion* (New York: Free Press, 1977), 216-17.

give it identity and boundaries. Matthew suggests an alternative understanding and practice of Jewish law. Finally, the last two woe oracles bring to a climax the attack against the personal ethics and intentions of the leaders with the charges of lawlessness and murder.

Blunting Matthew's Polemics

How then shall we read Matthew in this post-Holocaust world? Every line and every word should be read and explained so that, if a Jewish friend were sitting next to you in church or a lecture, you would not feel embarrassed or need to apologize. Matthean anti-Jewish texts have been deadly and still retain their potential for harm. They misrepresent Jewish leaders and the 1st-century Jewish commitment to God. The real cure for traditional Christian anti-Semitic interpretations of Matthew is to know one another and each other's traditions concretely, in all their particularities and peculiarities. Despite living side by side for centuries, Jews and Christians do not know one another very well. If we speak of "them" or "Jews" or "Judaism" with no sense of the diversity in Jewish communities and nuances in their traditions, then we paint all Jews with a broad brush and no individual detail. If we can speak with sophistication, dispute stereotypes, debate things we "always knew" about others, then we can change, slowly, communally, institutionally, fundamentally, deeply, spiritually.

In recognition of the pastoral nature of this conference, let me give six concrete rules for preaching and teaching about Judaism and about Jews.

1. Never talk about Jews and Judaism as a whole. Distinguish which Jews, which type of Judaism. According to 28:15, the story that Jesus' body was stolen by his disciples is still told among the Jews "to this day." Which Jews? Jews who are misled by false leaders? Some Judeans?
2. Never talk about the Pharisees or Sadducees or high priests or any other Jewish group without a thorough and fair historical understanding of the origins, goals, outlooks, behavior, accomplishments, and failures of each group.
3. Interpret authoritative statements concretely within the narrative, not according to some predetermined theological scheme. The

crowds/people in Matthew cry, "His blood be upon us and our children" (27:25). Which people, which crowds? Not the whole Jewish people. "People" in Matthew is not a technical theological term weighted with salvation history, but a concrete group of people in the early 1st century.

4. Read loaded, "anti-Jewish" texts briefly and carefully and preach about them extensively. Matt. 23 has seven powerful curses against the scribes and Pharisees as hypocrites. Matthew has been so successful that in English "pharisaic" means "hypocritical." Read just two of the curses, to show the pattern involved. Then explain this polemical attack in great detail and correct it by an empathetic and fair assessment of the Pharisees. In general, we do not read boring genealogies, nor shocking, violent scenes, nor (for Christians) the laws of sacrifice from the pulpit. We should accord the same treatment to polemically dangerous, obnoxious, or (for Christians today) meaningless anti-Jewish texts. Polemical texts have killed people. All texts read have an effect. All texts do things; they are, in the argot of literary criticism, performative. If they function in an anti-social way in our society, they contradict the purposes of the Bible and should not be read.

5. Change the translations of generic words for Jews into more specific terms. Not "Jews," but Jewish leaders, or Judeans, or a specific crowd or group within Judaism. Not "Jews" who can easily and unconsciously be identified with Jews today, but the actual narrative characters in the Bible.

6. Avoid artificial salvation history schemes which proclaim the end of Judaism as a viable, legitimate religion. Judaism in all its lively and creative forms is still a living religion with more than 1900 years of history since Jesus. Affirm that and the mystery of Israel's relation with God as it is found in Rom. 9-11.[33]

One final theological note. During the last 35 years many Christian churches have affirmed the authenticity, legitimacy, and integrity of the Jewish community as the people of God. After 19 centuries of denial, such admissions are a relief. However, Christian theology has not caught up with its social and pastoral practice. The standard model of Christian salvation — that God created humans, humans sinned, God called Israel

---

33. See Anthony J. Saldarini, "Demonization and Polemics," *JES* 34 (1997): 339-40.

through whom God sent Jesus his Son, and Jesus saves all human beings, Jew and Gentile, through his death and resurrection — tends to nullify any continuing role for Israel in God's world and implicitly supports some kind of Christian supersessionist, replacement theology. In popular theology, preaching, and religious education simplistic schemes of how God saves humans in history exalt the Christian Church and subordinate all other religions, Judaism included. The complexity of God's world and the profundity of God's will to save all humans, including the four and a half billion who are not members of the Christian Church and will not become so in our lifetimes, require a new Christian theology of how God works through Jesus Christ and his Church in the world today.

General Bibliography

Anderson, Janice Capel. *Matthew's Narrative Web: Over, and Over, and Over Again.* JSNTSup 91. Sheffield: JSOT, 1994.

Ascough, Richard S. "Translocal Relationships among Voluntary Associations and Early Christianity." *JECS* 5 (1997): 223-41.

————. *What Are They Saying about the Formation of Pauline Churches?* New York: Paulist, 1998.

Balch, David L., ed. *Social History of the Matthean Community: Cross-Disciplinary Approaches.* Minneapolis: Fortress, 1991.

Barton, Stephen C. "The Communal Dimension of Early Christianity: A Critical Survey of the Field." *JTS* 43 (1992): 399-427.

Bauckham, Richard J. *The Gospels for All Christians: Rethinking the Gospel Audiences.* Grand Rapids: Wm. B. Eerdmans, 1998.

Bauer, David R. *The Structure of Matthew's Gospel.* JSNTSup 31. Sheffield: Almond, 1989.

———— and Mark Allan Powell, eds. *Treasures New and Old: Recent Contributions to Matthean Studies.* SBL Symposium 1. Atlanta: Scholars, 1996.

Betz, Hans Dieter. *The Sermon on the Mount.* Hermeneia. Minneapolis: Fortress, 1995.

Boring, M. Eugene. "The Gospel of Matthew." *The New Interpreter's Bible* 8. Nashville: Abingdon, 1995.

Bornkamm, Günther, Gerhard Barth, and Heinz-Joachim Held. *Tradition and Interpretation in Matthew.* 2nd ed. Philadelphia: Westminster, 1982.

Byrskog, Samuel. *Jesus the Only Teacher: Didactic Authority and Transmission in*

Ancient Israel, Ancient Judaism and the Matthean Community. ConBNT 24. Stockholm: Almqvist & Wiksell, 1994.

Carter, Warren. "Community Definition and Matthew's Gospel." Pp. 637-63 in *SBL 1997 Seminar Papers.* SBLASP 36. Atlanta: Scholars, 1997.

Collins, John J., and Michael Fishbane, eds. *Death, Ecstasy and Other Worldly Journeys.* Saratoga Springs, N.Y.: State University of New York Press, 1995.

Cotter, Wendy J. "The Collegia and Roman Law: State Restrictions on Voluntary Associations 64 B.C.E.–200 C.E." Pp. 74-89 in *Voluntary Associations in the Graeco-Roman World*, ed. John S. Kloppenborg and Stephen G. Wilson.

Crosby, Michael H. *House of Disciples: Church, Economics, and Justice in Matthew.* Maryknoll: Orbis, 1988.

Davies, Alan T., ed. *Antisemitism and the Foundations of Christianity.* New York: Paulist, 1979.

Davies, W. D., and Dale C. Allison. *A Critical and Exegetical Commentary on the Gospel According to Saint Matthew.* 3 vols. ICC. Edinburgh: T. & T. Clark, 1988-1997.

Duling, Dennis C. "The Matthean Brotherhood and Marginal Scribal Leadership." Pp. 159-82 in *Modelling Early Christianity,* ed. Philip F. Esler.

Esler, Philip F. *Modelling Early Christianity: Social-Scientific Studies of the New Testament in Its Context.* London: Routledge, 1995.

Freyne, Sean. "Vilifying the Other and Defining the Self: Matthew's and John's Anti-Jewish Polemic in Focus." Pp. 117-43 in *"To See Ourselves as Others See Us": Christians, Jews, "Others" in Late Antiquity,* ed. Jacob Neusner and Ernest Frerichs. Chico: Scholars, 1985.

Gamble, Harry Y. *Books and Readers in the Early Church: A History of Early Christian Texts.* New Haven: Yale University Press, 1995.

Garland, David E. *Reading Matthew: A Literary and Theological Commentary on the First Gospel.* New York: Crossroad, 1993.

Gerhardsson, Birger. *The Mighty Acts of Jesus according to Matthew.* Lund: Gleerup, 1979.

Guardiola-Sáenz, Leticia A. "Borderless Women and Borderless Texts: A Cultural Reading of Matthew 15:21-28." *Semeia* 78 (1997): 69-81.

Gundry, Robert H. *Matthew: A Commentary on His Handbook for a Mixed Church Under Persecution.* 2nd ed. Grand Rapids: Wm. B. Eerdmans, 1994.

Hagner, Donald A. *Matthew 1–13.* WBC 33A. Waco: Word, 1993.

———. *Matthew 14–28.* WBC 33B. Waco: Word, 1995.

Harrington, Daniel J. *The Gospel of Matthew.* Sacra Pagina 1. Collegeville: Liturgical, 1991.

Heil, John Paul. "Significant Aspects of the Healing Miracles in Matthew." *CBQ* 41 (1979): 274-87.

van der Horst, Pieter Willem. *Hellenism, Judaism, Christianity: Essays on Their Interaction.* Kampen: Kok Pharos, 1994.

Howell, David B. *Matthew's Inclusive Story: A Study in the Narrative Rhetoric of the First Gospel.* JSNTSup 42. Sheffield: Sheffield Academic, 1990.

Kingsbury, Jack Dean. *Jesus Christ in Matthew, Mark, and Luke.* Proclamation Commentaries. Philadelphia: Fortress, 1981.

————. *Matthew: Structure, Christology, Kingdom.* Philadelphia: Fortress, 1975.

————. *Matthew as Story.* 2nd ed. Philadelphia: Fortress, 1988.

Kloppenborg, John S., and Stephen G. Wilson, eds. *Voluntary Associations in the Graeco-Roman World.* London: Routledge, 1996.

Krentz, Edgar. "Community and Character: Matthew's Vision of the Church." Pp. 565-73 in *SBL 1987 Seminar Papers.* SBLASP 26. Atlanta: Scholars, 1987.

LaVerdiere, Eugene A., and William G. Thompson. "New Testament Communities in Transition: A Study of Matthew and Luke." *TS* 37 (1976): 567-97.

Levine, Amy-Jill. *The Social and Ethnic Dimensions of Matthean Salvation History.* Studies in the Bible and Early Christianity 14. Lewiston: Edwin Mellen, 1988.

————, ed. *A Feminist Companion to Mark and Matthew.* Sheffield: Sheffield Academic, 1999.

Luz, Ulrich. *Matthew 1–7.* Continental Commentary. Minneapolis: Augsburg, 1989.

————. *The Theology of the Gospel of Matthew.* Cambridge: Cambridge University Press, 1995.

McNicol, Allen J., ed. *Beyond the Q Impasse: Luke's Use of Matthew.* Valley Forge: Trinity, 1996.

Malina, Bruce J. "Early Christian Groups: Using small group formation theory to explain Christian organizations." Pp. 96-113 in *Modelling Early Christianity,* ed. Philip F. Esler.

Massaux, Edouard. *The Influence of the Gospel of Matthew on Christian Literature before Saint Irenaeus.* Ed. Arthur J. Bellinzoni. Macon: Mercer University Press, 1993.

Meier, John. *The Vision of Matthew: Christ, Church and Morality in the First Gospel.* 1979; repr. New York: Crossroad, 1991.

Mounce, Robert H. *Matthew.* New International Biblical Commentary. Peabody: Hendrickson, 1995.

L'Orange, Hans Peter. *Apotheosis in Ancient Portraiture.* 2nd ed. 1947; repr. New Rochelle, N.Y.: Caratzas Brothers, 1982.

Overman, J. Andrew. *Church and Community in Crisis: The Gospel According to Matthew.* Valley Forge: Trinity, 1996.

————. *Matthew's Gospel and Formative Judaism: The Social World of the Matthean Community.* Minneapolis: Fortress, 1990.

Patte, Daniel. *The Gospel According to Matthew: A Structural Commentary on Matthew's Faith.* 1987; repr. Valley Forge: Trinity, 1996.

Pilch, John J. "The Health Care System in Matthew: A Social Science Analysis." *BTB* 16 (1986): 102-6.

————. "Reading Matthew Anthropologically: Healing in Cultural Perspective." *Listening* 24 (1989): 278-89.

Powell, Mark Allan. *God With Us: A Pastoral Theology of Matthew's Gospel.* Minneapolis: Fortress, 1995.

Ringe, Sharon H. "A Gentile Woman's Story." Pp. 65-72 in *Feminist Interpretation of the Bible,* ed. Letty M. Russell. Philadelphia: Westminster, 1985.

Roberts, Colin H., and T. C. Skeat. *The Birth of the Codex.* London: Oxford University Press, 1983.

Saldarini, Anthony J. *Matthew's Christian-Jewish Community.* Chicago: University of Chicago Press, 1994.

Van Segbroeck, Frans, et al. *The Four Gospels 1992: Festschrift Frans Neiryack.* BETL 100. Leuven: Leuven University Press, 1992.

Senior, Donald. "Between Two Worlds: Gentiles and Jewish Christians in Matthew's Gospel." *CBQ* 61 (1999): 1-23.

————. *The Gospel of Matthew.* Interpreting Biblical Texts. Nashville: Abingdon, 1997.

————. *What Are They Saying about Matthew?* Rev. ed. New York: Paulist, 1996.

Skeat, Theodore C. "The Oldest Manuscript of the Four Gospels?" *NTS* 43 (1997): 1-34.

Stanton, Graham N. "The Communities of Matthew." *Int.* 46 (1992): 379-91.

————. "The Fourfold Gospel." *NTS* 43 (1997): 317-46.

————. *A Gospel for a New People: Studies in Matthew.* Louisville: Westminster John Knox, 1992.

————. "Revisiting Matthew's Communities." Pp. 9-23 in *SBL 1994 Seminar Papers.* SBLASP 33. Atlanta: Scholars, 1994.

————, ed. *The Interpretation of Matthew.* 2nd ed. Edinburgh: T. & T. Clark, 1995.

Stewart-Sykes, Alistair. "Matthew's 'Miracle Chapters': From Composition to Narrative and Back Again." *Scripture Bulletin* 25/2 (1995): 55-65.

Stock, Augustine. *The Method and Message of Matthew.* Collegeville: Liturgical, 1994.

Theissen, Gerd. *The Gospels in Context: Social and Political History in the Synoptic Tradition.* Minneapolis: Fortress, 1991.

Thompson, William G. *The Gospels for Your Whole Life: Mark and John in Prayer and Study.* Minneapolis: Winston, 1983.

————. "An Historical Perspective in the Gospel of Matthew." *JBL* 93 (1974): 243-62.

————. *Matthew's Advice to a Divided Community (Mt 17,22–18,35)*. AnBib 44. Rome: Pontifical Biblical Institute, 1970.

————. *Matthew's Jesus*. London: Sheed & Ward, 1989.

————. *Matthew's Story: Good News for Uncertain Times*. New York: Paulist, 1989.

————. *Paul and His Message for Life's Journey*. New York: Paulist, 1986.

————. "Reflections on the Composition of Mt 8:1–9:34." *CBQ* 33 (1971): 365-88.

Viviano, Benedict T. "Social World and Community Leadership: The Case of Matthew 23:1-12, 34." *JSNT* 39 (1990): 3-21.

Wainwright, Elaine M. "The Gospel of Matthew." Pp. 635-77 in *Searching the Scriptures* 2: *A Feminist Commentary,* ed. Elizabeth Schüssler Fiorenza. New York: Crossroad, 1994.

————. *Shall We Look for Another? A Feminist Rereading of the Matthean Jesus*. Maryknoll: Orbis, 1998.

————. *Towards a Feminist Critical Reading of the Gospel according to Matthew*. BZNW 60. Berlin: de Gruyter, 1991.

Wilson, Stephen G. *Related Strangers: Jews and Christians 70-170 C.E.* Minneapolis: Fortress, 1995.

Contributors

Richard S. Ascough is Assistant Professor of New Testament at the Queen's Theological College (Kingston, Ontario)

David E. Aune is Professor of New Testament at the University of Notre Dame (Notre Dame, Indiana)

Wendy Cotter, C.S.J., is Associate Professor of New Testament at Loyola University (Chicago, Illinois)

Daniel J. Harrington, S.J., is Professor of New Testament, Weston Jesuit School of Theology (Cambridge, Massachusetts)

Jack Dean Kingsbury is Aubrey Lee Brooks Professor of Biblical Theology at Union Theological Seminary of Virginia (Richmond, Virginia)

Amy-Jill Levine is E. Rhodes and Leona B. Carpenter Professor of New Testament Studies and Director of the Carpenter Program in Religion, Gender and Sexuality at Vanderbilt University (Nashville, Tennessee)

Anthony J. Saldarini is Professor of New Testament at Boston College (Chestnut Hill, Massachusetts)

Donald Senior, C.P., is President and Professor of New Testament at Catholic Theological Union (Chicago, Illinois)

Graham N. Stanton is Lady Margaret's Professor of Divinity at the University of Cambridge (England)

Thomas H. Tobin, S.J., is Associate Professor of New Testament at Loyola University (Chicago, Illinois)

Elaine Wainwright, R.S.M., is Professor of New Testament at Pius XII Seminary (Banyo, Australia)